THE MEXICAN-AMERICANS:
an awakening minority

The Insight Series
Studies in Contemporary Issues
from Glencoe Press

PROBLEMS OF AMERICAN FOREIGN POLICY
Martin B. Hickman

THE OPPENHEIMER AFFAIR:
a political play in three acts
Joseph Boskin and Fred Krinsky

THE POLITICS OF RELIGION IN AMERICA
Fred Krinsky

THE WELFARE STATE:
who is my brother's keeper?
Fred Krinsky and Joseph Boskin

OPPOSITION POLITICS:
the anti—new deal tradition
Joseph Boskin

IS AMERICAN DEMOCRACY EXPORTABLE?
Edward G. McGrath

PROTEST FROM THE RIGHT
Robert A. Rosenstone

DEMOCRACY AND COMPLEXITY:
who governs the governors?
Fred Krinsky

FERMENT IN LABOR
Jerome Wolf

AMERICAN ANTI-WAR MOVEMENTS
Joseph Conlin

THE POLITICS AND ANTI-POLITICS OF THE YOUNG
Michael Brown

URBAN RACIAL VIOLENCE IN THE TWENTIETH CENTURY
Joseph Boskin

POSTWAR AMERICA:
the search for identity
Donald G. Baker and Charles H. Sheldon

BLACK POWER:
the radical response to white America
Thomas Wagstaff

THE MEXICAN-AMERICANS:
an awakening minority
Manuel P. Servín

THE SUPREME COURT:
politicians in robes
Charles H. Sheldon

Series Editors: Fred Krinsky and Joseph Boskin

THE MEXICAN-AMERICANS:
an awakening minority

Manuel P. Servín

Associate Professor
Department of History
University of Southern California

GLENCOE PRESS
A Division of The Macmillan Company
Beverly Hills
Collier-Macmillan Ltd., London

GLENCOE PRESS
A Division of The Macmillan Company
8701 Wilshire Boulevard, Beverly Hills, California 90211
Collier-Macmillan Canada, Ltd., Toronto, Canada

Library of Congress catalog card number: 78-104866

First printing, 1970
Second printing, 1970

Contents

Although the Mexican-American is not the most deprived or the most oppressed minority in the United States, nevertheless he is the most historically neglected and ignored group of all the peoples who make up our great nation. While excellent historical surveys and monographs have been written about other minorities—the Indian, the Negro, the Irish-American, and the Italian-American, for example—the Mexican-American possesses not one embracing historical survey concerning his overall urban and rural role in the development of the United States. Indeed, there are only one or two scholarly articles in historical journals that have been thoroughly researched and that merit the attention of history students.

This lack of scholarly historical works, especially of succinct articles, does not however mean that the Mexican-American has not been studied, or even overstudied, by researchers in other disciplines. Even before the recent rush to study this supposedly ignored minority, many pioneer studies were made by the economists, sociologists, and educationists in the 1920's and 1930's. Some studies, such as those of Professor Paul S. Taylor of the University of California at Berkeley and of Dean Emory S. Bogardus of the University of Southern California in Los Angeles (see Chapter Three), were indeed penetrating. The vast majority of the studies, however—especially the master's degree theses and the doctoral dissertations which happily remained unpublished— were generally mediocre and exceedingly biased. Consequently it is not an exaggeration to state that during these decades of the twenties and the thirties nearly all studies concluded, either explicitly or unconsciously, that the life which the Mexican or the Mexican-American endured was the result of his inherent lack of ambition, his innate violence, his racial make-up, or his religious beliefs.

Fortunately for the Mexican-American, and also for the other Americans, this derogatory attitude changed with the coming of World War II. After the Pachuco or Zoot-Suit Riots during the war, American writers began viewing the unhappy plight of the Mexican-American from a sociological viewpoint that exonerated him and attributed the cause of his downtrodden position to various aspects of American society. It was in this vein that Ruth D. Tuck published her *Not with the Fist: Mexican-Americans in a Southwest City* in 1946; Pauline R. Kibbe, her *Latin-Americans in Texas* also in 1946; Beatrice Griffith, her *American Me* in 1948; and Carey McWilliams, his *North from Mexico: The Spanish-Speaking People of the United States* in 1949.

After this initial phase, in which the plight of the Mexican-American was viewed as resulting not from his supposed inferiority but from his treatment by white Americans, there was a lull during the fifties. The publication of scholarly books and articles on this silent, uncomplaining minority group came to a standstill.

Although sociologists and educationists continued to produce theses and dissertations on social and educational problems presented by the Mexican-American, it was not until the 1960's that a sudden new concern—both altruistic and self-seeking—became apparent. Yet despite the large amounts of grant money that have accompanied this sudden concern, there has appeared little if any real historical literature in published form. Thus the Mexican-American, the Southwest's most populous minority, still lacks a sizeable scholarly literature. Furthermore, he has never received adequate treatment in surveys of western American and of American history. It is to overcome this lack of historical study, which is so necessary to understand the present-day Mexican-American, that this textbook is published.

This anthology, which attempts to trace and analyze the various aspects of the life and society of the Mexican-American, is not a mere collection of previously published articles or chapters. In addition to various outstanding, previously published selections, there are included six new historical studies by trained historians from the staff and graduate students of the University of Southern California. These new selections present events which have been studied by historians for the first time. The new articles and the previously published selections have been arranged chronologically. Consequently this volume, although it is a compilation of brief studies by authors in various disciplines and fields, is a historical work treating in chronological order the racial, cultural, educational, economic, and political development of the Mexican-American in the United States.

M.P.S.

Los Angeles, California
August, 1969

THE MEXICAN-AMERICANS:
an awakening minority

Chapter One

The Background of
Mexican-American Discrimination

Precedents for the treatment of the Mexican-American in the United States antedate the experience of any European-descended minority in the nation. Moreover, the discrimination suffered by the Mexican and the Mexican-American, unlike that of such later arrivals in North America as the Irish, Italian, Slovak, Jew, or Hungarian, is based on reasons other than differences in social habits and religion. The Mexican, who preceded even the English colonists and who later inherited the traditional Britannic hatred of things Spanish and Roman Catholic, is plagued by an even deeper prejudice.

The Mexican, and consequently the Mexican-American, is in the vast majority not a pure European. He is, whether he admits it or not, a mixture of two or three racial stocks—the once-hated Hispanic European, the American Indian who was nearly exterminated, and the supposedly inferior Negro who was brutally exploited. It is this racial mixture, deriving from previously despised peoples, that accounts for the white American's exploitation and mistreatment of the early Mexican immigrant and of the present-day Mexican-American.

The first selection in this chapter treats the racial development of Hispanic America, giving a fine analysis of race mixture in New Spain. The second selection presents the American attitude of superiority prior to the Mexican War. The reading of both selections will give the student of Mexican-American history a succinct understanding of the origin of the discrimination that continues today.

First Meeting of the Races in the Americas*

Magnus Mörner

The Conquest of Women

When they went ashore, Columbus and his men found that often the Indians of the Antilles tried to hide their women from the white strangers. On other occasions the Indian women showed themselves and were even importune in their admiration for the newcomers. Naturally enough, the discoverers thought that the first attitude was due to the jealousy of the Indian husbands, whereas the women, of course, were only expressing their love. Such a romantic interpretation of the first meeting of the races can also be found in the accounts of contemporary chroniclers and later historians. But in 1924 a Spanish historian made the sobering observation that the Indian attitudes would be better explained by their animist belief. At first they had to resist the alien spirits. When this was no longer possible, they had to surrender entirely. In addition, the Arawaks were not aware of any relationship between copulation and pregnancy. The latter was explained merely in an animistic way.[1] However true this may be, perhaps the boldness of the alien spirits at last succeeded in arousing the jealousy of the Indian husbands — when Columbus returned to Hispaniola on his second voyage, he found that the men he had left there had been killed. The Indians explained, an eyewitness reports, that one of the Spaniards "had taken three women to himself, and another four; from whence we drew the inference that jealousy was the cause of misfortune that had occurred."[2]

---

*From "First Meeting of the Races in the Americas," pp. 21–31 in *Race Mixture In The History Of Latin America* by Magnus Mörner. Copyright © 1967, by Little, Brown and Company (Inc.). Reprinted by permission of the author and publisher.

[1]Francisco Maldonaldo de Guevara, *El primer contacto de blancos y gentes de color en América: Estudio sobre el dario del primer viaje de Cristóbal Colón* (Valladolid: 1924); Christopher Columbus *The Journal of Christopher Columbus,* trans. C. Jane (New York: 1960), p. 111.

[2]Christopher Columbus, *Four Voyages to the New World: Letters and Selected Documents* (New York: 1961), p. 51.

From the very beginning, Spanish and Portuguese eyewitnesses and chroniclers devoted enthusiastic accounts to the beauty of the Indian girls. Also, a tough German mercenary, Ulrich Schmidel, who took part in the conquest of Río de la Plata, sounds inspired when talking about the Jarayes women: "Very handsome and great lovers, affectionate and with ardent bodies, in my opinion."[3] I would be the last to deny that such expressions in the otherwise not overly romantic chronicles might sometimes be sincere and based on experience. In fact, the female type of the forest tribes is rather close to the feminine ideal in Europe during the Renaissance and later. But I suspect that the sixteenth-century authors sometimes dwelt on the beauty and enchantment of the Indian women in order to satisfy the literary taste of the times. Therefore there is little reason to take these accounts very seriously, or to refer to them, as some historians do, as explaining the rapidity and character of the process of race mixture. Above all it would, as I see it, be absurd to consider them as evidence of a lack of prejudice on the part of the conquistadores. The basic explanation of the rapidity with which race mixture proceeded after the first contact is undoubtedly to be found in the lack of white women at the time of the first expeditions, and the months of abstention during the passage. The satisfaction of a natural instinct should not be confused with social and esthetic attitudes. In fact, the seventeenth-century Dutch did not hesitate to mix with the Bushmen of South Africa, probably the ugliest females to be found in the world, from the European point of view.[4]

In a way, the Spanish Conquest of the Americas was a conquest of women. The Spaniards obtained the Indian girls both by force and by peaceful means. The seizure of women was simply one element in the general enslavement of Indians that took place in the New World during the first decades of the sixteenth century. Indian slavery was finally prohibited categorically in the New

---

[3]U. Schmidel, *Derrotero y viaje a España y las Indias*, trans. with comments by E. Wernicke (Santa Fe, Argentina: 1938), p. 113.

[4]The account by José Pérez Barradas, *Los Mestizos de América* (Madrid: 1948), is romantic and uncritical. Angel Rosenblat, *La población indígena y el mestizaje en América* (Buenos Aires: 1954), vol. II, also attributes mestizaje partly to a supposed lack of racial prejudice on the part of Spaniards and Portuguese. Even Richard Konetzke, "El mestizaje y su importancia en el desarrollo de la población hispanoamericana durante la época colonial," *Revista de Indias*, VII (Madrid: 1946), p. 28ff, does not seem critical enough in this respect. Cautious reservation made by Alberto M. Salas, *Crónica florida del mestizaje de las Indias: Siglo XVI* (Buenos Aires: 1960), p. 24–25.

Laws of 1542. It then gradually disappeared, at least in most areas of Spanish America.[5] But Schmidel tells us about a campaign in Gran Chaco in 1547 that rendered him no fewer than fifty slaves: men, women, and children.[6] In Chile, where the Spaniards faced the stubborn resistance of the warlike Araucanos, the enslavement of the Indians, including that of their women, was once again made legal in 1608.[7] Bernal Díaz, that remarkable eyewitness of the conquest of Mexico, presents a lively account of the actual enslavement of women. Cortés had decided that all the slaves taken by the soldiers should be branded, so that the royal fifth (the Crown's share) and his own share of the human booty could be taken. When the soldiers returned the following day to recover the remaining slaves, they discovered to their dismay that Cortés and his officers had "hidden and taken away the best looking slaves so that there was not a single pretty one left. The ones we received were old and ugly. There was much grumbling against Cortés on this account. . . ."[8] Military campaigns have no doubt always been accompanied by rape and other brutalities against the defenseless. It seems, however, that violence possess special characteristics during warfare between peoples representing widely different civilizations. Critical, then, is the lack of common ethical norms,[9] as in the wars between Christians and Moslems in the Iberian Peninsula, and also during the conquest of the Americas.

Perhaps the element of violent rape should not be overemphasized. Though prematrimonial virginity was highly considered by certain tribes, the opposite was true among others. Probably the Indian women very often docilely complied with the conquistadores' desires.[10]

The Spaniards also obtained women in the form of gifts and as

---

[5]The best study of Indian slavery is Richard Konetzke, "La esclavitud de los indios como elemento de la estructuración social de Hispanoamérica," *Estudios de Historia Social de España*, I (Madrid: 1949).

[6]Quoted by Konetzke, *Revista de Indias*, VII (Madrid: 1946), p. 19.

[7]Alvaro Jara, *Los asientos de trabajo y la provisión de mano de obra para los no-encomenderos en la ciudad de Santiago, 1586–1600* (Santiago de Chile: 1959), p. 205–207.

[8]Bernal Díaz del Castillo, *Historia verdadera de la conquista de la Nueva España* (Mexico: 1955), vol. I, p. 428.

[9]Franklin Frazier, *Race and Culture Contacts in the Modern World* (New York: 1957), p. 46.

[10]Virginia Guitiérrez de Pineda, *La familia en Colombia* (Bogotá: 1963), vol. I, p. 67ff.

tokens of friendship from the Indian caciques. This kind of hospitality has existed in many other environments and ages. Bernal Díaz tells us how the cacique Xicotenga offered Cortés his virgin daughter and four other pretty girls to his captains. Similar episodes abound in the chronicles of the times.[11] From Paraguay, Rui Díaz de Guzmán reports that the Guaraní caciques considered the gift of women to be an excellent means of allying themsleves with the Spaniards. "They called all of them brothers-in-law. This is the origin of the existing custom of calling the Indians entrusted to you *Tobayá* which means brother-in-law. And it so happened that the Spaniards had many sons and daughters with the Indian women they received."[12] Once confirmed by the gift of women, the alliances between Spaniards and Indians were likely to be strong and lasting. This could very well be of greatest importance for the success of a small group of conquistadores. As Inca Garcilaso de la Vega puts it, "as soon as the Indians saw that a woman had been begotten by a Spaniard, all the kinsfolk rallied to pay homage to the Spaniard as their idol and to serve him because they were now related to him. Such Indians were of great help during the Conquest of the Indies."[13]

Another way of obtaining women was provided by the *encomienda*, the famous institution by which Indians were distributed among Spaniards who were granted their tribute. In his turn, the recipient of an *encomienda* was supposed to protect and civilize his Indians and see to it that they were Christianized. At least until the New Laws (1542), the Indians usually paid their tributes to the *encomendero* in days of work. It is not surprising that the *encomenderos* often asked for female domestic servants. As Bishop Juan de Zumárraga of Mexico observed, in his well-known letter to Emperor Charles in 1529, such servants were used as concubines more often than not. Near Cuenca in present Ecuador, Cieza de León reports, the Indians sent their wives and daughters to carry the Spaniards' luggage, while they stayed at home. The chronicler remarks that these women were "beautiful, and not a little lascivious, and fond of the Spaniards."[14] It also happened that the

---

[11]Díaz del Castillo, vol. I, p. 222.

[12]Quoted by Konetzke, *Revista de Indias*, VII (Madrid: 1946), p. 24–25.

[13]Quoted by José Varallanos, *El cholo y el Perú* (Buenos Aires: 1962), p. 45.

[14]C. E. Marshall, "The Birth of the Mestizo in New Spain," *The Hispanic American Historical Review*, XIX (1939), p. 173; Pedro de Cieza de León, *La crónica del Perú* (Buenos Aires: 1945), p. 145.

Indians paid their tribute in slaves, men or women. Slavery already existed among many Indian tribes on different cultural levels. The Indians also occasionally sold female slaves to the Spaniards. This traffic was prohibited by the New Laws.[15]

However the Spaniard and the Portuguese of the early sixteenth century had obtained them, by force, purchase, or gift, he lived surrounded by Indian women. Sometimes they were his slaves or the kind of serfs called *naborías* in the Caribbean and *yanaconas* in Peru; sometimes they were, theoretically, free servants. This way of life often produced the impression of a real harem, though some accounts of contemporary observers seem exaggerated, perhaps because they were shocked or too enthusiastic. We should not take as a statistically verified fact the report that in Paraguay, called the Paradise of Mohammed, every Spaniard had an average of twenty to thirty women.[16]

The Church, of course, by no means approved of this situation, but it was certainly not easy to do anything about it. The Bishop of Santo Domingo wrote to the Emperor in 1529 that when his Spanish parishioners were living in sin the concubines were their own Indian servants "and nothing can be found out about it." Furthermore, the results of such unions were often born in faraway places. As another report from Santo Domingo during the same period put it: "there are a great many mestizos here, sons of Spaniards and Indian women who are usually born in *estancias* [ranches] and uninhabited places."[17] The civil authorities during the Conquest were often satisfied with having the Indian women baptized prior to coition. Thus, the commander of an expedition in Cartagena in 1538 was instructed that he should see to it that "no soldier slept with any Indian who was not a Christian."[18] The conquistadores themselves seem to have taken the reproaches for being promiscuous very lightly, whether they were aware of fulfilling a "civilizing" mission or not. Accused by the Inquisition of a great many blasphemous utterances, the old conquistador Fran-

---

[15]*Recopilación de Leyes de los Rienos de las Indias* (Madrid: 1680), VI-I-6. See also Díaz del Castillo, Vol. II, p. 387–388.

[16]As does, e.g., Salas, p. 189ff.

[17]Quoted by Konetzke, *Revista de Indias*, VII (Madrid: 1946), p. 22–23; for Brazil, see Manoel da Nóbrega, *Cartas do Brasil e mais excritos . . . com introdução e notas históricas e críticas de S. Leite* (Coimbra: 1955), *passim*.

[18]Guitérrez de Pineda, vol. I, p. 183; the same custom reported from Brazil by Nóbrega, pp. 30–31.

cisco de Aguirre, governor of Tucumán, confessed among other things to having declared that "the service rendered to God in producing mestizos is greater than the sin committed by the same act."[19]

Concubines and Intermarriage

There can be no doubt that casual intercourse and concubinage accounted for most of the crossing during the conquest.[20] And polygamy was more than frequent. But it should not be forgotten that marriage also brought about race mixture. Intermarriage was explicitly permitted by the monarch in 1501. Two years later Governor Ovando of Santo Domingo was instructed to see to it that "some Christians [i.e., Spaniards] marry some Indian women and some Christian women marry some Indian men, so that both parties can communicate and teach each other and the Indians become men and women of reason." We shall discuss this decree in its legal context later. Here, we are interested in how such a policy was received in the American environment. The colonial authorities were far from enthusiastic about it, but there were always some churchmen around who put pressure on them to permit or even promote intermarriage. Spanish-Indian couples living in concubinage should be persuaded to marry. According to a chronicler, Governor Ovando ordered the Spaniards in Santo Domingo either to marry their Indian partners or to part company: "In order not to lose their authority over the Indian women and their services they married them."[21] But even with such methods rather little was achieved. A census taken in Santo Domingo in 1514 revealed that only 171 of the 689 Spaniards living there were married. The wives of 107 were Spanish (5 of them having been left behind in Spain), and only 64 were natives. Those married to Indian women usually belonged to the lower social stratum.[22] The

---

[19]J. T. Medina (ed.), *Colección de documentos inéditos para la historia de Chile*, 2nd series (Santiago: 1959), p. 85.

[20]The assertion of J. M. Ots Capdequí, *El estado español en las Indias*, 3rd ed. (Buenos Aires: 1957), p. 80, that most Spanish-Indian concubinages ended in marriage, seems to be completely groundless.

[21]*Colección de documentos para la formación social de Hispanoamérica, 1493–1810* (Madrid: 1953–62), vol. I, pp. 12–13; Konetzke, *Revista de Indias*, VII (Madrid: 1946), pp. 215–216.

[22]*Ibid.*, p. 218.

policy of the Crown also vacillated a great deal with regard to intermarriage. By its order, numbers of white female slaves were sent to the Indies. The royal decree of 1514 explained that the very lack of women there was such that it had caused some Spaniards to marry Indian women, "people far from possessing reason."[23] And many Spaniards preferred to marry a white prostitute rather than a native woman. This is why Cervantes called the Americas the "great lure of licentious women."[24] As soon as Spanish women were available, the Spaniards were likely to reject their Indian spouses or favorites. This also happened to "princesses," such as the mother of Inca Garcilaso de la Vega. The famous writer himself sadly states: "In Peru there have been few who have married in order to legitimize their natural offspring enabling them to inherit."[25]

It seems fair to draw two conclusions on the basis of what we know about race mixture during the conquest. In the first place, the color of the sexual partner was of no importance, as well stated by Juan de Carvajal, a conquistador of Venezuela. When accused of promiscuity he flatly replied: "No one in these parts who has a homestead can live without women, Spanish or Indian."[26] Second, it is obvious that the Spaniards preferred to marry Spanish women, above all, probably because of their desire to provide their descendants with a good lineage.

To the Indian women, association with the conquistadores offered many advantages, even though they were not allowed to marry. But many seem to have become aware of their inferiority to their white rivals. Chronicler Gonzalo Fernández de Oviedo tells a pathetic story of how Indian girls tried to bleach their skin. The Indian women could hope that the children they had with the whites would be accepted as free "Spaniards."[27]

In the beginning, such expectations seemed to be fulfilled. As a rule, the first generation of mestizos was accepted as "Spaniards." This is easy to understand for mestizos born in marriage, but, as

---

[23]*Ibid.*, p. 235.

[24]Miguel de Cervantes Saavedra, *Obras completas*, A. Valbuena Prat, ed. (Madrid: 1949), p. 902.

[25]Inca Garcilaso de la Vega, *Comentarios Reales de los Incas* (Buenos Aires: 1959), I: 2, ch. I.

[26]Juan Friede, *Los Welser en la conquista de Venezuela* (Caracas: 1961), p. 405.

[27]Quoted by Salas, p. 57.

we have pointed out, these were not at all frequent. On the other hand, during this early period many mestizos were recognized by their fathers. The process of legitimization seems to have been frequently used at this time both in Spain and Portugal.[28] A very tolerant attitude, indeed, was that of a certain Diego de Ocaña in sixteenth-century New Spain. In his will he confesses that the Indian servant Antonica had been his mistress. Since she also lived with an Indian, however, he did not know for sure who was the father of her child, even if the color made it likely that it was Diego. Be this as it may, he found he had better recognize the child and ask his legitimate children to instruct him and to take good care of him.[29] In another will, that of Domingo Martínez de Irala, a famed conquistador of Paraguay, the list of children sired with seven Indian women comprises three boys and six girls. Whereas six of the mothers were servants of Irala himself, the seventh was "the servant of Diego de Villalpando." Irala had married his daughters to other conquistadores, providing them with the best possible dowry, he declares.[30]

The Early Mestizos

Mestizos of this accepted and well-treated category must, as a rule, have felt strong solidarity with the paternal group. In the beginning, mestizo sons were even able to inherit the grant of an *encomienda* from their Spanish fathers.[31] And the first generation of mestizos took an active part in the last stages of the conquest. In the River Plate region it was Juan de Garay and his fellow mestizos from Asunción who founded Santa Fé and, finally, Buenos Aires in 1580. In Chile the mestizos were active in the struggles against the Araucanos. In an interesting letter from the Governor of Chile to the King in 1585, the former acknowledges receipt of a royal decree restricting the rights of the mestizos. Barely able to suppress his anger, the Governor refers to the fact there are 150 mestizos in the army, most of them sons of the conquistadores. Without them Chile would have been lost, he exclaims: "I should

---

[28]Gutiérrez de Pineda, vol. I, pp. 160–161.

[29]Herbert I. Priestly, *The Coming of the White Man, 1492–1848* (New York: 1929), pp. 111–112.

[30]R. De Lafuente Machain, *El gobernador Domingo Martínez de Irala* (Buenos Aires: 1939), pp. 560–561.

[31]Ots Capdequí, pp. 125–126.

pray to God that there were as many good people among those sent to us from Spain as there are among those Mestizos."[32] In Brazil, it is well known that two shipwrecked Portuguese, "Caramurú" and João Ramalho, with their numerous progeny, helped Governor Tomé de Souza to found the settlements of Baía and São Vicente respectively. The Governor wrote to the King that Ramalho had so many children that he did not dare to put down the number. "Caramurú," for his part, is said to have had at least sixty. However savage and primitive were these Brazilian mestizos (*mamelucos*, as they were called), the future explorers of the inland, they obviously remained loyal to the cause of their fathers.[33]

But there were exceptions from the general solidarity of the early mestizos with the paternal group. Some mestizos of the first generation chose to stay with the maternal group or, later in life, came to join it. Most of the "Spanish deserters" who went over the Araucanos in Chile were probably mestizos. But this phenomenon was not confined to mestizos. Quite a few native Spaniards, some of them involved in shipwreck or captivity, also switched sides, and were assimilated with the Indians. As distinguished from "Caramurú" and Ramalho, some could not revive the original loyalty even by direct contact with compatriots later on. Thus we have the pathetic Francisco Martín, a member of an expedition of conquest in Venezuela, who "went native" after almost incredible adventures and hardships. Years later he was found by a group of compatriots and was forced to return to "civilization" with them. He soon fled to join his Indian tribe and family but was fetched away for a second time and exiled to New Granada. Chronicler Fernández de Oviedo says that "his love for the wife and children he had in captivity was such that he lamented and wept for them. The Indian ceremonies and customs were also so deeply ingrained in him that by carelessness he sometimes made use of them among Spaniards."[34] Another interesting story is that of two Spaniards, Jaime Aguilar and Gonzalo Guerrero, who had been taken prisoner in Campeche. When Cortés arrived at Cozumel years later he got to know about them, and forwarded to Aguilar the ransom required to set both of them free. Aguilar,

---

[32]Medina, vol. III, pp. 268–269.

[33]On Ramalho see also Nóbrega, pp. 183–184.

[34]Friede, pp. 198–202; Juan Friede, "La extraordinaria experiencia de Francisco Martín (1531–1533)," *Fundación John Boulton, Boletín Histórico*, no. 7 (Caracas: 1965), pp. 33–46.

who had come to be more than happy, went to Guerrero to break the news. But the latter replied: "Brother Aguilar, I am married and have three children, and they look on me as a *Cacique* here, and a captain in time of war. Go, and God's blessing be with you. But my face is tattooed and my ears are pierced. What would the Spaniards say if they saw me like this? And look how handsome these children of mine are . . ." And Guerrero's wife angrily added, storyteller Bernal Díaz says: "Why has this slave come here to call my husband away? Go off with you, and let us have no more of your talk."[35] As an example of acculturation and assimilation, Aguilar was the "misfit," the man incapable of assimilation, whereas Guerrero had been successful in assimilating. In fact, the poor sailor had climbed the social ladder, becoming chieftain and captain of war.

To return to the mestizos of the first generation, we have seen that, obviously, most were absorbed by the paternal group, whereas others joined the Indians. Certainly there were also those who led a marginal existence between the two groups without being accepted by either. But this phenomenon was to occur on a large scale only later on. It is a simple sociological fact that persons of mixed origin tend to be absorbed by either parental group when they are few in number. When they are numerous, though, they are likely to form a group of their own.[36]

The Negro and Early Race Mixture

The conquest witnessed the beginning of an extensive process of crossing between Caucasoid and Amerindian. Ever since the early years of the sixteenth century, the Negroid element was present, too, though small in numbers.

The first Negroes who appeared in the Indies were Hispanicized ladinos, who accompanied their masters as slaves or free servants all the way from Spain. Practically all the conquistador leaders and higher functionaries were able to obtain licenses to bring some slaves with them. Many slaves took an active part in the conquest; some obtained their freedom in that way.[37] There

---

[35]Díaz del Castillo, vol. I, p. 98.

[36]UNESCO (1956), p. 315.

[37]Rolando Mellafe, *La esclavitud en Hispanoamérica* (Buenos Aires: 1964), pp. 22–27; Gonzalo Aguirre Beltrán, *La población negra de México, 1519–1810: Estudio etnohistórico* (Mexico: 1946), chaps. XI-XIV.

were also some female Negro slaves around. We know, for instance, that Diego de Almagro Senior set his Negro slave Margarita free. Years later this lady endowed a *capellanía* or pious foundation in 1553 in order to honor and perpetuate the name of the Almagros and that of "other gentlemen and friends of mine who accompainied my master during the expedition that we made to the provinces of Chile."[38] In the open society of the conquest, it seems that similar spectacular social ascents among the Negroes took place now and then. Many Negro slaves were placed as foremen, *calpisques,* by the *encomenderos* in the villages of their Indians. The Negroes were urged to find an outlet in racial mixture by the same basic factor that was instrumental among the Europeans: the lack of due proportion between the sexes. Perhaps there were as many as three times as many men as there were women among the Negroes brought to the Indies; the ratio may have been even more unequal. At the same time, the slave status often was a severe handicap in their pursuit of sexual satisfaction. The vigorous efforts that they had to make thus earned the Negroes a reputation for being "boundlessly voluptuous." Logically, their partners were usually Indian women. In fact, it seems as if many Indian women preferred them to their own husbands.[39] Leaving aside possible sexual or psychological factors, this may also have a social explanation. Despite their legal slave status the Negroes, by being associated with the Spanish conquerors, automatically came to occupy a position superior to that of the vanquished Indians. There can be no doubt that the Afro–Indian unions during this period almost always took place outside wedlock being usually of a casual character.

Demographic Disaster

We can be rather sure that the relatively small groups of Europeans and Africans who arrived in the Indies during the first half of the sixteenth century carried on miscegenation as extensively as was feasible, and the opportunities were certainly present. Since most of the offspring joined their fathers and the other Europeans, this dynamic biological activity also opened the way for acculturation and assimilation into the Western civilization.

[38]Mellafe, p. 45.

[39]See, e.g., a letter from the Viceroy of New Spain to the King in 1574, Medina, p. 299.

But the advance of the mestizaje during the conquest would have been much less conspicuous if the Indian masses had remained as numerous as they evidently were prior to contact with the Europeans. . . .

Race and Regeneration*

David T. Leary

During the first half of the nineteenth century, along with motifs such as concern for moral rectitude, enthusiasm for popular rule, belief in work, and the like, the United States' ethos included superabundant confidence in the country's future. An observant Scot named Alexander Mackay, who toured North America in 1846 and 1847, remarked on the trait when he wrote:

> Many of what some regard as the more inflated peculiarities of the American character, may be attributed to the faith which Americans cherish in the destiny of their country. Whatever may be its future social and political influence, they have no doubt that, as regards territorial extension, it will yet embrace the continent. The issues which such a consummation involves are enough to make a people feel proud of their country.[1]

Although there was doubtless some merit in Mackay's concern for "territorial expansion," the careful student must pause at his minimizing of "social and political influence," because it appears there was a close link between geographic expansion and the sway of missionary zeal. Yankee extension surely had a territorial element, but in point of fact it had an ameliorative one as well. The fifteen writers [who are subjects] of this study gave themselves up to a good deal of racial thought. And if they are good evidence,

---

* Based on David T. Leary, "The Attitudes of Certain United States Citizens Toward Mexico, 1821–1846" (Ph.D. dissertation, University of Southern California, 1970). Copyright © 1970 by David T. Leary.

[1] Alex Mackay, *The Western World*, 3 vols. (London: 1849), 3: 335–336.

there was a distinct belief afoot not only that the Anglo-Saxon was really a superior race, but also that the Anglo-Saxon peoples had a kind of regenerative function to perform in Mexico—if not elsewhere.

Racial Thought

There were about a million Caucasians in Mexico, Waddy Thompson estimated in 1846, mainly in the cities and on the great estates.[2] And while race imposed no political distinctions, there was an "aristocracy of color." Thompson said that "the pure Castillian [sic] is quite as proud that he is a man without 'a cross,' as was old Leather-stocking, even if that cross should have been with the Indian race however remote." Moreover, he asserted, "At one of those large assemblies at the President's palace, it is very rare to see a lady whose color indicates any impurity of blood. The same remark is, to a great extent, true of the gentlemen, but there are a good many exceptions."[3]

There were, Thompson believed, between 4 and 4.5 million Indians in Mexico.[4] Although smaller in stature, they were physically very like those of the United States. But, Thompson averred, they lacked pride of bearing. "In a word," he declared, "I am by no means sure that in exchanging the peculiar civilization which existed in the time of Montezuma for that which the Spaniards gave them, that they have improved the condition of the masses; they have lost little of the former but its virtues, and acquired little of the latter but its vices." Still, he said that "in travelling the country it would be safe to wager that forty-nine of every fifty persons you might meet would be Indian."[5]

Thompson estimated between 1.5 million and 2 million Mexicans were of mixed ancestry—a great many of whom were mestizos—people of Spanish and Indian blood.[6] Interestingly, however, Thompson found a reluctance on the part of the Indians to mingle with the Spaniards. "Although everything admonishes them that the European is the superior race," he said, "they are generally averse to alliance with them, and whenever such are formed, they are

---

[2]Waddy Thompson, *Recollections of Mexico* (New York: 1846), pp. 187–188.

[3]*Ibid.*, pp. 6, 166.

[4]*Ibid.*, p. 187.

[5]*Ibid.*, pp. 166, 188.

[6]*Ibid.*, pp. 187–188.

prompted more by interest than inclination." Thompson considered the history of Spanish oppression fostered this reluctance. There were fewer mulattos and *zambos*—the latter being people of Indian and Negro ancestry—but whatever the number, Thompson seemingly despised their Negro blood. "I have never looked upon any colour so horribly revolting as that of the Zambo," he said.[7]

Thompson indicated Negroes were few but stated:

> The negro, in Mexico, as everywhere else, is looked upon as belonging to a class a little lower than the lowest – the same lazy, filthy, and vicious creatures that they inevitably become where they are not held in bondage. Bondage or barbarism seems to be their destiny – a destiny from which the Ethiopian race has furnished no exception in any country for a period of time long enough to constitute an epoch.

Thompson went on to declare, "This may be called prejudice, but it is a prejudice which exists wherever the Caucasian race is found; and nowhere is it stronger than in Mexico."[8]

Albert Gilliam, too, commented on the subject of race. Said he:

> The Mexicans are a motley race, reflecting a complexion in proportion with their mixture with the European blood, and exhibiting, as it were, numberless hues in the same crowd. At the city of Mexico, I beheld every imaginable colour of skin that human beings possess, excepting that of the African; for of this latter race I met with none, as negroes are hardly ever to be seen at any distance from the coasts; and also, from an early antipathy of the Mexicans to the black man, but few had ever been imported into that country.[9]

In certain respects this account was quite similar to Waddy Thompson's.

Yet Gilliam offered his own view. He declared that "there is no blood so pure in Mexico, but what is in some degree mixed with the native aboriginal Indian." More significantly, however, he stated, "I have been taught to believe that a mingling of the European with

---

[7] *Ibid.*, pp. 187–189.

[8] *Ibid.*, pp. 5–6.

[9] Albert M. Gilliam, *Travels over the Table Lands and Cordilleras of Mexico in 1843 and 1844* (Philadelphia: 1846), p. 158.

the Indian blood in North America, and particularly in my own state of Virginia, was a good cross of the human species."[10]

Brantz Mayer, too, delivered several comments on race. About the Indians he said,

> Notwithstanding the brilliant pages which Aztec history contributed to the annals of America and the civilization which prevailed, not only in the valley of Mexico, but also in other portions of the territory now within the limits of the republic, we find that the indigenous descendants of these heroic and intelligent ancestors have degenerated to such a degree that they are at present, in general, fitted only for the servile toils to which they are commonly and habitually devoted.[11]

As for the historic association of the two great elements of the Mexican population, Mayer stated, "The Spaniard and Indian lived together in a spirit of lordly dominion on the one hand, and of crushed dependence on the other, whilst the Castilian derived from the native nothing but his habits of savage life, and the Indian, in turn, learned nothing from the Castilian but his vices."[12] Mayer, nevertheless, was perceptive enough to observe that the Indians possessed talents and that, had the Spaniards but cultivated them, the nation would have been different.[13]

Mayer discussed racial fusion, but his scheme of classification—confusing status with race—was so odd as to render it unsatisfactory. Among the "mixed breeds" he put "1st, the educated and respectable Mexicans dwelling in towns, villages or on estates; 2d, the Leperos; and 3d, the Rancheros." He disparaged the *lépero* and praised the *ranchero*.[14] Yet by precise definition—irrespective of race—*léperos* were any kind of wretched folk and *rancheros* small farmers.

Mayer had scant sympathy for the Negro. He went once or twice to some carnival amusements but said that "I had quite enough of

---

[10]*Ibid.*, pp. 35, 156.

[11]Brantz Mayer, *Mexico; Aztec, Spanish and Republican*, 2 vols. (Hartford, Conn.: 1852), 2: 29.

[12]Brantz Mayer, *History of the War between Mexico and the United States* (New York: 1848), p. 9.

[13]Brantz Mayer, *Mexico, As It Was and As It Is* (New York: 1844), pp. 197-198.

[14]Mayer, *Mexico; Aztec, Spanish and Republican*, 2: 22, 26–29.

them, when, on venturing once to stand up in a quadrille with some unknown fair one, I found an unmasked *negro* (the leader of one of the orchestras in the city) take the place of my *vis-à-vis with a white woman!* I plead guilty to a prejudice against such exhibitions!"[15]

John Lloyd Stephens' racial attitudes were perhaps a bit inconsistent. At one point he declared, "The accounts of the Indians were never reliable. When they gave us reason to expect much we found but little, and, on the other hand, when we expected but little a great field presented itself." Only shortly thereafter, nonetheless, he reported meeting an Indian landowner whose Indian workers were of fine appearance and discipline. Said Stephens, "This produced on my mind a strong impression that, indolent, ignorant, and debased as the race is under the dominion of strangers, the Indian even now is not incapable of fulfilling the obligation of a higher station than that in which his destiny has placed him."[16]

Stephens' attitude toward racial fusion was equally ambivalent. He declared the *toreros* at a bullfight in Yucatan were the worst looking men he had seen in the country or anywhere else. "They were of mixed blood," he stated, "which makes, perhaps, the worst race known, vis., the cross of the Indian and African, and called Pardos." Yet after the *corrida,* Stephens attended a ball for which the ladies had discarded mestiza dress in favor of European. This disappointed Stephens. "It wanted the piquancy of the báyle de las Mestizas; the young ladies were not so pretty in their more fashionable costume."[17]

Anthony Ganilh, also, seemed to have a complex attitude—in his case about the status of the Negro. At one point in *Ambrosio de Letinez,* the quadroon Flambeau found Ambrosio moping over his love for Miss Quinton. Flambeau urged Ambrosio to unburden his heart, saying, "If we were in a country where the line of demarcation between your race and mine is rigorously drawn, I would abstain from urging my petition, but a perfect equality prevails here, and you have been so kind to me, that I cannot

---

[15]Mayer, *Mexico, As It Was and As It Is,* p. 149.

[16]John Lloyd Stephens, *Incidents of Travel in Yucatan,* 2 vols. (New York: 1843), 2: 49, 69–70.

[17]*Ibid.,* 2: 109–110, 112.

suppose you lack confidence in my probity."[18] On the other hand, Ambrosio had earlier exclaimed to a Texan:

> And how does it happen that so moral and chaste a people as your Anglo-saxon [*sic*] race, have so many mulattoes among them? You may travel the whole extent of Mexico, without meeting with half the number of individuals of mongrel breed, though marriages between the different castas, among us, are neither prohibited by law, nor stigmatised by public opinion.[19]

One suspects Ganilh approved equality for the Negro without sanctioning racial fusion, although the possibility exists that certain characters of the novel did not voice the author's personal opinions.

Thomas Jefferson Farnham was pronouncedly negative about two elements of California's citizenry. He said:

> That part of the population which by courtesy are called white, are the descendants of the free settlers from Mexico and the soldiers of the garrisons and Missions, who were permitted by his most Catholic Majesty to take wives. Their complexion is a light clear bronze; not white, as they themselves quite erroneously imagine; and, withal, not a very seemly color; not remarkably pure in any way; a lazy color; and for that reason rather out of place, associated as it is, with large dark flashing eyes, a finely chiselled Roman nose, and teeth as clear and sound as pearl.[20]

Evidently Farnham believed the Caucasians of California were really often of mixed descent. But in any case, when he spoke directly about the mestizos, he had little good to say. "The half-breed," he declared, "as might be expected, exhibits much of the Indian character; the dull suspicious countenance, the small twinkling piercing eye, the laziness and filth of a free brute, using freedom as the mere means of animal enjoyment." And, he went on, "The intelligence of these mestizos, as they are called, is quite limited; and what little they do possess, is of very doubtful utility."[21]

---

[18]Anthony Ganilh, *Ambrosio de Letinez, or The First Texian Novel*, 2 vols. (New York: 1842), 2: 82–83.

[19]*Ibid.*, 2: 27.

[20]Thomas Jefferson Farnham, *Travels in the Californias* (New York: 1844), p. 358.

[21]*Ibid.*, p. 356.

Lieutenant Wilkes had something to add on the subject of race relations in California. He described how one of the Mexican governors supposedly trained a company of Indian soldiery to such proficiency that, becoming fearful of their competence he directed they all be shot. Wilkes opined the substance of the story might be true because the Mexicans valued Indians scarcely more than cattle. "The commandant-general is frequently said to hunt them," declared Wilkes, "and by his prowess in these expeditions he had gained some reputation."[22]

Josiah Gregg noticed that the complexions of the New Mexicans were often dark. "Their darkness has resulted," he said, "partly from their original Moorish blood, but more from intermarriages with the aborigines. An occasional Indian, and sometimes an entire village, have abandoned their wonted seclusion, and become identified with their conquerors."[23] And, he continued, "The present race of New Mexicans has thus become an amalgam, averaging about equal parts of the European and aboriginal blood." The mix of races apparently did not trouble Gregg too much, however, because he declared, "The females, although many of them are about as broad-featured as the veriest Indian, not unfrequently possess striking traits of beauty."[24]

Nonetheless, Gregg experienced a sense of uneasiness over the status of the Negro. "There are no negroes in New Mexico," he said at one point, "and consequently neither mulattoes nor *zambos*."[25] Even so, he met a free Negro from the United States at Durango—George, by name. Leaving Gregg unnoticed, a custom-house officer's wife showed considerable deference to "Señor Don Jorge." Gregg asserted that "the popularity of negroes in Northern Mexico has ceased to be a matter of surprise to the traveller."[26] He was, custom notwithstanding, clearly disturbed by the episode.

Anglo-Saxon Supremacism

Informing the thought of several of the Yankee writers in their discussions of race was the spirit of Anglo-Saxon supremacism.

---

[22]Charles Wilkes, *Narrative of the United States Exploring Expedition*, 5 vols. (Philadelphia: 1844), 5: 197–198.

[23]Josiah Gregg, *Commerce of the Prairies*, 2 vols. (New York: 1844), 1: 217.

[24]*Ibid.*, 2: 218.

[25]*Ibid.*, 1: 149.

[26]*Ibid.*, 2: 90–91.

Joel Poinsett, in the 1820's, hinted at what was to come. He admitted there were qualities of solidity and grandeur of appearance in Mexico. But he felt impelled to continue that in the United States "a stranger does not see that striking and disgusting contrast between the magnificence of the wealthy and the squalid penury of the poor, which constantly meets his view in Mexico."[27] If Poinsett's remarks were not so explicit as those of others, they opened the way.

Thomas Jefferson Farnham was much more direct. Telling of Juan Bautista Alvarado's revolution against California Governor Nicolás Gutiérrez in 1836—a successful coup in which certain foreigners participated—Farnham said, "Since the 'Revolution' of '36 the Californian Spaniards had been convinced that the Americans and Britons were vastly their superiors in courage, and skill in war."[28] Farnham had special praise for Isaac Graham, a Yankee mountain man who had taken a prominent part in the events of 1836. Farnham called Graham "a stout, sturdy backwoodsman, of a stamp which exists only on the frontiers of the American States —men with the blood of the ancient Normans and Saxons in their veins—with hearts as large as their bodies can hold, beating nothing but kindness till injustice shows its fangs, and then, lion-like, striking for vengeance."[29] The record does not bear out Farnham's generous estimate of Graham's character, but in this case the total attitude is the important thing.

Amos Parker exhibited Anglo-Saxon supremacism of a sort in an account of relations between Yankees, Mexicans, and Indians in Texas. "In hunting parties composed of both Americans and Spaniards," he said, "when attacked by the Indians in their excursions along the Rocky Mountains, they [the Indians] have been known to spare the Americans, when they have killed all the Spaniards." According to Parker, at least, there was a reason for this: "They consider the Spaniards lawful game; but do not care about fighting the Americans. They say, the Americans are a brave people, and fight most desperately; and from them, they obtain their chief supplies."[30] The Indians might certainly have stood off from the Yankees because it was simply good business to do so, although

[27]Joel R. Poinsett, *Notes on Mexico* (Philadelphia: 1824), p. 48.

[28]Farnham, *Travels*, p. 67.

[29]*Ibid.*, p. 61.

[30]Amos A. Parker, *Trip to the West and Texas* (Concord, N.H.: 1835), p. 133, 156.

it seems clear Parker did not believe this the primary consideration.

James Ohio Pattie entertained similar supremacist notions about the Mexicans. While he and his companions were at Santa Fe, he said, word came that Comanche Indians had attacked certain outlying estates—robbing, kidnapping, and murdering. The Yankees joined the Mexicans in seeking to bring the marauders to justice; the Mexicans, however, allegedly fled at the crucial moment. But, said Pattie, he and his friends stood their ground and managed to rout the Indians. The Mexicans returned to the fray only when the enemy was retreating—and even then, Pattie claimed, did not approach enough to risk danger.[31]

Pattie's account of another incident exhibited similar supremacist thinking. According to the story, on the way to Mexico City, Pattie met an officer and ten soldiers. One of the officer's remarks drew the Yankee's ire. And Pattie told the Mexican that "if himself and his men did not conduct themselves properly when they were among the Americans, the latter would soon despatch them to another country, which they had not yet seen; as the Americans were not Mexican, to stand at the corner of a home, and hide their guns behind the side of it, while they looked another way, and pulled the trigger."[32] Although little more came of the exchange, one must note Pattie's presumption of cowardice in the Mexican, of bravery in the Yankee.

Mary Austin Holley, too, was convinced of Yankee superiority. She called the Mexicans of Texas "very ignorant and degraded, and generally speaking, timid and irresolute." Still, she reassured her readers, "The great majority of the population of Texas, and the most valuable portion of it, consists of emigrants from the United States."[33]

Anthony Ganilh's *Ambrosio de Letinez* fairly abounded with the concept of Anglo-Saxon supremacism. The general drift of the thought became clear in the description of the Battle of San Jacinto. Said Ganilh,

> The foolhardiness of Santa Anna, who, after having seen one thousand of his soldiers killed at the taking of the Alamo, by

---

[31]James Ohio Pattie, *The Personal Narrative of James Ohio Pattie* (Cincinnati: 1833), p. 44–48.

[32]*Ibid.*, pp. 240–241.

[33]Mary Austin Holley, *Texas* (Lexington, Ky.: 1836), pp. 128–129.

a garrison of two hundred backwoodsmen, still persisted in the notion that the Texians were inferior in bravery and intelligence to the peasantry of his own country, prompted him to rush headlong with his vanguard, into the very snare prepared for him; and the fatal twenty-first of April taught him the difference between the two races.[34]

Ganilh stated he would not expatiate on "the more advanced state of civilization enjoyed by the Anglo-Americans...." Nonetheless, he indulged himself a bit, remarking, "Mexico is behind hand by, at least, three centuries, in politics, religion and civil economy."[35] And in exclamation he called the Texans, "A people of twenty five [sic] thousand souls, at most, resisting one of eight millions, and, by means of that coolness and indomitable spirit of freedom, inseparable from the genius of English civilization, making their resistance good!"[36]

Ambrosio, the central figure in the novel, garnered praise for his ancestry—albeit indirectly. In describing the hero's relations with the military, and particularly with General Urrea, Ganilh said that "his gallant bearing, together with his intelligence, so far superior to that of his brother officers, had rendered him a special favorite with the general, who frequently honored him with his conversation." And when it came to command, Ambrosio disobeyed orders so as to pursue "civilized warfare."[37] The point of significance here is that Ambrosio was half-Yankee, and by implication the source of all the gallantry, intelligence, and civilization was the Anglo-Saxon side of his ancestry!

By the same token, Ganilh's description of Yankee women carried in it an element of Anglo-Saxon supremacism. Conversing with Ambrosio, a brother officer exclaimed, "It must be confessed that those women of the northern people are handsomer than ours, and somewhat better bred. What complexions! what features!" The officer, however, went on to say that "they are no better than animals, you know, being unbaptized! A Christian cannot possibly think of such creatures, as long as they remain obstinate." Ambrosio took the man for a "block head"—but, it was clear, only because of the religious objections.[38]

---

[34]Ganilh, *Ambrosio de Letinez*, 2: 9.

[35]*Ibid.*, 2: 30–31.

[36]*Ibid.*, 2: 23.

[37]*Ibid.*, 1: 116, 118.

[38]*Ibid.*, 1: 139.

Ganilh even got round to the conduct of the Comanches. Enemies of the Mexicans, he averred, these Indians were on a better basis with the North Americans. It was thus that the Comanches did not harm Ambrosio and his friend Flambeau, whom they took to be "Texian" spies.[39]

Regeneration

Together with Anglo-Saxon supremacism, there was in the Yankee writing a belief that Mexico needed improvement. Not all the writers called for regeneration through the aegis of the supposedly superior people of the United States, but enough did to make the concept truly worth mentioning.

Albert Gilliam was one who spoke to the subject of regeneration. The typical Mexican, he asserted, "believes that his people are the most learned and pious in the world; hence his prejudice to foreigners, and opposition to improvement." But, he said,

> I am persuaded in the opinion, that if the present race of Mexicans were taught a just abhorrence of fraud and crime, so that a committal of such deeds could be reached and punished by the laws of the country; and if they were instructed to dread the anger of heaven for such acts of wickedness, his mildness of disposition, and native sincerity of manners, would make him one of the most amiable of the human species.[40]

Certainly Gilliam's words must have fired missionary zeal in some of his North American readers.

On the other hand, although he wanted to see the United States expand in the Southwest, Gilliam did not yield to the cry for "all Mexico." He thought the land south of the Californias and the Rio Grande too dry for agriculture and hence unsuitable for the North American or European. "It is necessary, for those races to live happily," he said, "that the land should be cultivated; and that there should be water-power and fuel for the uses of machinery, and these are not to be found in Mexico, south of the boundaries above spoken of." Moreover, Gilliam offered, mining would prove morally deleterious, and the Mexicans would resist Yankee traditions of religious freedom.[41] In sum, Gilliam wanted none of the

[39]*Ibid.*, 2: 66, 70.

[40]Gilliam, *Travels*, pp. 157–158.

[41]*Ibid.*, p. 360.

southern Mexicans unless they became "Americanized." Other
Yankees, however, were not so reserved!

Brantz Mayer was occupied, for instance, with thoughts about
the improvement of Mexico. He said that the Mexicans "want but
peace and the stimulus of foreign emulation, to bring them forward among the nations of the earth with great distinction."[42]
The "emulation" would presumably occur through immigration.
What was necessary, he stated, was "the infusion of a new and
energetic blood into the system."[43] He did not specify Anglo-Saxon
immigration, but given the remarks of other writers, one suspects
this was on his mind.

Waddy Thompson clearly coupled the themes of race and regeneration. "That the Indian race of Mexico must recede before
us," he said, "is quite as certain as that that is the destiny of our
own Indians, who in a military point of view, if in no other, are
superior to them." Indeed, as he viewed it, the best people in
Mexico looked forward to the event. Said he, "The feeling is becoming a pretty general one amongst the enlightened and patriotic,
that they are not prepared for free institutions, and are incapable
themselves of maintaining them."[44]

Thompson, however, had even a grander design for the United
States; he pictured nothing short of the total occupation of North
America. "That our language and laws are destined to pervade
this continent," he declared, "I regard as more certain than any
other event which is in the future." In this respect his thinking
was rooted in pure Anglo-Saxon supremacism. "Our race," he
argued, "has never yet put its foot upon a soil which it has not
only not kept but has advanced. I mean not our English ancestors only, but that great Teuton race from which we have both
descended."[45]

But there was an economic element mixed — however subtly —
with Thompson's racialism. He thought Yankee occupation would
multiply Mexico's mineral production at least five times. About
this matter he said, "Recent manifestations of a rabid, I will not
say a rapacious, spirit, of acquisition of more territory on the part
of our countrymen may well cause a race so inferior in all the

---

[42]Mayer, *Mexico, As It Was and As It Is*, p. 295.

[43]*Ibid.*, p. 353.

[44]Thompson, *Recollections*, p. 239.

[45]*Ibid.*

elements of power and greatness to tremble for the tenure by which they hold this El Dorado."[46] Then, too, Thompson was aware Mexico did not raise enough cotton to supply even its own manufacturers. "If the country was occupied by a population from this country equal to that of Mexico," he remarked, "the amount of cotton produced in the world would be doubled."[47] But more than this, Thompson sensed Mexico's potential for agriculture. If a Yankee population dwelt in the Valley of Mexico, he said that "there is not a foot of it that would not be cultivated like a garden, and nowhere would the care and industry of the farmer meet a richer reward."[48] In short, while Thompson may have thought in terms of political stability resulting from Yankee penetration, the prospect of economic gain did not by any means escape him.

Thomas Jefferson Farnham was equally the disciple of Anglo-Saxon mission. Said he, "No one acquainted with the indolent, mixed race of California, will ever believe that they will populate, much less, for any length of time, govern the country." And he continued, "The old Saxon blood must stride the continent, must command all its northern shores, and must here press the grape and the olive, here eat the orange and fig, and in their own unaided might, erect the altar of civil and religious freedom on the plains of the Californias."[49]

So much for the destiny of California. But what of central Mexico? On this score Farnham stated:

> As the Indian and other inferior orders of the human family have ever given place to the Caucasian branch; so must, as a general law, all mixtures of that branch with these, fade before the greater intelligence of its pure blood — so certainly as the stars do before the sun. How interesting then does the fate of Mexicans become; and their country — the theatre of coming acts and scenes of untold influence over man — how important for Americans to know it well.[50]

Farnham's admonition to know Mexico could scarcely have been lost on readers sympathetic to Yankee expansionism.

---

[46]*Ibid.*, p. 204.

[47]*Ibid.*, p. 209–210.

[48]*Ibid.*, p. 34.

[49]Farnham, *Travels*, p. 413.

[50]Thomas Jefferson Farnham, *Mexico: Its Geography—Its People—And Its Institutions* (New York: 1846), p. 3.

Charles Wilkes also linked regeneration and race — but the result, as he saw it, was not what one might have expected. He argued Upper California would eventually join with Oregon and perhaps become a distinct nation, vitally important in the Pacific world. He said that "this western coast, enjoying a climate in many respects superior to any other in the Pacific, possessed as it must be by the Anglo-Norman race, and having none to enter into rivalry with it but the indolent inhabitants of warm climates, is evidently destined to fill a large space in the world's future history."[51] This was of course the theme of the "Pacific Republic" — dating at least from Jefferson. And while the concept was indeed plausible enough, Wilkes was unique among the fifteen writers of this study in discussing it.

Richard Henry Dana betrayed a bit of racial and regenerative thought in *Two Years before the Mast*. California, in his mind, was a near-paradise of boundless resources. Still, it wanted a vigorous population. "In the hands of an enterprising people, what a country this might be!" he exclaimed. And it was clear from the context that he thought the "enterprising people" would be Yankee or British. He had misgivings on this count, however, for he believed life in California sapped even these supposedly stalwart folk. The parents might be energetic and industrious enough; the children, nonetheless, lapsed into sloth.[52]

For all the fact that Alfred Robinson was quite sympathetic to Mexican life, he, too, entertained the notion that California would be better with different rule. He fairly glowed when he pictured the result of United States' annexation: "Every thing would improve; population would increase; consumption would be greater, and industry would follow."[53]

Mary Austin Holley certainly combined the twin concepts of improvement and Anglo-Saxon supremacy. She said of the Mexicans living in Texas, "They are held in great contempt by the American settlers, who assert that five Indians will chase twenty Mexicans, but five Anglo-Americans will chase twenty Indians." She declared as well, "The moral education of this people must be improved, before their political condition can be ameliorated."

---

[51]Wilkes, *Narrative*, 5:171–172.

[52]Richard Henry Dana, *Two Years before the Mast* (New York: 1840), pp. 215–216.

[53]Alfred Robinson, *Life in California* (New York: 1846), p. 226.

Who would undertake the endeavor? Her position was clear: "The active and enterprising New Englander — the bold and hardy western hunter — the high spirited southern planter — meet here upon common ground, divested of all sectional influence, to lend their combined energies to the improvement of this infant but delightful and prosperous country."[54]

Still and all, more than the regeneration of Texas lay in Mrs. Holley's mind. "Texas once emancipated," she asserted, "its moral influence will not stop short of the Pacific. She *must* be emancipated. What can resist the moral impetus already given? What stop the progress of the anglo-Saxon [sic] race?"[55] Although she did not phrase it clearly, she no doubt meant the process of regeneration through Anglo-Saxon influence was to progress to the Pacific. Indeed, one might suppose Mrs. Holley did not limit the effort to a purely western direction.

Anthony Ganilh's *Ambrosio de Letinez* clearly embodied the concept of Anglo-Saxon regeneration. Yankee society had established itself in Texas, winning its great victory at the Battle of San Jacinto. "In less than an hour," said Ganilh, "a country larger than France and Italy was lost to the Mexican republic, and an opening made for the Anglo-American race, to the immense mineral wealth of Chihuahua and Sonora, the far greater part of which is yet unexplored." This remark smacked of economic motive, but the book set forth the element of moral improvement, too. "The southern races must be renovated," a Texan declared, "and a new vigor infused into them, and the United States are the *officina gentium* for the New Continent."[56]

---

[54]Holley, *Texas*, pp. 128–129.

[55]*Ibid.*, p. 293.

[56]Ganilh, *Ambrosio de Letinez*, 2: 11, 26.

Chapter Two

The Hispanic and the American Southwest

Most students of the Southwest and California—the Spanish Border-lands described by Professor Herbert E. Bolton—have at least a basic knowledge of the Spanish and Mexican people of this vast area during the Hispanic Period of 1539–1848. These students are well acquainted with the Spanish expeditions of Francisco Vásquez de Coronado, Juan de Oñate, Alonso de León, and Gaspar de Portolá. Furthermore they are usually well grounded in the Hispanic development—missionary, military, and civil—of New Mexico, Arizona, Texas, and California. They possess a knowledge of the achievements of the Spanish pioneers, the chaotic Mexican rule, and the American acquisitorial designs. Yet they neither know, nor can they obtain, any substantial history of the Mexican-American for the century that followed United States acquisition of the Borderlands.

While one can somewhat rationalize the historians' omission in treating the 1848–1900 Mexican-American, there is no excuse for not studying the post-1900 immigrant. After 1900 Mexican immigration began in earnest and almost flooded the Southwest. It was from this immigration that the great majority of today's Mexican-Americans is descended. Since this immigration, as well as the life of the immigrants, has been studied by scholars of other disciplines, there is no satis-factory reason that explains why United States historians, especially those in Western America, have tended to ignore the role of the Mexican-American in the Southwest during the period beginning in 1900 and ending with the Great Depression. Those few works which have been written are generally accessible only to scholars. It is to fill this lack of historical treatment that the following two publications were selected for reprinting here.

In the first piece Carey McWilliams, a distinguished editor and lawyer and a true humanitarian, traces the history of the Mexican and the Mexican-American during this period in a most adequate and sympathetic manner. In the second Raymond A. Mulligan, a historian, describes an incident of Anglo-American prejudice and Mexican-American suffering. It is hoped that the reader may come to understand better, both intellectually and emotionally, the conditions under which the Mexican-American lived during the pre-Depression days in the Southwest and in other areas of the United States.

The Borderlands Are Invaded*

Carey McWilliams

Captain Luis de Velasco, who accompanied [Juan] de Oñate on the *entrada* of 1598, had a most remarkable wardrobe. It consisted, according to Bolton, of one suit of blue Italian velvet trimmed with wide gold passementerie, with green silk stockings, blue garters, and points of gold lace; a suit of rose satin; one of straw-colored satin; another of purple Castilian cloth; another of chestnut-colored cloth; a sixth, and daintier, suit of Chinese flowered silk; two doublets of Castilian dressed kid and one of royal lion skin gold-trimmed; two linen shirts; six linen handkerchiefs; fourteen pairs of Rouen linen breeches; forty pairs of boots, shoes, and gaiters; a raincoat; three hats including one of purple taffeta trimmed with blue, purple, and yellow feathers and a band of gold and silver passementerie. His equipment naturally matched the splendor of his wardrobe: four saddles; three suits of armor, three suits of horse-armor, a silver-handled lance with gold and purple tassels, a sword and gilded dagger, a broadsword, two

---

*From Carey McWilliams, *North From Mexico: The Spanish-Speaking People of the United States* (Philadelphia and New York: J. B. Lippincott Company, 1948). Reprinted with permission of the author.

shields; a bedstead, two mattresses, numerous sheets, pillows, and pillowcases; a bevy of servants; thirty horses and mules, and a silken banner. Indeed, the first Spaniards to invade the borderlands did so with plumes waving, banners flying, and armor gleaming.

But when Spanish-speaking people re-invaded the borderlands three hundred years later, their leaders were landless peons who forded across the Rio Grande in the dead of night. Their wardrobe — indeed their wordly possessions — consisted of the clothes they wore. No taffeta-trimmed hats for them; no blue, purple, and yellow feathers; no gold and silver ornaments; no mattresses, sheets, and pillowcases. For these latter-day conquistadores were Mexican *cholos* [half-breeds] who came to chop brush, to build railroads, to work in copper mines, and to pick cotton in lands which De Oñate and Juan Bautista de Anza had mapped and charted, explored and colonized. The first *entrada* was made up of Spanish hidalgos and caballeros; the second of Mexican peons. The first invaders came in search of gold and silver; the second in search of bread and a job. What the second invasion lacked in color, splendor, and majesty, was more than offset by the capacity of the peons for hard work and endurance.

Those colorful murals that one can see nowadays throughout the Southwest in which figures like Captain Luis de Velasco are depicted in all their finery might well be balanced by a few murals showing Mexican migratory workers sweating in desert cement plants, in the copper mines of Morenci, the smelters of El Paso, and the great farm-factories of the San Joaquin Valley. Captain de Velasco and his colleagues may have discovered the borderlands but Spanish-speaking immigrants from Mexico have built the economic empire which exists in the Southwest today.

No one knows precisely how many Mexican immigrants came to the United States in the period from 1900 to 1930 but it is generally agreed that the number was in excess of a million. Prior to 1900 there had been a trickle of Mexican immigration to the borderlands: Texas had an immigrant population of 71,062 in 1900; Arizona, 14,172; California, 8,096; New Mexico, 6,649. The bulk of these earlier immigrants, of course, were concentrated in the Southwest; and, of the post-1900 immigrants, nine-tenths settled in the borderlands. At first the immigration was largely restricted to Texas, for the use of Oriental labor, particularly the Chinese, barred the way to Mexican immigration in California until about 1917. The rapid increase of Mexican immigrants in the border states after 1900, however, can be seen in the following table:

	1900	1910	1920	1930
Arizona	14,171	29,987	61,580	114,173
California	8,086	33,694	88,881	368,013
New Mexico	6,649	11,918	20,272	59,340
Texas	71,062	125,016	251,827	683,681

Three facts should be noted about the great wave of Mexican immigration which brought to the Southwest after 1900 nearly ten percent of the total population of Mexico: it was overwhelmingly concentrated in the old Spanish borderlands; in point of time it coincided with the birth of the Southwest as an economic empire; and, in each instance, Mexican immigrants labored in the building of industries in which there had been an earlier Spanish–Mexican cultural contribution. The industries in which Mexicans were concentrated, moreover, were those vital to the economic development of the Southwest. In all essentials, therefore, the story of the invasion of the borderlands can be told in terms of railroads, cotton, sugar beets, and truck or produce farming.

Spanish Trails, American Rails

The Spanish introduction of the horse, mule, burro, and ox to America marked the longest stride that so many people, in so short a time, have ever taken in the arts of transportation.
— CHARLES FLETCHER LUMMIS

The terrain of the Southwest is rugged, mountainous and semi-desert; waterholes are few and far between; and great reaches have remained wholly uninhabited for centuries. To establish a system of transportation in such a region was infinitely more difficult than to build a flatboat at Pittsburgh and float down the Ohio and the Mississippi to New Orleans. Spain is also a country of elevated mountain ranges, of narrow, winding defiles, of rocky trails, and stretches of torrid plain. From the eighth century, when the Spaniards had acquired the *aparejo* or packsaddle from the Moors, mules and burros had been used as transport. Washington Irving records that in 1486 [Queen] Isabella organized, equipped and maintained pack-trains consisting of fourteen thousand mules and burros which were used to supply an army of fifty thousand in the conquest of Granada. This efficient system of transport the

Spanish brought to the Americas, where, for three hundred years, the pack-train was the lifeline of their colonies.

The trails that later became rail lines and highways in the Southwest were first discovered, charted, and travelled by Spaniards and Mexicans. The historic trail that De Anza blazed from Tubac to San Gabriel might well be regarded as the initial survey for the present-day Southern Pacific line. Long before the rail lines were built, the Spaniards and Mexicans had organized an elaborate system of pack-trains which operated over the endless trails blazed by the conquistadores. In the early days, "King's Wagons"— the famous *Carros del Rey* — made the long journey from Mexico City to Santa Fe, from Santa Fe to Veracruz, carting merchandise, supplies, and silver from the mines. Crisscrossing the deserts and mountain ranges, these pack-trains were the principal means of transportation as late as the 1880's, transporting merchandise to the towns, supplying the army posts, carrying the mail. The tinkling of the pack-train bell was heard throughout the West until the whistle of the locomotive began to echo in the mountain passes and canyons.

Mule and burro transport, so well adapted to desert conditions, was a Spanish invention and Southwestern pioneers were in complete agreement that no one could handle burros or mules as skilfully as Mexicans. For efficient service, pack-trains had to be thoroughly organized. The form of organization and the type of equipment were well established when Columbus discovered America. A typical pack-train consisted of the packmaster or *patrón;* the head loader or *cargador;* a blacksmith; a cook; and eight or ten packers or *arrieros.* The duties of each man in the pack-train were defined by custom in the most precise detail. Operating from Tucson to San Diego, from Santa Fe to El Paso, from Tucson to Guaymas, pack-trains constituted an extremely efficient and economical mode of transportation for the time and place.

Santiago Hubbel, a famous pack-master of New Mexico, freighted heavy mining equipment overland from Lavaca, Texas, to the Heintzelman mine in Arizona — a distance of 1,200 miles — and his pack-trains carried ore to the Missouri River in rawhide bags. Freight rates ranged from thirty to seventy cents per ton per mile and the mules, carrying an average load of 250 pounds, often made thirty miles a day. It was not uncommon for desert pack-trains to travel three hundred miles in four days and, in 1881, a pack-train, loaded two hundred pounds to the pack mule, travelled eighty-five miles in twelve hours. Pack-trains carried supplies to mining camps throughout the West and New Mexico *arrieros* made their appearance as far north as the Salmon and Frazer rivers.

The operation of these pack-trains was based on the most elaborate and intricate lore. In Spain the pack mules had housings, similar to those of the cavalry, of rich cloth embroidered with gold; halters brocaded with silk; and bridles, headpieces, and harnesses that glittered with silver. The *arrieros* of the Southwest kept this great tradition alive. In odd moments they decorated their equipment with figures of animals and birds, insignia and legend, woven with silken threads of various colors. A pack saddle, stock and all, often cost $100 and was beautifully stamped and engraved by hand, trimmed with Mexican silver dollars, cut and chased in various designs; while the bridles were inlaid with silver and gold. The *arrieros* dressed like their grandfathers in Spain: with high-heeled top boots and tiny spurs, silken *banda* or sash wrapped around the waist two or three times, embroidered shirt front, and conical sombrero with a silver snake around the crown, the underside of the brim being trimmed with silver braid.

"Such was the holiday costume of the packer of thirty-five or forty years ago," wrote H. W. Daly in 1910, "when, mounted on his favorite mule, he would sing some Spanish ditty when visiting friends in some nearby hamlet; a man who never turned his back on a foe or forsook a friend in moments of peril, honest and honorable in all his dealings with his fellow men, kind to animals in his care, with a love for his calling and thoroughly imbued with an 'esprit de corps' for the pack service." "I cannot recall," wrote Charles Fletcher Lummis, "hearing of any *arriero* that ever robbed his employer."

Used by General Crook in the sixties in campaigns against the Shoshones in Nevada, pack-trains played an important part in his later campaigns against the Apaches in the Southwest; in fact, some historians believe they were the decisive factor. Among the famous muleteers who operated these supply trains for the army were such names as Chileno John, José de Leon, and Lauriano Gómez. Later the army used this same pack-train system in the Spanish-American War, both in Cuba and in the Philippines, and it became a standardized unit in army transport. Just how intricately organized and delicately articulated the whole system was can be seen by reference to a manual of pack transportation which the army issued in 1910. The technique of roping packsaddles, for example, was highly intricate and the most elaborate lore existed about hitches, knots, and splices. Prepared by Chief Packer H. W. Daly, the manual points out that the whole system, in its every detail, was taken over from the Mexicans intact, including its vocabulary.

The load was, of course, the cargo, from the Spanish *cargar*, to load. The pack-train was the *atajo;* the pack-cushion, or saddle, the *aparejo;* the sweat-cloth, the *suadera;* the crupper, the *grupera;* the saddle cloth, the *corona;* the cover for the harness was the *sobre-en-jalma* or *sobre-jalma;* the bell, the *cencerro;* the canteen, the *gerafe;* the saddlebags, the *alforjas;* the bell-mare, the *acémila;* the eye-blind, the *tapaojo;* the currycomb, the *almo-haza.* Much of the vocabulary of the pack-train was Arabic in origin; but its organization was Andalusian.

Estevan Ochoa, whose family had come from Spain to Mexico in the days of Cortez, was born in the cathedral city of Chihuahua in 1831. As a young man, he had journeyed to Independence, Missouri, where he lived for a time, learning the English langauge. Returning to the Southwest in 1859, by way of the Santa Fe Trail, he established a chain of stores and a well-organized pack-train system that supplied them. When troops of the Confederacy under Captain Hunter seized Tucson during the Civil War, Ochoa was given the alternative of taking an oath of allegiance to the Confederacy or of leaving Tucson. He answered this ultimatum by climbing on his horse and riding out alone through the Apache territory to Mesilla. A partner in the famous early-day freighting firm of Tully and Ochoa, his pack-trains freighted throughout the Southwest and deep into Mexican territory. As a pioneer resident of Tucson, he led the fight that finally resulted in the establishment of the first public school system in the territory.

Member of the territorial legislature and mayor of Tucson, Estevan Ochoa was perhaps the first citizen of Tucson in the 1870's. At his beautiful home in Tucson, scores of friends annually assembled from points as distant as El Paso and Guaymas for the ten-day celebration of the festival of Saint Augustine. When the railroad finally reached Tucson on March 25, 1880, Don Estevan Ochoa presented Charles Crocker with the silver spike used in the dedication ceremonies. As a pioneer freighter in the Southwest, Don Estevan was, in effect, presenting his competitor with a spike to be driven into his own coffin. For the coming of the railroads spelled the end of the pack-trains and proved to be the undoing of Ochoa, who died, a few years later, a ruined man.

Life in a Boxcar

Mexican labor was extensively used in the construction of the Southern Pacific and Santa Fe lines in the Southwest in the eighties, particularly on the desert sections built by the Southern Pacific. From that day to this, Mexicans have repaired and maintained Western rail lines. As watchmen of the rails, section hands must live near their work, while the extra crews literally live on the rails in boxcars which are shunted about the divisions. "Their abode," as one railroad executive tersely phrased it, "is where these cars are placed." Hundreds of Mexican families have spent their entire sojourn in the United States bouncing around the Southwest in boxcar homes.

Since 1880 Mexicans have made up seventy percent of the section crews and ninety percent of the extra gangs on the principal western lines which regularly employ between 35,000 and 50,000 workmen in these categories. In 1930 the Santa Fe reported that it was then employing 14,000 Mexicans; the Rock Island, 3,000; the Great Northern, 1,500; and the Southern Pacific, 10,000. According to the census of 1930, 70,799 Mexicans were engaged in "transportation and communication" mostly as common laborers on the western lines and as maintenance workers on the streetcar systems of the Southwest. In Kansas and Nebraska, Mexican settlements will be found to extend along the rail lines while the colonies of Kansas City and Chicago are outgrowths of Mexican railroad labor camps. As late as 1928 the boxcar labor camps of the railroads housed 469 Mexican men, 155 women, and 372 children in Chicago.

The principal large-scale importers of Mexican labor, the rail lines of the Southwest constantly fed workers to other industries since so much railroad labor is seasonal in character. Forever losing labor, the railroads kept recruiting additional workers in Mexico. This process was greatly accelerated as increased freight and passenger traffic paralleled the economic development of the region. Railroad employment naturally stimulated migration, since the companies provided transportation to various points along the line. Just how important the railroads were in setting the tide of Mexican immigration in motion can be seen from a statement made by an investigator for the Department of Labor in 1912. Most of the Mexicans then in the United States, he said, had at one time or another worked for the railroads. For years the prevailing wage for section hands in the Southwest was a dollar a day — considerably below the rate paid for similar labor on the middle western and eastern lines.

Recruited by labor agents and commissary companies, Mexicans were assembled in El Paso and from there sent out on six-month work contracts with the Southern Pacific and Santa Fe. In 1908 some sixteen thousand Mexicans were recruited in El Paso for railroad employment. Two years later as many as two thousand Mexicans crossed the border into El Paso in a single month at the instigation of the commissary companies. Starting around 1900, railroad recruitment reached its peak in 1910 and 1912. Originally recruited by the Southwestern lines, Mexicans were used after 1905 in an ever-widening arc which gradually extended through Colorado, Wyoming, Utah, Montana, Idaho, Oregon, and Washington.

As early as 1900 the Southern Pacific was regularly employing 4,500 Mexicans on its lines in California. By 1906 the Southern Pacific and the Santa Fe were importing as many as two and three carloads of *cholos* a week to Southern California. The rapid extension of the Pacific Electric interurban system in Southern California also greatly stimulated the demand for Mexican labor. Wherever a railroad labor camp was established, a Mexican *colonia* exists today. For example, the Mexican settlement in Watts — called *Tajauta* by the Mexicans — dates from the importation of a carload of *cholos* in 1906. While the lines were being built, the *cholos* lived in boxcars and tents. Later the company built row-houses on its property and rented these houses to the employees. Thirty or forty such camps are still to be found in Los Angeles County. Around the initial camp site, Mexicans began to buy lots at $1 down and $1 a week and to build the shacks in which their children live today.

In the sparsely settled semi-arid Southwest, the construction of the rail lines was well in advance of actual settlement. Elsewhere in the West and Middle West, settlers had promoted railroads; but here railroads promoted settlement. The first great land "boom" in Los Angeles, for example, was strictly a railroad promotion. In the economic development of the region, railroads have played an all-important role. Prior to the completion of the Southern Pacific and Santa Fe lines in the eighties, the Southwest was hardly a part of the United States. In every state in the region, the modern phase in its development dates from the arrival of the first passenger or freight train. Largely built by Mexican labor along routes first explored and mapped by Spanish-speaking people, the railroads of the Southwest have been maintained by Mexicans from 1880 to the present time. All the products of the region — copper, cotton, lettuce, produce, wool, beef, and dairy products — move to markets on desert lines dotted at regular intervals by small, isolated clusters of Mexican section-crew shacks lost in time and space.

Cotton in Texas

As early as the 1890's, Mexican labor from both sides of the Rio Grande was following the cotton harvest on foot into the old cotton-producing sections of east Texas. East Texas was then devoted to cotton; south and west Texas to cattle. Since the Negroes were concentrated in the eastern section, Mexicans remained a secondary source of labor. But from 1890 to 1910 the cattle industry began to retreat before the forces of King Cotton, first in middle Texas and later (1910–1930) in west Texas. In these areas the plantation system had never been firmly established and large land units and inflated land values demanded a more "efficient" type of labor at lower costs. This was achieved largely through an increasing use of mechanized methods and the substitution of transient Mexican labor for Negro and "poor white" sharecroppers and tenants. Writing in *Current History* for February, 1930, Remsen Crawford observed that "in the unirrigated plains regions of Texas and Oklahoma millions of acres formerly used as ranges for cattle and sheep and goats are being cultivated in cotton, mainly for non-resident landlords, by Mexican tenants, or hired workers, living in miserable shacks. . . . New cotton gin plants have sprung up everywhere. Old towns have greatly increased in size, and new ones have been built. The bulk of the work of making and gathering this cotton is done by Mexicans imported from over the border."

With the coming of cotton, middle and west Texas were inundated with hordes of people who, in the words of one observer, "planted cotton, talked cotton, thought cotton, sold cotton, everything but ate cotton." It so happened that the expansion of cotton in these new areas coincided with the first rumblings of the social revolution which began in Mexico in 1910. Thus as cotton pushed its way into the Southwest, Mexicans from across the border came to meet it. "It was in Southwest Texas," writes Dr. Edward Everett Davis, "that fourteenth century feudalism met the southern plantation" and from this meeting came the large-scale cotton farming of Texas based on the use of migratory Mexican labor. As early as 1908, writes Dr. Davis, the Mexican invasion "had driven itself like a wedge into the heart of Texas beyond San Antonio, veering to the south of the Balcones Escarpment and the ranch country, and sticking close to the cotton fields of Comal, Hays, and Caldwell counties."[1] Coming through the ports of Laredo, Eagle Pass, and Brownsville, the Mexicans had concentrated at San Antonio, and that city, "like the small end of a funnel, poured them out into the cotton fields with such speed that by 1920, the greatest density of rural Mexican population in Texas was not along the Río Grande but in Caldwell County in sight of the dome of the State Capitol."

In the story of Keglar Hill, Dr. Robert H. Montgomery has given a graphic account of what happened in one Texas community when this invasion began. Keglar Hill had moved from cattle to cotton in one generation. As cotton supplanted cattle, the first Mexicans began to arrive in 1887 and 1888. At first they returned to their homes across the Rio Grande after the cotton harvest. But each year a few stayed over at the end of the season and, as the number increased, they gradually began to displace the white tenants, not as tenants, however, but as day laborers. The white tenants were the first to leave, around 1900, but were soon followed to the towns by their former landlords. Since the Mexicans did not speak English and were not in the habit of sending their children to school, the rural schools vanished with the white tenants and landlords. Of some three hundred-odd white settlers who had made up this small rural community in 1895, writes Dr. Montgomery, not one remained on the land by 1910.[2]

Obviously it was the joint appearance of cotton *and* Mexicans that brought about this disintegration of rural life. But the white tenants and sharecroppers, resenting the new dispensation, tended to blame Mexican labor for the transition, whereas the Mexicans were as much victims of the transformation as the tenants they displaced. "Before the incoming hosts of Mexicans," writes Dr. Davis,

three rural institutions — the home, the church, and the school — fell like a trio of staggering tenpins at the end of a bowling

---

[1] Edward Everett Davis, *The White Scourge* (New York: 1940).
[2] *Survey-Graphic* (May 1, 1931).

race. White tenants could not compete with cheap Mexican labor. Prosperous owners moved to town, leaving the menial work for Mexicans to do. Rural dwellings, orchards, and yard fences went to wreck; deserted country churches made excellent hay barns and tool sheds for absentee landlords; and the large rural schools packed with happy white children dwindled into sickly institutions for a few indifferent Mexican muchachos, as a wilderness of rag-weeds and cockleburs grew on the school grounds. . . . The Mexican did not hit the interior cotton lands with the impact of a hurricane, but seeped in silently and undermined the rural social structures like termites eating out the sills of a wooden house.

Needless to say, I quote this passage for its revealing explanation of the basis of much anti-Mexican sentiment in Texas rather than to describe the transformation that took place. Actually new modes of production and new social forces had "undermined the rural social structures" of Texas; the appearance of the Mexicans was a symptom, not a cause, of this process. Mexicans did not "seep" into Texas: they were recruited for employment. To charge them with responsibility for the disappearance of rural schools and churches, while exonerating their employers, was certainly to give a vulgar and misleading interpretation to a familiar economic process.

By 1940 nearly four hundred thousand workers, two-thirds of whom were Mexicans, were following "the big swing" through the cotton-growing regions of Texas. Starting in the southern part of the state in June, the migratory army sweeps eastward through the coastal counties and then turns west for the later harvest in the central section. It then splits into three units: one moves into east Texas; another proceeds to the Red River country; and a third treks westward to the San Angelo–Lubbock area. Organized in the south, the army gains recruits as it proceeds along the line of march. From the Lower Valley, where the season starts, comes the initial vanguard of about twenty-five thousand Mexican migratory workers. As the army marches through the Robstown–Corpus Christi area, an additional twenty-five thousand recruits join the procession. By the time the army has reached central Texas it has probably grown to two hundred thousand workers. During the Depression, as many as four hundred thousand Mexicans made this great circle, traveling distances of from eighteen hundred to two thousand miles. Over this long and wearisome route, Mexican families travel "like the starlings and the black-birds."

The generals of this tatterdemalion army are the Mexican labor contractors and truckers. About sixty percent of the cotton-picking, in fact, is contracted through these *jefes* or *papacitos*. The contractor, who usually speaks English, knows the routes, deals with the employer, and organizes the expedition. He is really a *capitán* or *jefe* because he happens to own a truck. Paid to transport workers, he is also hired to weigh the cotton, take charge of the commissary, and oversee the work. The trucks are often loaded with fifty or sixty workers as well as quantities of bedding and equipment. Thoroughly mechanized, the cotton-picking army moves on wheels in open or stake trucks. In an accident at McAllen, Texas, in 1940, forty-four Mexicans riding in one of these trucks were injured: twenty-nine were killed and of these, eleven were children under sixteen years of age—a tragedy memorialized in a famous border *corrido*. In depression years the army, of course, is inflated to fantastic proportions. The growers are anxious to have their crops harvested as rapidly as possible and, with the pay on a piecework basis, total labor costs remain the same regardless of size of the crew.

Here is a picture of what happens, and has been happening for years, on this great circle (from a report by Pauline Kibbe to the coordinator of Inter-American Affairs, December 29, 1944):

> On one Saturday afternoon in October, 496 migratory labor trucks were counted on the streets of Lubbock. Lubbock is a city of between 40,000 and 50,000. Each truck carries an average of 15 migrants, of all ages which means an estimated total of 7,440 migrants who had come to Lubbock to spend the weekend, seek new employment, purchase their groceries, and other supplies, find a little recreation, etc. . . . Suppose each of the 496 trucks in Lubbock spent an average of $25.00. . . . That is a total of $12,400.00 income to the business places of all kinds for one weekend. Yet Lubbock had made no provision whatever for taking care of this influx of people which occurs regularly every fall, and every weekend during each fall. There is no place provided where they may park their trucks, take a bath, change their clothes, even go to the toilet. In Lamesa it was stated . . . that toilet facilities in the City Hall, which the migrants could use most conveniently, were locked up at noon on Saturdays, and filling station facilities were used except where the owners prohibited it because of the objections of customers.

Of 117 complaints of discrimination against Mexicans in public places filed with the Texas Good Neighbor Commission in 1944, two-thirds of the total involved mistreatment in towns of less than five thousand population. These towns were scattered over the general area through which the migratory labor movement passes. It would seem to be obvious, therefore, that a degree of correlation exists between migration and discrimination.

Cotton Moves West

With the First World War creating a sharp demand for long-staple cotton, the cotton kingdom jumped from west Texas to the Salt River Valley in Arizona. Agents of the Arizona Cotton Growers Association recruited thousands of workers in Mexico for employment on the large-scale irrigated cotton farms. In most cases, the costs of transportation and of subsistence en route were later deducted from earnings. Up to June 30, 1919, 5,824 Mexicans had been imported into Arizona and 7,269 were specifically recruited for cotton-picking, not including those who came without contracts or special inducements. When the cotton boom exploded after the war, thousands of these workers were stranded in Arizona. In the Salt River Valley alone, ten thousand Mexicans were destitute in the winter of 1921 and the Mexican consul had to seek an appropriation of $17,000 to provide temporary relief. When four thousand imported Mexicans went on strike in the cotton fields in 1920, the growers had their leaders deported and arrested scores of the strikers. At about the same time, the development of irrigated cotton in the Mesilla Valley of New Mexico also began to attract Mexican workers from across the border.[3]

In 1910 the first cotton was planted in the Imperial Valley in California. As the cotton acreage expanded in response to wartime demands, the Imperial Valley growers began to bring in truckloads of Mexicans, in units of fifteen hundred and two thousand, from such communities as San Felipe and Guaymas. After the war, cotton production declined for a time and then soared to new heights as the center of production shifted to the huge farm-factories of the San Joaquin Valley. With 5,500 acres planted in cotton in 1919, the acreage in the San Joaquin increased to 172,400 acres in 1931. As the cotton acreage expanded, more and more Mexicans were imported, with the year 1920 being referred to in

---

[3]*Economic Geography* (January, 1931), 1.

the farm journals as the first "Mexican harvest." From 1924 to 1930, an average of 58,000 Mexicans trekked into the San Joaquin Valley each year, principally for the cotton harvest. In the middle 'twenties, over a hundred trucks loaded with Mexicans were counted crossing the Ridge Route in a single day. The townspeople would provide the Mexicans stranded in the valley towns at the end of the season, from public funds, with just enough gasoline to make the trip back over the Ridge Route to Los Angeles, where welfare and charitable agencies took care of them during the winter months.

Commanding a premium price, with a yield-per-acre nearly twice the national average, cotton soon became a $40 million crop in California. Largely produced on high-priced irrigated lands which had been capitalized on the basis of five decades of cheap labor, the expansion of cotton in California was premised upon the availability of a large supply of low-cost labor exclusively earmarked for the cotton growers. Consistently opposed to Mexican immigration, the labor unions failed to note that the cotton fields of the Imperial and San Joaquin valleys were a major factor in the location of large automobile tire factories in Los Angeles which, in turn, stimulated the demand for industrial labor.

Vitamins and Mexicans

Irrigation equals Mexicans.
— DR. PAUL S. TAYLOR

Twice the size of Germany and larger in area than the thirteen original states, the Southwest had a population in 1902 about half the size of the city of Chicago in the same year. Irrigation was the magic key that unlocked the resources of the region. Irrigated farming is intensive farming: with high yields per acre, heavy labor requirements, year-round production, and crop specialization. Small in area, the "winter gardens" of the Southwest have off-set, by their exceptional productivity, many of the disadvantages of an arid environment. Throughout the region, the distribution of Mexicans in rural areas is largely determined by the location of irrigated crops. As an economic empire, the Southwest dates from the passage of the Reclamation Act in 1902 which outlined a development policy for the arid West and made possible the use of federal funds in the construction of large-scale irrigation and reclamation projects. Irrigation has had more to do with the economic growth of the Southwest than any single factor.

Today a visitor from the North, driving into the Lower Rio Grande Valley in midwinter, would have the illusion, writes Hart Stilwell,

> of moving into a modern version of the Garden of Eden. As he drove along the Valley's "Main Street," a 65 mile highway, he would see stately palms and green citrus-fruit trees laden with golden orange fruit; bougainvillea vines in full bloom; bright green papaya plants. . . . And when he came to the level, rich fields he would see bronze-skinned people by the thousands harvesting vegetables — red beets with their green tops, white and purple turnips with their green tops, golden carrots with their green tops — everything green. He might see other laborers harvesting cabbage, broccoli, endive, peppers, beans, tomatoes, new potatoes, peas, anise, cauliflower or squash.

In the valley today Mexican laborers—forty thousand of them illegal entrants or "wetbacks"—plant, cultivate, and harvest fruit and vegetable crops worth $100 million a year. Virtually none of this development existed in 1904 when the St. Louis, Brownsville, and Mexico Railway finally completed its line to Brownsville.[4] A miraculous transformation, indeed; but just how was it brought about?

"The hand of the Mexican laborer," wrote Dr. Paul S. Taylor in 1927, "is grubbing out the chaparral of south Texas." Before the lands could be levelled, planted, and irrigated, the brush had to be cut away for this was the *brasada* or brush country of Texas. While an occasional tractor was used to pull out small trees, Mexicans grubbed most of the brush by hand with the use of grubbing hoes. "Grubbing brush," the Texans said, "is a Mexican job." And properly so, perhaps, for the Mexican alone knew and understood the brush country. To the Anglo-Americans, writes J. Frank Dobie, the *brasada* vegetation was just "brush," an all-encompassing term; but generations of Mexicans had learned to distinguish, and had named, the endless varieties of shrubs and plants to be found in this section. When these varieties are distinguished today, it is by their Spanish–Mexican names: *mogotes,* or thick patches of evergreen; *coma,* with its dirk-like thorns; the *cejas* or thickets; the wand-like *retama* with its yellow flowers called *lluvia de oro* ("showers of gold"); *grandjero* with its yellow berries; the *agarita*

---

or wild currant; the bitter *amargosa;* the black chaparral or *chaparro prieto;* and the *tasajillo* or rat-tail cactus. Thousands of acres of this densely thicketed brush had to be grubbed out by hand to make way for the fabulously rich "winter garden" that exists today in the Lower Valley.

After 1900 the increasing urbanization of population, the disappearance of the backyard garden, the development of new canning processes, and the introduction of refrigerator cars, brought about an enormous increase in the production of fruits and vegetables on large-scale commercial farms in the irrigated portions of the Southwest. "Citrus fruit output," writes Dr. Harry Schwartz, "jumped more than five fold in the first decades of this century, while grape tonnage increased four times. Between 1919 and 1939 production of fresh market spinach, lettuce, cauliflower, snap beans, and carrots increased five times or more, while celery output tripled. In 1900 most fruits and vegetables were not considered sufficiently important to justify extensive collection of statistics regarding them. By 1940 they contributed more than a billion dollars to cash farm income, roughly 30 percent of the total *from all crops.*[5] (Emphasis added.) It should be emphasized that this increased production represented a net addition to the total American agricultural income.[6]

Virtually all of this phenomenal increase occurred in the Southwest and was made possible by the use of Mexican labor. In the growth of commercial fruit and vegetable production in the Southwest between 1900 and 1940, there is not a single crop in the production and harvesting of which Mexicans have not played a major role. This fabulous increase in production—which set the Southwest on its feet financially—could never have taken place so rapidly without the use of Mexican labor. To grow and harvest an acre of wheat, during the 1930's, required on the average only about 13 man-hours of labor; but an acre of lettuce required 125 man-hours and an acre of strawberries 500 man-hours. Unorganized Mexican labor in inexhaustible quantities made this production possible.[7]

---

[5] Harry Schwartz, *Seasonal Farm Labor in the United States* (1945), p. 29.

[6] *Commercial Survey of the Pacific Southwest* (Washington, D.C.: Department of Commerce, 1930), pp. 224–254.

[7] Lawrence Leslie Walters, "Transient Mexican Agricultural Labor," *Southwest Social and Political Science Quarterly* (June, 1941).

It should be noted that the increased production took place on irrigated acreage within the confines of the old Spanish borderlands. It was here that the Spanish and the Mexicans had first demonstrated the value of irrigation and had developed an understanding of irrigation techniques. Prior to the development of the Southwest, as Ray Stannard Baker pointed out, Anglo-Saxons had never attempted irrigation on a large scale and irrigation "means a complete change of many racial institutions and customs." Thus the contribution of Mexican laborers related back to a much earlier cultural contribution which had been made by the Spanish and Mexican settlers. Reclaimed and irrigated at enormous costs, much of this land was overcapitalized. Overcapitalization, in turn, had created a terrific pressure for cheap labor. But the years during which the Southwest became an economic empire saw a great increase in living standards for the American working class brought about by the use of more efficient machines. It was precisely in the production of truck crops, fruit, cotton, and sugar beets that the least progress had been made in the introduction of machines. Thus the use of Mexican labor fitted into the economic cogs of the Southwest in perfect fashion.[8]

To appreciate what Mexican labor meant to the economy of the Southwest, one simple, obvious fact needs to be stressed, namely, the desert or semi-desert character of the region. In the San Joaquin, Imperial, Salt River, Mesilla, and Lower Rio Grande valleys, temperatures of 100, 110, and 112 degrees are not uncommon. Those who have never visited the copper mines of Morenci in July or the cotton fields of the San Joaquin Valley in September or the cantaloupe fields of Imperial Valley in June are hardly in a position even to imagine what Mexican workers have endured in these areas. It should be remembered that the development of the Southwest occurred at a time when the living and working conditions of American workmen were undergoing rapid improvement. It was not easy to find in these years a large supply of labor that would brave the desert heat and perform the monotonous stoop-labor, hand-labor tasks which the agriculture of the Southwest demanded. Under the circumstances, the use of Mexican labor was largely non-competitive and nearly indispensable.

---

[8]See article by Dr. Max Handman, *American Journal of Sociology* (January, 1930).

Coyotes and Man-Snatchers

Spearheaded by the completion of the rail lines, the westward movement of cotton, the spread of "winter garden" fruit and vegetable production, and the phenomenally rapid economic expansion of the Southwest after 1900 created an enormous demand for unskilled labor. Mexicans poured into Texas by the thousands. "Farming is not a profitable industry" said John Nance Garner the Uvalde millionaire, "and in order to make money you have to have cheap labor." From 70,981 in 1900 the number of Mexicans in Texas shot up to 683,681 in 1930. With enforcement of the contract-labor law being suspended from 1918 to 1921, over 50,000 workers were directly recruited in Mexico for employment in the United States. By the time the border patrol was established in 1924, and administrative restriction adopted as a policy in March, 1929, the great labor pool of Texas had been filled to overflowing with Mexican immigrants. From this reservoir Mexican labor was siphoned off in all directions as the war and the Immigration Act of 1924 drastically reduced the volume of European immigration. The tip of the wave of Mexican immigration reached as far north as Detroit and as far east as Pittsburgh. "Mexicans," said a California grower in 1927, "scatter like clouds. They are all over America." From Texas, Mexicans were recruited, in small numbers, for employment on the plantations in the Mississippi Delta; thousands were recruited for employment in the northern and western sugar-beet fields; and an entire trainload was at one time shipped from Texas to Seattle for employment in the Alaska canneries.

Throughout the borderlands prior to 1924 the contract-labor law of 1885 was more often honored in the breach than in its observance. For a quarter of a century, Texas growers had recruited labor in Mexico whenever they needed it. In large measure this traffic had been made possible by the activities of labor smugglers who developed a lucrative racket in Mexicans. The labor smuggler or "coyote" crossed the border, not only to round up crews, but to get workers across the line in violation of the immigration regulations. For a fee of ten or fifteen dollars, the coyote would arrange to get Mexicans across the line, by having them "jump the fence" at La Colorado; or come across concealed in automobiles, carts, or trucks; or by fording the Rio Grande at night. In many cases, forged passports and head-tax receipts were provided.

Once across the line, the Mexican was turned over by the coyote to a labor contractor (*enganchista*), who sold him for a fee of fifty cents to one dollar a head to some agricultural, railroad, or mining employer. Labor agents operating out of Laredo and El Paso had forwarding agents elsewhere in Texas, notably in San Antonio. Charging the employers a fee for supplying the labor, the contractors charged the workers for transportation and subsistence en route. The profits in this racket were really enormous and the smugglers and coyotes and labor-contractors constituted an intimate and powerful alliance from Calexico to Brownsville.

Another type of agent, the man-snatcher, also figured in this dubious traffic. The man-snatchers made a business of stealing Mexican labor and selling the same crew to several different employers. Delivering a crew to an employer, they would steal the crew at night and resell it to still another employer. In this manner, the same crew would often be sold to four or five employers in the course of a few days. Frequently the man-snatchers raided crews imported by the labor contractors and made off with them by force of arms. Shipments of workers en route to employers were often kept locked up at night in barns, warehouses, and corrals, with armed guards posted to prevent their theft. Crews of imported Mexicans were marched through the streets of San Antonio under armed guard in broad daylight and, in Gonzales County, workers who attempted to breach their contracts were chained to posts and guarded by men with shotguns.[9] "Large planters," wrote James L. Slayden, "welcome the Mexican immigrant as they would welcome fresh arrivals from the Congo, without a thought of the social and political embarrassment to their country."

Los Betabeleros

Mexicans have been identified with the sugar-beet industry since its inception; the phrase "Mexican sugar-beet worker" is as common as "Mexican sheepherder." Prior to the tariff of 1897, the sugar-beet acreage in this country was insignificant; but, by taxing foreign sugar 75 percent of its value, the Dingley Tariff immediately created a great demand for sugar beets. States paid bounties, offered tax exemption, and otherwise encouraged the growing of sugar beets as a matter of official policy. From 135,000

---

[9]See testimony of Emilio Flores before the Industrial Relations Commission, 1915.

acres in 1899, the sugar-beet acreage increased to 376,000 acres in 1906 and, for the last decade, has averaged about 750,000 acres. With each increase in the sugar-beet acreage, of course, the demand for Mexican labor has been stepped up.

The production of a large acreage in sugar beets has consistently required, until the last few years, a large amount of labor, for blocking and thinning in the spring and for harvesting in the fall. To induce labor to stay over in the area, so as to be available for the harvest, the sugar-beet companies have always used the device of contract-labor in which workers, more often families, contract to block, thin, and harvest beets for a stipulated sum per acre. For many years, the major companies included in the contract a hold-back provision to insure that the workers would be present in the fall for the harvest. The growing of sugar beets is unique in that it represents "a curious union of family farms and million dollar corporations." The sugar-beet refineries, rather than the individual farmers, have long assumed responsibility for the recruitment, distribution, and control of the labor supply.

The principal growing areas are to be found in California, Michigan, and Colorado. From the beginning of the industry, Mexican workers were used in California. Elsewhere the sugar-beet companies at first experimented with other types of labor: Japanese in Colorado; the so-called Volga-Germans in Nebraska and other areas; and Belgians and Poles in Michigan. But these non-Mexican groups showed a tendency to aspire to farm ownership and, in some areas, by dint of unbelievably hard effort, succeeded in achieving their goal. It was to curb this tendency that the companies shifted to Mexican labor, particularly after the First World War and the passage of the Immigration Act of 1924. In fact, it was at the insistence of the sugar-beet companies that the contract-labor law was suspended from 1918 to 1920 to permit direct recruitment in Mexico. By 1927 it was estimated that, of 58,000 sugar-beet workers, 30,000 were Mexicans. Today sixty-six percent of the 100,000 workers in the industry are Mexicans. In states such as Ohio, Michigan, Minnesota, and North Dakota, Mexicans constitute from seventy-five to ninety percent of the labor supply.

In Colorado the Great Western Sugar Beet Company began to recruit Mexican labor in 1916, at first from southern Colorado and New Mexico, and, later, from Mexico. In 1920 the company spent $360,000 in the recruitment of Mexican labor. In one year alone, 1921, some ten thousand Mexican workers were imported, most of them from Texas; and, between 1910 and 1930 a total of at least thirty thousand Mexicans were brought to the Colorado sugar-beet areas. Throughout its history, the company has shown a marked preference for the "unspoiled" Mexican, "fresh from Mexico clad in the sombrero, light cotton clothing, and even sandals of the Mexican peon." Even during the Depression years, the company attempted to recruit Mexican labor from outside the state. In an effort to prevent this practice, the Governor of Colorado on April 20, 1936, proclaimed a state of martial law and stationed Colorado National Guardsmen along the Colorado–New Mexico border to turn back Mexican workers from New Mexico.

At the outset, the sugar-beet companies sought to anchor the imported labor in the sugar-beet areas: first, by some feeble efforts at colonization; then by offering a bonus to those families who agreed to waive the payment of transportation back to the point of recruitment; and, more frequently, by simply stalling on final settlement under the contract at the end of the season. The earnings of the Mexican beet workers were, in not a few cases, so low that they were compelled to stay over during the winter months. Thus wherever Mexican labor has been imported for sugar-beet employment, small Mexican colonies have developed. In the South Platt area of Colorado, the number of stay-overs rose in a six-year period from 537 to 2,084. El Paso was the principal place of recruitment for Mexican sugar-beet workers in the Rocky Mountain states, with San Antonio being the center from which they were recruited for the principal middle western areas. Over the years, however, Denver has come to occupy, in relation to the sugar-beet areas in Utah, Wyoming, and Montana, much the same relationship that El Paso and San Antonio occupied at an earlier period. There are today some 14,631 Spanish-speaking residents in Denver.

Needless to say, the Texas growers became extremely annoyed when the agents for the sugar-beet companies began to tap their great reservoir of Mexican labor. Noting that more and more Mexican labor tended to stay over in the sugar-beet areas, the cotton growers took matters into their own hands. Holes were shot in the tires on the trucks of the sugar-beet agents and Mexicans, in any number of cases, were prevented by force from keeping their rendezvous with the sugar-beet agents. In a final effort to stop this out-of-state recruitment, the cotton growers secured the passage of the Texas Emigrant Agent Law of 1929 which, in effect, barred outside agents from recruiting labor in Texas. The principal consequence of this law was to make of out-of-state recruitment a kind of illegal, underground conspiracy. For, despite the law, thousands of Mexicans continued to leave every year for out-of-state employment. For example, it has been estimated that nearly sixty thousand Texas-Mexicans leave the state every year. Originally this movement was organized by the sugar-beet companies through the use of special trains but for the last decade it has been handled by Mexican truckers and contractors.

Most of the trucks are open, stake trucks, never intended for passenger transportation. Planks or benches are placed on the truck, which is then loaded with passengers and equipment. Frequently fifty or sixty Mexicans are huddled like sheep in these trucks. Once the Mexicans have crowded into the back of the truck, a heavy tarpaulin is thrown over them and fastened down around the edges so that the passengers are concealed. The reason for this conspiratorial atmosphere is, of course, that perhaps two-thirds of the Mexicans who leave the state have been recruited in violation of the Emigrant Agent Law. Outwardly the truck looks as though it were loaded with a cargo of potatoes. Before climbing into the driver's seat, the trucker tosses a couple of coffee cans into the back of the truck which are used as urinals during the long journey north. Then, usually around midnight, the truck rolls out of San Antonio and heads north.

With a relief driver in the cab, the truckers drive straight through to Michigan, and other equally remote destinations, stopping only for gas and oil. By driving night and day, they can make the trip in forty-five to fifty hours. Paid ten dollars a head to deliver Mexicans in Michigan, which is ultimately charged up by the sugar-beet companies against earnings, the average trucker can make about three thousand dollars a season. Naturally the truckers are in a hurry; they want to make, if possible, two or three trips. Instead of travelling the main highways, they pursue a crazily zigzag course, making many detours, zooming along country roads and minor highways, in an effort to avoid highway patrolmen. Almost every season since this traffic developed serious accidents have occurred along the line of march.

Wherever sugar beets are grown—in Michigan and Minnesota, in Colorado and Montana—the same pattern can be traced. In the sugar-beet area around Findlay, Ohio—dominated by the Great Lakes Sugar Company—nearly three thousand Mexican workers are imported each year from Texas. Telesforo Mandujano and his six sons made the trip to Ohio from San Antonio in a truck that carried forty Mexican workers. Here is his abbreviated statement before the Tolan Committee: "The truck did stop a few times for bowel evacuations and eating, when the truck needed gas or oil; but on most occasions cans were used as urinals and dumped out of the truck. Passengers had to stand all the way and one man tied himself upright to a stake so he could not fall out if he should happen to fall asleep." After deducting all expenses, Telesforo and his six sons made $200.10 for the season. Catarino Ramirez also made the trip from San Antonio to Findlay —in a truck that carried thirty-seven adults and eight children, making the trip in two days and three nights. "No stops were made unless the truckers were forced to," he testified, "and when such stops were made we ate if we had time."

No aspect of Mexican immigration has been more frequently or more thoroughly investigated than the history of their employment in sugar beets. The documentation is voluminous and covers every aspect of their employment in every sugar-beet area in the United States. It would serve no purpose, here, to attempt a summarization of this data, with its appalling revelation of low earnings, miserable health and housing conditions, child labor, sickness and disease. The data, for those who are interested, is summarized in Part 19 of the Tolan Committee Hearings (the "Detroit Hearings," September 23, 24, 25, 1941). Suffice it to say, that from 1916 to the present time, between thirty thousand and sixty thousand Mexican workers have been directly dependent upon sugarbeet employment with average annual earnings of from five to six hundred dollars *per family*.

In Midwest Industries

Beginning around 1916, Mexican laborers began to appear in the Chicago industrial area, in Gary, Indiana Harbor, and Calumet. Most of these workers were from such states as Jalisco, Michoacan, and Guanajuato, having leap-frogged from the interior of Mexico to the midwest industrial centers, "literally passing through and beyond," writes Dr. Paul S. Taylor, "their compatriots of the Mexican northern border states who have made the shorter migration to the adjacent southwestern United States." Appearing first as track laborers, they were later employed in the steel mills, the packing plants, and the tanneries. From 1920 to 1930 the Mexican population of Chicago increased from 3,854 to 19,362 and is today generally estimated at about 25,000.

The small Mexican colony in Detroit had its beginnings in 1918, when several hundred Mexican workers were brought to work in the automobile industry as student-workers. From eight thousand in 1920, the Mexican colony in Detroit rose to a peak of fifteen thousand in 1928, and then declined during the Depression years, when many workers returned to the Texas communities from which they had been recruited or were repatriated by welfare agencies to Mexico. Today the colony is estimated to number about 6,515 residents. Throughout the Midwest there are similar colonies, usually quite small, in most of the industrial centers, totaling perhaps seventy thousand for the region. In 1923 the National Tube Company, an affiliate of U.S. Steel, brought 1,300 Mexicans from Texas to work in its plant at Lorain, Ohio. And, in the same year, the Bethlehem Steel Company imported about one thousand to work in its plant at Bethlehem, Pennsylvania. When the first trainload arrived from San Antonio, police were on hand to escort the workers to their barracks as the "Mexicans in their broad plain sombreros" marched stoically through the streets.

The movements to import Mexican labor for industrial employment would have reached large proportions after 1923 had it not been for two factors. Both the sugar-beet companies and the southwestern agricultural interests were strenuously opposed to any attempt to establish a pattern of Mexican employment in industry and also feared that, if Mexicans spread into new territory, the agitation for a quota on Mexican immigration would immediately assume serious proportions. Hence the passage of the Texas Emigrant Agent Law in 1929, and the Depression of that year, brought the movement to a halt. The second factor had to do with immigration policy. The first bill aimed at placing Mexican immigration on a quota basis was introduced in 1926 and was supported by a rapidly growing exclusionist sentiment. Largely for diplomatic reasons, the federal government in March, 1929, adopted a policy of "administrative restriction" by simply tightening up the enforcement of existing immigration regulations with the aid and cooperation of the Mexican government. Thus the northbound movement of Mexican immigrants had virtually ceased by 1930; and, in the Depression years, some sixty-five thousand Mexican immigrants were repatriated, some voluntarily, some with the aid of the Mexican government, some being summarily shipped back to Mexico by welfare agencies of this country.

This pattern of events has a twofold bearing on the so-called "Mexican Problem" in this country. It explains, to some extent, the concentration of Mexicans in the old borderlands region; and it also explains why so many immigrants have been involved in cul-

de-sac types of employment. For the doors of middle western industrial employment were closed almost as soon as they were
opened; and, in the Southwest, employment opportunities were
restricted, by custom, by discrimination, and by other factors, to
a few limited types of employment. It is not surprising, therefore,
that the 1930 census should show that of Mexicans gainfully employed, ten years of age or over, 189,005 should have been employed
in agriculture, 150,604 as common laborers.

New York Foundlings at Clifton–Morenci:
Social Justice in Arizona Territory, 1904–1905*

Raymond A. Mulligan

Of all the themes employed by students of the frontier, few
deal with children—and practically none with dependent or or-
phaned children. Buried, however, among the records of children's
aid societies and foundling homes are interesting and dramatic
accounts that point up the role these agencies played in the history of the American West. Particularly revealing of the operations, and the difficulties, involved in the placing of children in
foster homes was the attempt in 1904 by the New York Foundling
Hospital to settle forty of its charges in the Clifton–Morenci area
of Arizona.[1] As it happened, this episode proved to be more than a
simple matter of placing travel-weary foundlings in foster homes.
Before the children were settled satisfactorily, the home-finding
process was interrupted by howling mobs, armed deputies, and
angry lawyers, and by pronouncements of the Territorial Supreme

*In *Arizona and the West: A Quarterly Journal of History* (Summer 1964).

[1]*New York Foundling Hospital* v. *William Norton, in the custody of John C.
Gatti*, in *Reports of Cases Argued and Determined in the Supreme Court of the
Territory of Arizona 1904 to 1906 Inclusive* (San Francisco: Bancroft-Whitney
Company, 1908) 9:105–121. In the court action that developed in this affair,
William Norton, adopted by John C. Gatti of Clifton, was selected as the object
of a test case brought by the Foundling Hospital. This case hereafter will be
cited as *Foundling Hospital* v. *Gatti, Arizona Reports.* For newspaper accounts,
see the *Phoenix Republican* (November 5, 1904; January 13–22, 1905); and

Court. President Theodore Roosevelt, as well as Governor Alexander O. Brodie, became involved in the affair, and for a time it appeared that even the Arizona Rangers would be called into action to restore order and recover the children. The case of the New York foundlings not only illustrates some of the problems that characterized the history of child welfare in the United States, but also offers insights into the workings of formal and informal justice in Arizona at the turn of the century.

The agency that sent the foundlings to Arizona in 1904 was only one of the many such organizations that long had been engaged in locating homes for dependent children. As early as 1852 the New York Children's Aid Society[2] had pioneered the use of the free foster home system. This organization was founded by Charles Brace, who had been greatly moved by the conditions of the children of the poor in New York City, many of whom were growing up in idleness, vice, and crime. At that time, and for many years afterward, thousands of homeless, neglected, and dependent children thronged the streets of the larger Eastern cities, with very few individuals concerned with their plight. It was an age of deadening poverty for the poor, with concomitant high birth, death, and infant mortality rates, sprawling slums, rampant vice, few compulsory school laws, and an almost complete absence of welfare programs of any significance.

Although an advocate for the shelter, religious training, recreation, schooling, and remunerative work for dependent children, Brace felt that the one solution for the homeless child, and even the children of the poor, was the placing of these children in foster homes in rural areas of America. In 1853 he began writing to farmers, mechanics, and manufacturers in rural areas, requesting that they take children into their homes. From responses to this appeal, and to others which followed, he obtained a list of applicants, and was soon making individual placements. In 1854, Brace expanded his operations to include the sending of large groups of

---

Tucson *Citizen* (October 5, 6, 19, November 4, 1904; January 21, 1905). Also see "Babies Sold Like Sheep," *Los Angeles Examiner* (October 6, 1945) ; John D. Lyons, "Foundling Case Was Strange," Tucson *Star* (October 31, 1957) ; W. R. Ridgway, "Clifton Opens Its Homes," *Arizona Days and Ways* (August 21, 1955) ; and James M. Patton, "The History of Clifton" (M.A. thesis, University of Arizona, 1945), pp. 209–213.

[2]Miriam Z. Langsam, *Children West: A History of the Placing-Out System of the New York Children's Aid Society, 1853–1890* (Madison: U. of Wisconsin Press, 1964).

children to one locality—a practice that continued until 1929. From 1853 to 1894 the Society placed more than twenty thousand children, a majority of them being accepted by families living in southern and western states. Indeed, these areas appeared to have offered the most hospitable welcome, as well as the right combination of Christian charity and need for youthful labor.[3]

That the placing-out process did not operate without unforeseen difficulties was vividly borne out in the case of the New York foundlings sent to the mining towns of Clifton and Morenci, Arizona, in the fall of 1904.[4] The Foundling Hospital had learned of the availability of desirable homes in these towns from Father Constant Mandin, who temporarily was in charge of the Clifton–Morenci parish during the absence of Father Peter Timmerman, the resident priest.[5] Father Mandin had only been in the United States ten months, spoke English with difficulty, and being a true Frenchman apparently had all the Gallic obliviousness of his countrymen to racial and ethnic distinctions that were not generally appreciated in Arizona in 1904. He had announced the contents of a circular from the agency to his congregation, and soon had requests for children of both sexes. The priest is alleged to have informed the agency that forty children could be placed in the homes of his congregation, which he represented to be of Spanish background, but who spoke English.[6]

In response to the application, the Foundling Hospital made

---

[3]Charles L. Brace, *The Dangerous Classes of New York*, 3rd ed. (New York: 1880), pp. 84–96. Also see Henry W. Thurston, *The Dependent Child* (Columbia U. Press, 1930). The New York Children's Aid Society was not the only agency that transported dependent children to other states. In fact, the American Female Guardian Society of New York City preceded Brace in this method of placement. Other agencies that used similar techniques, but on a more limited scale, were the New York Juvenile Asylum, the New England Home for Little Wanderers, the New York Orphan Home, and the New York Foundling Hospital.

[4]*Foundling Hospital* v. *Gatti, Arizona Reports*, 9:109. By 1904 this institution was placing an average of 450 children per year in foster homes.

[5]*Ibid.*, pp. 109–110; *Phoenix Republican* (January 13–22, 1905); *Arizona Days and Ways* (August 21, 1955); and Patton, "History of Clifton," p. 209.

[6]*Foundling Hospital* v. *Gatti, Arizona Reports*, 9:109. Tucson *Citizen* (October 5, 1904). After being harried out of Clifton, Father Mandin arrived in Tucson, and was interviewed through an interpreter. He stated: "Some time ago the institution [Foundling Hospital] sent me a circular asking if I knew of any families in my parish that cared to adopt children. I paid no notice to the circular, but a second came, which I read from the altar, both in English and

arrangements to send forty children to Arizona. The children were of "Anglo-Saxon race," and, as requested by the priest, were chosen from among those in the institution who were fairest and lightest in complexion. They were said to have been of unusual beauty and attractiveness, and varied in age from eighteen months to five years. Attached to the clothing of each child was a tag which carried a number, his name and date of birth, and the name of the person to whom he was consigned. In addition, on each child's shirtwaist his name was beautifully embroidered. To the family receiving a child, the Sister Superior sent a letter, instructing the head of the household, within a week after the child arrived, to fill out and return an enclosed blank, giving the name of the child, and the name, occupation, and post office address of the foster parents. The foster parents also were asked to write yearly, about May 1, concerning the child's progress.[7]

Late Saturday evening, October 1, 1904, forty children, accompanied by three members of the Sisters of Charity order, three nurses, and G. Whitney Swayne, agent for the Foundling Hospital, reached Clifton in a special railroad car.[8] At that time, the towns of Clifton and Morenci were not well-ordered communities. For example, the residential district in Morenci was called Helltown, while the business section was composed principally of saloons and dance halls. It was referred to as the toughest town in the Territory. One writer referred to the inhabitants with a few exceptions

---

Spanish. I requested anyone caring to adopt one of these orphan children to send me his or her name. I received some sixty applications, of which thirty-three, after proper investigation, were approved. Among them was one American family. I then wrote to Mr. Swayne, the official agent of the institution, setting forth what I had done. It was well understood that the arrangement for adoption of the children was merely tentative, as nothing could be done officially until the Sisters in charge of the children had personally investigated. . . . I wrote Mr. Swayne that I myself doubted the wisdom of granting these American children to the Mexican families, but stating that he being an American and of much experience in such matters, could decide for himself, as I had not been in country long and of course was not as familiar with manners and customs as he was. He accepted the responsibility and brought forty children, though I had informed him that I had only recommended the adoption of thirty-three."

[7]*Foundling Hospital* v. *Gatti, Arizona Reports*, 9:109–10; *Phoenix Republican* (January 13–22, 1905).

[8]Sister Anna Michella was accompanied by Sister Anna Eloyisa and Sister Louisa Liguori, and Misses Reynolds, Dixon, and Bowen. Tucson *Citizen* (October 5, 1904); *Phoenix Republican* (January 17, 1905); and *Foundling Hospital* v. *Gatti, Arizona Reports* 9:110.

as somewhat less refined than the copper smelters found in the area. During the previous year, 1903, twenty-five of the twenty-six Arizona Rangers then in service had been called to Morenci to keep order during a strike in the mines.[9]

Gathered at the station awaiting the arrival of the train was a crowd of Spanish-speaking and English-speaking residents, together with several Chinese. The news already had circulated that a number of foundlings were to arrive, and would be distributed to "Mexican" families.[10] When Father Mandin came into the special car, he was met by a barrage of questions. Sister Anna Michella immediately inquired as to what sort of people the foster parents were, and he is alleged to have replied that they were all good moral American citizens who had no children of their own. Their homes were all that could be wished for. Noticing that some of the people were not as fair in color as she had hoped for, or expected, the nun is purported to have asked if there were any "half breeds" among them—and he said, "No." The Foundling Hospital, Sister Michella than stated, had a rule that the children always were placed on trial until such time as the homes could be visited by the sisters. If any of the homes were not as expected, the children would be removed. Apparently satisfied by the priest's replies, the hospital representatives began taking the children from the car. When the question of the disposition of the foundlings was raised by persons in the crowd, Swayne stated that there would be no decisions made that night. It was later stated that he even assured one of the women who pressed him on the matter that the following morning she would have an opportunity to make an application for one of the children.[11]

---

[9]Tucson *Star* (October 31, 1957) ; Tom Foust, "Admen Blush: It's Arizona Rangers—Not Texas Ones," *Ibid.* (August 26, 1962).

[10]*Foundling Hospital* v. *Gatti, Arizona Reports,* 9:110. The families may have been partially or wholly Mexican-American, but the reports make no distinction, calling them "Half-breed Mexican Indians" or "Mexicans." *Arizona Days and Ways,* (August 21, 1955).

[11]*Foundling Hospital* v. *Gatti, Arizona Reports,* 9:110. According to Father Mandin, he called out the names of those who had made application for children, and one of the nuns selected the child for each of the applicants. While this was going on, several "American ladies" approached the priest and asked to be given children, but he politely refused their verbal petitions. Father Mandin later explained: "Not having made application previously, as the others had, and not knowing them, I could not in conscience grant them any of the children, nor could the good Sisters in charge." Tucson *Citizen* (October 5, 1905).

That night, however, sixteen children were placed with foster parents in Clifton. As required by the Foundling Hospital, the parents had purchased clothes for the children and had agreed to pay part of their fare from New York. The total expenses varied from $30.00 to $40.00 per child. Because money changed hands during the course of the transfer of the children from hospital authorities to parents that evening, a story became widespread that the children were sold like cattle.[12] The following morning, Sunday, Swayne secured wheeled conveyances and with Father Mandin and the sisters took the remaining twenty-four children to Morenci for distribution among the families there who had agreed to accept them.[13]

At a later date it was claimed that the persons in Clifton and Morenci who received the children were wholly unfit to be entrusted with them. They were said to have been of the lowest class of "half-breed Mexican Indians"—persons who were impecunious, illiterate, unacquainted with the English language, vicious, and in several instances, prostitutes and persons of notorious character. Many had children of their own, whom they were unable properly to support. Sister Michella, who was responsible for carrying out the instructions of the hospital, was said to have been so struck by the unfitness of the foster parents that in three instances she gave them up "with tears streaming from her eyes." Apparently she was not satisfied with the families to whom the foundlings were delivered, but felt that she could not override the authority of the priest.[14]

On Sunday morning, while Swayne and his party were en route to Morenci, the residents of Clifton learned that the children had been placed in Mexican homes. An informal conference of citizens hurriedly was called to discuss the matter, and a committee of two

---

[12]The priest was aware of the rumor, and tried to explain the cause: "I utterly deny the preposterous assertion that was traffic in children.... How this arose was in this way: Some Americans heard a Mexican say, 'Who will give back the $40 I expended on this child?' This is explained by the fact that I insisted on provision being made for the proper clothing of the children, and some of the Mexicans had purchased fully three suits of clothes complete for the child awarded them. When the children were taken away by force they asked who would recompense them for the outlay." Tucson *Citizen* (October 5, 1905). Also see *Arizona Days and Ways* (August 21, 1955); and *Los Angeles Examiner* (October 6, 1945).

[13]*Foundling Hospital* v. *Gatti, Arizona Reports*, 9:110–111.

[14]*Ibid.*, p. 111; Tucson *Citizen* (October 19, 1904).

was appointed to go to Morenci and ascertain from Father Mandin and Swayne their purposes. They also were to be informed of the excitement caused by the children being placed with "half-breed Indian" families. This committee was composed of Jeff Dunagan, a deputy sheriff, and Thomas Simpson.[15] Dunagan and Simpson arrived in Morenci shortly after two o'clock in the afternoon, and went immediately to see Charles E. Mills, the superintendent of the Detroit Copper Company and one of the leading citizens of the town. With him they went in search of Swayne, whom they found at the hotel. Dunagan and Simpson later testified that in response to their inquiries, Swayne said that he knew his business, and did not propose to be dictated to by others. The children "had been placed, and would stay placed." Dunagan telephoned the information to Clifton that they had seen Swayne, and that the agent would do nothing.[16]

Dunagan's report resulted in a second meeting being called that day in Clifton. Hundreds of persons, including women and children, crowded into Liberty Hall, which stood on the present site of the Phelps Dodge store. After several speeches, it was decided that a committee of twenty-five should be chosen to take possession of the foundlings in Clifton, regardless of the objections of the foster parents. This vigilante group, some of whom were armed, acted swiftly and ruthlessly, although it was later stated that the children were "voluntarily" surrendered to the committee. When taken from their foster homes, the children were said to have been in a filthy condition, covered with vermin, and with two or three exceptions, ill and nauseated from the effects of coarse Mexican beans, chiles, watermelons, and other "improper" food which had been fed them. In some instances beer and whiskey had been given them to drink.

By evening the children had been collected at the Clifton Hotel. It was raining, and the crowd had increased and was in an angry mood. There was talk of lynching both the priest and the agent. The women present took charge of the foundlings, and secured medical care and attention for them. An informal selection process then began. A Morenci doctor picked out a child, a Clifton official selected another. When one wide-eyed little girl looked at the wife of the hotel owner and said, "Mama," the woman opened her arms

---

[15]*Foundling Hospital* v. *Gatti, Arizona Reports*, 9:111.

[16]*Ibid.*, pp. 111–112. Swayne's testimony in court qualifies the statements of Dunagan and Simpson as to what he said on that occasion.

and claimed the child as her very own. On the next day, the remaining children were placed with Anglo families in Clifton.[17]

Early Monday morning, October 3, Swayne and Father Mandin reached Clifton with Dunagan and Simpson. They found that more than two hundred citizens had assembled. That evening there was another meeting. There was a great deal of excitement manifested at the gathering, but there was no act of violence. Many persons, however, did crowd around Swayne, hurling threats of a general character—threats such as "Make him leave town!" "Tar and feather him!" and "Hang him!" Only the intervention of deputies John (Hard Times) Parks and Lee Hobbs saved Swayne from violence. Both Swayne and Father Mandin made statements to the group. Apprehensive that he might receive bodily harm, Swayne assured the citizens that the children had been placed only temporarily. The sisters would remain for two or three weeks, and if they found any of the children in improper homes, they would remove them. He protested against the seizing of the children without his consent or that of the sisters. The following day more meetings were held at which both the priest and the agent were present. At the conclusion of the proceedings, the citizens chose to be firm, and not give up the foundlings to the hospital representatives. It was feared that if so returned, the children might be again placed in equally unfit homes of Mexican families elsewhere.

In Morenci the same indignation arose among the Anglo citizens, and much the same course was pursued as in Clifton. Charles E. Mills and others called upon the sisters and upon the agent, remonstrating against permitting twenty-four of the children to remain in Morenci with the people to whom they had been distributed. As a result of these remonstrances, and a strong statement by Mills that the local residents would not suffer the children so to remain, Father Mandin and Swayne visited the Mexicans having the children, obtained a surrender of them, and brought them to the local hotel. These foundlings, with the exception of the three who were turned over at Dunagan's request to certain Morenci residents, were then delivered to the sisters. Sister Michella and Swayne later stated that they would not have left the three children in Morenci except that they believed that the citizens would have refused to release the children to them.[18] Sev-

[17]*Ibid.*, pp. 112–113; *Phoenix Republican* (January 13–22, 1905); and *Arizona Days and Ways* (August 21, 1955).

[18]*Foundling Hospital* v. *Gatti, Arizona Reports*, 9:113; *Phoenix Republican* (January 13–22, 1905); and *Arizona Days and Ways* (August 21, 1955).

eral days later, the nuns, the nurses, and twenty-one of the children boarded the train at Clifton for the East.

On October 18, the sisters arrived in New York City mentally and physically exhausted, having been delayed en route by washouts on the railroads. They said that they had had a terrifying experience. Mobs in Arizona had threatened to shoot them because they had sought to place the foundlings with Catholic Mexican families. Swayne had narrowly escaped lynching. On October 5 a "committee of citizens" had accompanied the agent to the train advising him not to return. Father Mandin had been forced to leave Clifton the day before.[19] One of the nuns gave the following story to a reporter:

> At Clifton we left 16 children, and the others at Morenci, 18 miles distant, and over a hard mountain road. Some of the children were taken to refined, dependable, prosperous Spanish people, whose homes were neat and clean.
>
> On Sunday night we were called from the rooms of our hotel in Morenci. In the street a sheriff sat on horseback, armed with a revolver, like the other men. Women called us vile names, and some of them put pistols to our heads. They said there was no law in that town; that they made their own laws. We were told to get the children from the Spaniards and leave by Tuesday morning. If we did not we would be killed. We got the children, but nineteen of the twenty-four were taken from the nurses by force and put, I understand, into the families of Americans.
>
> When we reached Clifton we were compelled to take once more that trying journey to Morenci and obtain the five children left there. When we left Arizona we had 21 children, who were taken by Dr. Swain (Swayne) into Illinois, where we had many applications for them.[20]

The Foundling Hospital, it also was reported, planned to make an appeal to the federal authorities for recovery of the children.

As early as October 16, the families in Clifton and Morenci holding the foundlings began making application in the probate court at Solomonville, the county seat of Graham County, for letters of guardianship. These requests for adoption papers were granted in the matter of a few days by Probate Judge Peter C. Little. Arizona attorneys familiar with the case were of the opinion that the Foundling Hospital had lost all right to the children by

---

[19]Tucson *Citizen* (October 5, 6, 19, 1904); *Phoenix Republican* (January 13–22, 1905).

[20]Tucson *Citizen* (October 19, 1904).

abandoning, or placing, them with incompetent and unworthy people. The Mexican foster parents were the only ones who had a standing in court, but as they now probably did not want the children, it was unlikely that they would try to recover them.[21]

On November 5 Governor Brodie arrived in Clifton. Although his purpose was to speak before a political rally, the rumor quickly spread that he had come with instructions from President Roosevelt to collect the children and send them back to New York. It was stated that Brodie was expecting trouble, and had instructed Captain Tom Rynning, of the Arizona Rangers at Douglas, to be ready to quell any disturbances. The Governor met the women who had assumed charge of the children, and visited the homes of the Mexican families where the children originally had been placed. At the conclusion of his investigation, he wired an informal report to Washington.[22]

When news of the happenings in Clifton reached New York, the Foundling Hospital went into the court to recover the children. An appeal of Judge Little's decisions was filed in the district court at Solomonville, and pending this appeal the institution made application through its Arizona attorneys, Eugene S. Ives, of Tucson, and Thomas D. Bennett, of Bisbee, to the Supreme Court of Arizona for writs of habeas corpus to secure custody of the children.[23]

On January 12, 1905, in Phoenix a hearing was begun before the Supreme Court regarding the writs.[24] The attorneys waxed eloquent before a courtroom crowded with anxious residents from Clifton and Morenci, the children under question, and interested spectators. Walter Bennett, of the influential firm of Kibbey, Bennett, and Bennett, paraded a host of witnesses before the court.

---

[21]*Foundling Hospital* v. *Gatti, Arizona Reports*, 9:114; *Phoenix Republican* (November 5, 1904; January 13–22, 1905) ; and *Clifton Copper Era* (November 24, 1904)....

[22]Tucson *Citizen* (November 4, 1904)....

[23]*Foundling Hospital* v. *Gatti, Arizona Reports*, 9:114....

[24]The seventeen applications by the Foundling Hospital for writs were listed as cases 202–218. Each petition requested that the party filed against be directed "to make return by what right he holds said infant in his possession and under his custody and control." One of the respondents, John C. Gatti, through his counsel moved that the writ to secure his young charge, William Norton, be quashed, but the motion was denied. Because of the similarity in the seventeen petitions, the opposing attorneys agreed that the proof adduced and decision reached in the Gatti case would be applied to the other cases.... *Foundling Hospital* v. *Gatti, Arizona Reports*, 9:353–354.

The nuns, Swayne, and the parents who had filed adoption papers for the children were asked to testify. The nuns, it was reported, broke down under questioning and blamed the priest. Swayne was evasive. According to one Mexican parent who had received a child, several of the Mexican families had been forced to take children "under the orders of the padre."[25] As the hearing dragged on, the local papers made much of the plight of the children:

> One woman, the possessor of a beautiful little girl, sat at lunch in a restaurant and cried when she thought of the possibility of an adverse decision. "I would rather," she said, "give up my right arm than lose her." One little boy, stopping with his foster father and mother at a hotel, grew sleepy ... and when his father told him to go to sleep, he said: "Won't you watch me so the Mexicans can't get me."[26]

Scrubbed and in their Sunday best, the children were seen frequently on the streets of Phoenix. Wherever they went they found "admiring crowds." In the courtroom, several of the foundlings were seated in conspicuous locations for all to see. Toward the end of the hearing Bennett injected the issue of religion into the discussion. To neutralize any attempt by opposing counsels to raise the question of religious discrimination, he pointed out that several of his clients were Catholics and that they had applied for, but had been refused children by the priest.

Thomas D. Bennett presented the argument for the Foundling Hospital. While the attorney for the Clifton residents had based his case on the welfare of the children, the counsel for the institution pressed for consideration of the legal points involved. His statements were brief, and noticeably lacking in fervor. Few witnesses appeared. The fact that the better known of the two attorneys retained by the Foundling Hospital, Eugene S. Ives, failed to enter the hearing until near the end, added to the feeling of futility that pervaded the statements made before the court by his partner.[27]

After a week of hearings, the Court took the case under advisement. On January 21 decision was rendered. In his pronouncement, Chief Justice Edward Kent took issue with the point made by counsel that it would be to the interest of the children "to take them to the East, and there place them in homes far removed from

---

[25]*Phoenix Republican* (January 13–17, 1905). . . .

[26]*Ibid.* (January 13, 1905).

[27]*Ibid.* (January 13–19, 1905).

the knowledge of their antecedents. . . ." In strong rhetoric, he asserted:

> . . . these present foster parents — persons of some means and education — from the day when with humanitarian impulse, and actuated by motives of sympathy for their pitiful condition, they assisted in the rescue of these little children from the evil into which they had fallen, down to the time of their attendance at this trial, at cost of much time and money, in their loving care and attention, have shown that more than ordinary ties of affection bind them to the children, and that in no other homes that can be found for them are they so likely to fare as well. We feel that it is for their best interests that no change be made in their custody, and that, if anywhere, here in the changing West, the land of opportunity and hope, these children, as they grow to manhood and womanhood, will have the fullest opportunity that it is possible for them to have to be judged, not upon the unfortunate condition of birth, but upon the record they themselves shall make, and the character they shall develop.[28]

Kent stated that at the time of the controversy, neither the Foundling Hospital nor the Clifton families had a right to the children. The Foundling Hospital certainly had no right because its charter specified they were to care for, not dispose of, the children. The new parents had legally adopted the foundlings and now legally owned them, he asserted.

Although Judge Kent dismissed the writs filed in the case, the Foundling Hospital, because of the interstate nature of the litigation, was able to appeal the decision to the United States Supreme Court. The appeal was based on the question of "personal freedom" arising from the habeas corpus petitions.[29] Both John Gatti, whose charge William Norton, was the object of the test case, and Henry Hill, the wealthiest parent involved, went east to attend the hearing; Hill furnished most of the money to fight the Foundling Hospital.[30]

The task of preparing for the appeal proved tedious. By March 3, Ives had received the stenographic minutes of the proceedings

[28]*Foundling Hospital* v. *Gatti, Arizona Reports*, 9:121. Kent's full statement is on pp. 114–121. The Tucson *Citizen* (January 21, 1905) quoted Ives as saying the decision was "eminently just and fair and perhaps humane," but not "well fortified in strict legality."

[29]See *New York Foundling Hospital* v. *John C. Gatti*, in *Cases Argued and Determined in the United States Supreme Court, October Term, 1906* (St. Paul: West Publishing Co., 1907), p. 53. . . .

[30]See Patton, "History of Clifton," p. 213.

at Solomonville, and had prepared a statement of facts "in the nature of a special verdict for our supreme court to find. . . ."[31] He sent this statement to Charles E. Miller, the attorney for the Foundling Hospital in New York, who made certain alterations and returned it.[32] On March 17, Ives forwarded the statement to Justice Kent in Phoenix. Kent suggested changes, and late in March, attorney Walter Bennett corrected the statement further.[33] Finally, early in April Ives sent the revised statement to Miller.[34] The efforts of the Foundling Hospital, however, came to naught. On December 3, 1906, the Supreme Court dismissed the case as "not appealable" to the high court, thereby reaffirming the decision of the lower court. The Anglo families in Clifton and Morenci had won final custody of the children.[35]

In reviewing the court decisions and the newspaper accounts in Arizona of the foundling case, it is interesting to note that the question of religion received little attention. Each party in the case resorted to the legality of its own position, while the court based its decision on the welfare of the children involved. However, as the children were undoubtedly Catholics and originally were placed in homes of this faith, one cannot help but wondering if the Foundling Hospital were not fighting two battles: it not only was fighting the forceful removal of the children from its control, but also was fighting to preserve the religion of the children. In the history of child welfare in the United States, one of the reasons for the establishment of private institutions for dependent and neglected children, or even delinquent children, was to give children care under the religious auspices of their parents, and thus to keep them from losing their ancestral faith. The Foundling Hospital evidently was operating under this principle in its original place-

[31]Eugene S. Ives, Tucson, to Charles E. Miller, 32 Nassau Street, New York, March 1, 1905, Eugene S. Ives, Papers VII: 31; Special Collections, University of Arizona, Tucson. Ives to Thomas D. Bennett, Bisbee, March 3, 1905, Ives Papers VII: 44.

[32]Ives to Miller, March 3, 1905, Ives Papers VII: 45; and *Ibid.*, March 16, 1905, Ives Papers VII: 98. . . .

[33]Ives to Edward Kent, March 17, 1905, Ives Papers VII: 101; Ives to Walter Bennett, March 27, 1905, Ives Papers VII: 151.

[34]On April 9, Ives wrote Miller explaining his efforts: Ives to Miller, April 9, 1905, Ives Papers VII: 218. . . .

[35]The Court ruled that Congress had limited "the right of appeal" in habeas corpus cases involving personal freedom. Stating that "an infant is not entitled to his freedom," the Court recognized the right of the legal parent or guardian to enjoy the custody of the infant. *Foundling Hospital* v. *Gatti*, *U.S. Supreme Court Cases . . . 1906*, p. 55.

ment of the children, although it did not make an issue of it during the court procedures, nor did the court make mention of it in its paean to the ultimate foster parents.

In many ways, the circumstances surrounding the placement of the foundlings in the Clifton–Morenci parish was unfortunate. It was unfortunate because of the socio-economic background of the families and the contrasting ethnic social systems of the children and their foster parents. As foster home placement should represent an opportunity for the children involved, the original placements, considering all the factors in the case, did not appear to offer opportunities for the foundlings. Furthermore, the introduction of mob justice was unfortunate. Without this popular upheaval, the nuns perhaps would have visited the original foster homes, and according to the rules of the Foundling Hospital, could have reclaimed the children, if they found the homes and families unsuitable.

Finally, the Territorial Supreme Court was slightly ethnocentric in handling the case. Certainly the foundlings were forceably and illegally removed from the original foster parents and the Foundling Hospital representatives. The court chose to ignore this, referring to the mob action as "committee meetings" and the surrendering of the children to armed groups as "volunteer" action. The spirit of the frontier in all its ramifications played a larger role in the court decision than abstract justice. The collection and return of all the children in Morenci, except three, to the nuns, was a sane and civilized action—and perhaps the wisest solution to the case. If a similar plan had been followed in Clifton, little Phoebe would not have been dragged out in a rainstorm at night to become a candidate for pneumonia and death.

Contrary to the statistics carried by some of the newspapers, only seventeen of the original forty children were involved in the court cases. The Foundling Hospital recovered twenty-one and subsequently placed them in homes in the Midwest. One child died, as had been noted. These calculations leave one child unaccounted for. It was reported that a Mexican family disappeared with one of the children during the wild and rainy night the foundlings were being gathered up by the aroused residents of Clifton. The family was purported to have returned to the community some time later with a red-haired female child who upon maturity worked as a maid. The tale, which has been referred to as "The Mystery of the Red-Haired Maid," may account for the fortieth child.[36]

[36]Tucson *Star* (October 31, 1957)....

Chapter Three

The Status of the Mexican-American Before World War II

Most studies of the Mexican and of the Mexican-American prior to World War II dwelled upon the farm laboring groups, especially in the states of California, Texas, and Colorado. Not all Mexicans and Mexican-Americans, however, were farm laborers. As a matter of fact, the growth in urban population became so great that by the late 1920's Los Angeles had the second largest population of Mexican descent in all North America.

Consequently it is fortunate for the historian that Governor C. C. Young of California found it necessary to appoint a committee to study the Mexicans and the Mexican-Americans in the state. In the subsequent report that was published in 1930, the living and social conditions of these peoples, both the urban and the rural, were described and analyzed. Although this report was published in 1930, it is included here because it dealt mainly with the living conditions of the growing Mexican population of Los Angeles and because the lot of Mexicans and Mexican-Americans did not greatly change from 1900 until the 1941 entry of the United States into World War II.

The second selection, from a well-researched book by Dr. Emory Bogardus of the University of Southern California, also concerns both urban and rural Mexicans and Mexican-Americans. This selection treats an almost unknown historical event: the repatriation of these peoples to Mexico during the Great Depression. It is of utmost significance in viewing the treatment of pre–World War II Mexicans and Mexican-Americans.

Health, Relief, and Delinquency
Conditions among the Mexicans of California*

California Department of Social Welfare

Introduction

In gathering material concerning social welfare problems among the Mexicans of California, the Department of Social Welfare has drawn upon records and reports of the State Departments of Public Health, Education, Institutions, and Social Welfare, city and county records from the localities where the Mexicans constitute a considerable proportion of the population, and records of private social agencies in those districts. Some of this material has been issued in published reports, much is compiled from unpublished but official records, and part was secured by these agencies for the present survey. The bulk of the data from sources other than the state departments is from Los Angeles County for the reasons that, on account of its size and organization, far more record material is available in that county than elsewhere in the state, and also far more Mexicans reside in that county than in any other. In the smaller counties much of the data sought were not obtainable, since the keeping of records is not well developed in the smaller counties nor was it found possible to segregate social data relating to Mexicans. All pertinent data secured, except fragmentary and disconnected items, have been included.

Estimates as to the Mexican population of California vary widely. For the first six months of 1929 the State Bureau of Vital Statistics records over one-sixth of all births in the state as Mexicans. As the birth rate among Mexicans is undoubtedly higher than among the general population and as a large number of the Mexicans have come into the state in the child-bearing ages, the proportion of Mexican births to total births is doubtless far higher than the proportion of Mexicans in the population. Lack of recent

---

*From *Mexicans in California: Report of Governor C. C. Young's Fact-Finding Committee* (San Francisco: California State Printing Office, 1930).

census data as to the general population of California as well as to the Mexican population makes difficult any attempt to draw comparisons, but certain estimates of population will assist in arriving at a sense of the significance of the social data which follow.

The estimated Mexican population of Los Angeles County in 1928, as figured by the Los Angeles County Charities Department, the Mexican consul at Los Angeles and others working directly with the Mexicans, was approximately 250,000. The total population of the county at the same date was estimated as approximately 2,270,000 which would indicate that the Mexicans represented about 11 percent of the county population. At the same date the population of the city of Los Angeles was estimated by the Los Angeles City Police Department as 1,343,000. Of this total Mexicans were estimated to represent slightly over 10 percent. The Los Angeles city school system in the school census of 1928 accounted for 48,000 Mexican children, and according to a statement issued by the school department, Los Angeles has a larger population of Mexicans than any other city in the United States or even Mexico with exception of Mexico City.

Housing

The Mexican in California, like various other foreign-speaking immigrants in the United States, tends to live in colonies, retaining his traditions and a mode of life not always satisfactory to his American neighbors. How many or what proportion of the Mexicans live in distinctly Mexican districts can not be stated, but the existence of "'Little Mexicos," both urban and rural, is a matter of common knowledge.

The tendency of the Mexican to live in a racial group is strengthened by several conditions. On arrival he seldom speaks English and consequently is dependent upon the Spanish-speaking group for adjustment to his new environment. The Mexican commonly performs unskilled and consequently low-paid work, so that his choice as to quarters is restricted. In Mexico the laboring classes have been used to very simple living with only the most primitive sanitation, and owners are naturally reluctant to rent their buildings to Mexican tenants if others can be found. In addition, there exists a prejudice against the Mexican which manifests itself in the common classification of the Mexican as "not white."[1]

From an inquiry sent to realty boards in various cities of the state,[2] 47 replies were received, of which number the following twenty-four reported segregated districts composed of Mexicans, or Mexicans and other foreigners:

Azusa	Monrovia	San Bernardino
Bakersfield	Montebello	San Fernando
Bell	Napa	Santa Barbara
Compton	Ontario	Santa Maria
Huntington Park	Pomona	Santa Monica
Lankershim	Porterville	Van Nuys
Madera	Redlands	Visalia
Modesto	Riverside	Whittier

In addition, other boards cited clauses inserted in deeds and sales contracts calculated to confine Orientals, Mexicans, and Negroes to certain districts. Although most of these clauses seek to restrict the occupants of the premises to "persons of Caucasian race," in some instances the Mexican was definitely specified as prohibited from occupancy.

Further evidence of the concentration of Mexicans in separate localities and districts is presented in the following list of counties having regular elementary schools with an enrollment of over 90 percent Mexican. A total of fifty-eight elementary public schools appear on the record for the school year 1927–1928 as having from

---

[1]In his study of Mexican labor in the Imperial Valley, Paul S. Taylor discusses this domiciliary isolation: "One of the most striking aspects of the Mexican labor situation in Imperial Valley is the concentration of Mexican town population in colonies geographically apart from the American community.... Most of the Mexicans outside of Calexico are poor, and poverty leaves them little choice of residence outside of the cheapest quarters. Furthermore, there is the natural tendency to gravitate toward the places where, in a strange land, others of one's language, class, and culture may be found. Finally, there is the social pressure from the American community, which generally does not desire Mexicans as neighbors. A symptom of this pressure is the race restriction sometimes included in the deeds to property.... The Mexicans in the valley are sensitive to the social ostracism which they face, and do not force themselves in where they feel the pressure against them.... The separation of rural Mexicans from American neighbors is as clear as the separation prevailing in the towns." "Mexican Labor in the United States: Imperial Valley," by Paul S. Taylor, pp. 79, 80, 82.

[2]Inquiry sent out by Professor Elliott G. Mears of Stanford University in cooperation with the California Real Estate Association, February, 1927.

90 to 100 percent enrollment of Mexicans. It should be noted that these schools are not separate schools in mixed districts to which Mexicans must send their children, but are regular public schools, the almost exclusive enrollment of Mexicans being due to the fact that the district is inhabited by virtually none but Mexicans.

County	Number of schools having an enrollment 90 to 100% Mexican
Imperial	8
Kern	8
Orange	14
Los Angeles	10
Riverside	2
San Bernardino	16
Santa Barbara	2
Ventura	4

The older section of Los Angeles, around and east of the Plaza, is a distinctly Mexican settlement. Spanish is the language commonly heard, the signs in the shops are in Spanish, the goods on sale are distinctly for Mexicans, and the moving picture theaters show only Spanish titles. In the old mission are celebrated colorful and picturesque festivals with all the traditional Mexican games of chance. In a study of the home conditions of the Mexican families made by the principal of the Macey Street School, and including all families whether or not they had children attending school, the fact was brought out that virtually none of these families owned their own homes. The explanation given was that property in that district was held for industrial developments at prices too high to permit the Mexicans to purchase, and that the developments within the city have forced many of the Mexicans to move to districts farther out. The largest of these is in the Belvedere district, just outside of Los Angeles, known as Maravilla Park. The Mexican population in this district numbers about 45,000, and six large modern public schools have been built in which the enrollment is practically one hundred percent Mexican. One of these schools is a "development school" for subnormal children.

This district is just beyond the city limits and was built up without regard to the proper requirements for sanitation in congested districts. Two, and sometimes three, shacks are built upon one very small lot, leaving little unoccupied ground space. The shacks are flimsy shells, usually constructed of scrap lumber, old boxes, or other salvage.

At various times the city and county health departments have made housing surveys of the Mexican districts. Summary findings of two housing surveys made recently by the Los Angeles County Health Department[3] give a fair picture of life in the Mexican districts.

One district covered by the survey consisted of eight city blocks in Maravilla Park, containing 317 houses having a population of 1509 persons, or an average of practically 40 houses to the block and 4.8 persons to the house.

The average annual family income was $795, almost all of the workers being classed as unskilled laborers. Of the 317 houses, 199 were owned and 118 rented, of which number 211 were rated as mere shacks and the remaining 106 as bungalows or semibunga-lows. Light and ventilation were classed as reasonably good in 154 cases, and as poor in 163 cases. Sixty-two houses had good screens, and 255 had poor screens or none. Only 10 of the houses had cesspools connected up to flush toilets, 16 had cesspools not connected to flush toilets; 147 had privies in fair condition and 144 were classed as privies in poor condition. The attempt to maintain cleanliness under these difficult conditions was evidenced by the report that 227 of the houses were clean and 252 of the yards at least fairly clean.

A check on food supplies and diet showed 158 houses with sufficient food, 95 in which food was somewhat lacking, and 64 in which food was distinctly scant. For preserving food, only 9 had refrigerators, 128 had screened cupboards and coolers, and the balance of 180 had no provisions for keeping food in good condition.

On the home index score card,[4] with 25 as the standard, the district averages 8.3.[5]

A similar housing survey[6] made in a Mexican district in San Fernando covered 357 families, with a total of 1,668 persons—851 adults and 817 children. The income range of the families showed

---

[3]"The Mexican as a Health Problem" (unpublished report by Los Angeles County Health Department; June, 1928).

[4]Score card used in the inspection and rating of home conditions, numerical values being given in place of such rating as "excellent," "fair," or "poor." On such a card a rating of 25 would be given where all the itemized conditions were found "excellent." A score of 8.3 would be decidedly poor.

[5]Concerning the mode of life of the Mexicans of this district the following statement is made by Los Angeles County Charities Department: "Virtually

79 having less than $400 per year; 112 from $600 to $800 per year; 79 from $800 to $1,000 per year; and 87, $1,000 or over. A special study was made of their diet and food supplies which indicated that 35 percent had plenty of meat in their diet, 56 percent very little, and 9 percent none at all. Of vegetables, 40 percent had plenty, and 60 percent very few. Milk was received daily by 45 percent, while 25 percent took milk occasionally and 30 percent never bought milk. Automobiles of some description were owned by 39 percent and 37 percent possessed musical instruments. On the home index card the San Fernando district, with 25 as the standard, averaged 9.5.

In addition to the large settlements of Mexicans, there are smaller camps located on the outskirts of Whittier, Montebello, and El Monte [; these] were inspected by representatives of the Department of Social Welfare, accompanied by Los Angeles County Health, Charities, and School officials. In camps of this character as the renter has no security of tenure he naturally wastes no money on lasting sanitary improvements. These settlements are sources of constant annoyance to the localities, and only by continual inspection and vigilance on the part of the health authorities can the menace of widespread disease be held in check. Patches of ground are rented as small as twenty by thirty feet. Ground rent varies from one, two, three, five, even ten dollars a month, and in several camps inspected by the department the annual rental would amount to over a thousand dollars an acre, in return for which the owner had made no investment whatever in sanitation or road improvements.

In his study of Mexican labor in the Imperial Valley, Paul S. Taylor discusses the housing of agricultural labor in that district:

> In the more permanent camps one finds rough lumber houses of a room or two, often screened, seldom painted. Sometimes the kitchen is in one of the rooms, often [it] is in a separate shelter outside the house. A roof of brush or arrow weed may be built out across the front or rear for shade. The "ditch-bank camp"

---

all of the Mexicans, regardless of age and physical inability, migrate 'to the fruit' in early summer and return when the seasonal work is over. In good years they bring back enough funds to carry them into, and sometimes through the winter, but in poor years they return with no money, their clothes worn out, and worse off than when they left." And again: "There are possibly not ten homes in Maravilla where income is really adequate for the family needs."

[6]Figures for State Department of Public Health, Bureau of Vital Statistics, 928.

is the typical temporary camp for the seasonal labor forces which
harvest the crops (of course many permanent camps also are
located along ditch banks). This type of camp is usually located
among the trees that line the irrigation ditches. Its shelters are
commonly tents, which the Mexicans generally supply themselves,
or pieces of canvas stretched across a pole, with boxes, brush,
burlap or what-not across the end. Sometimes the shelters are
nothing more than the typical arrow weed *ramada*, consisting of
roof and from one to three sides, which provides shade and wind
protection. . . . The impermanent types of shelter, tents, *ramadas*,
etc. are, of course, not confined to the temporary camps, but may
be found also accommodating the seasonal influx in the permanent
camps. The inspectors of the State Housing Commission endeavor
to enforce certain minimum standards. These include tents
(floored during lettuce season, but not necessarily in the cantaloupe season), beds, screened cook houses and toilets, bathing
facilities, and garbage disposal. Employers are held responsible
for the cleanliness of the camps. Up to the present time (1927)
inspectors have experienced considerable difficulty in enforcing
these standards, which are by no means universally observed.

Birth Statistics of Mexicans in California

Beginning in 1926 the State Bureau of Vital Statistics began
segregating Mexican births in their records. In that year Mexican
births equaled one-seventh of the total. Two years later they rose
to one-sixth, and the first six months of 1929 indicate a continued
increase. The figures for these years are:

*Table 1. Total Births and Number of Mexican Births
in California, 1926–1929*

Year	Total births	Mexican births	Percent Mexican
1926	82,372	11,721	14.2
1927	84,334	12,688	15.0
1928	83,643	13,846	16.6
1929 (Jan.–June)	39,221	6,959	17.7

Most of these births occur in the southern part of the state.
In the rural districts of Imperial County, 52 percent of all births
in 1928 were Mexican. In the rural districts of San Bernardino
and Riverside counties, more than 40 percent of all births were
Mexican. In some of the cities of Imperial County, the Mexican
births in 1928 were between 60 and 70 percent of all births.

In the following table [omitted here] are given the total births in the counties and cities of California in 1928, the number of Mexican births and the percentage which Mexican births represented of the total. This distribution of Mexican births indicates the migration of Mexican families into the San Joaquin Valley and certain counties of northern California. Santa Barbara and Ventura indicate the presence of a large proportion of Mexicans. In the San Joaquin Valley, Madera, Kings, and the rural districts of Fresno and Kern counties indicate over one-fifth of all births to be Mexican; while an unexpectedly large proportoin of Mexican births are found in Amador (26 percent), Contra Costa rural (19.8 percent), Lassen (18.2 percent), Placer (19.7 percent), San Benito (18 percent) and Tuolumne (16.4 percent).

.   .   .   .

Since 1916 the Los Angeles County Health Department has been segregating its statistics of Mexican births and deaths, in the unincorporated area of the county, and the rapid increase in the number of Mexican births and the proportion which they represent of the total, as given in the following table, indicates the

Table 3. Total Births in Los Angeles County (Unincorporated Area), Number of White and Mexican Births, and Percentage which White and Mexican Births Represent of Total, 1916–1927.[7]

Year	Total births	Number white births	Number Mexican births	Percent white of total	Percent Mexican of total
1916	1,519	843	193	55.5	12.7
1917	1,571	830	196	52.8	12.5
1918	1,503	828	258	55.1	17.2
1919	1,474	776	276	52.6	18.7
1920	1,867	1,079	375	57.8	20.1
1921	2,300	1,374	458	59.7	19.9
1922	2,468	1,531	489	62.0	19.8
1923	3,229	1,999	806	61.9	25.0
1924	4.194	2,674	1,189	63.7	28.4
1925	4.044	2,461	1,222	60.8	30.2
1926	4,230	2,702	1,276	63.9	30.2
1927	4,435	2,827	1,406	63.7	31.7

[7]Figures [for Tables 3 and 4] from the Los Angeles County Health Department, 1929. The large number of Japanese births in the earlier years covered in this table accounts for most of the difference between the sum of the whites plus the Mexican, and the total.

increase of Mexican population in that district. It will be noted that in 1916 Mexican births represented one-eighth of the total but the proportion has increased to nearly one-third of the total in 1927.

Corresponding figures for Los Angeles city from 1918 to 1927 indicate a similar rapid increase in the number of Mexican births and in the proportion from approximately one-twelfth of the total in 1918 to nearly one-fifth in 1927.

Table 4. Total Number of Births and Mexican Births in Los Angeles City, 1918–1927, with Percentage which Mexican Births Comprise of Total

Year	Total Births	Number Mexican births	Percent Mexican of total
1918	8,581	733	8.5
1919	8,822	850	9.6
1920	10,439	1,313	12.6
1921	12,097	1,708	14.1
1922	13,473	1,869	13.9
1923	14,807	2,206	14.9
1924	18,425	3,140	17.0
1925	19,124	3,225	16.9
1926	18,207	2,976	16.3
1927	18,053	3,449	19.1

A tabulation of the white[8] and Mexican deaths in the unincorporated area of Los Angeles County from 1921 to the present time, and a comparison with the births for the same period, indicates a steadily increasing excess of births over deaths among the Mexicans from 247 in 1921 to 950 in 1927, but among the white population in three years out of the seven, the number of deaths exceeded the number of births and the total excess of births over deaths for the seven years is only 241. The rapid increase in all classes of the population by migration overshadows the importance of the increase through excess of births over deaths, but the trend should be noted.

Corresponding figures of the excess of births over deaths, or of deaths over births, for the general population and for the Mexican population of Los Angeles City from 1918 to 1928, indicates that the Mexican share of this increase has grown from

---

[8]In addition to the white (Caucasian) and Mexican figures, the total includes Negroes and Orientals. To simplify the table, detail figures for these other groups are not here given, as not significant to the present study.

one-sixteenth in 1918 to well over one-third in 1927, and during the period of ten years almost one-fourth of the natural increase in population has been Mexican.

. . . .

Infant Mortality

As has been demonstrated by the elaborate studies made by the United States Children's Bureau,[9] infant mortality may be accepted as an index of the standard of living and intelligence of the group. A comparison of the infant mortality rate[10] among the Mexican and white population of Los Angeles County's unincorporated area is significant. With a foreign language group the tendency towards incompleteness in the reporting of vital statistics always exists, but under the present maternal and infant hygiene service conducted by the Los Angeles County Department of Health, every precaution is taken to insure completeness and accuracy. During all this period the district has been within the birth registration area, which implies repeated checks upon the completeness and accuracy of reporting.

Table 7. Infant Mortality Rate of the White and Mexican Population of Los Angeles County (Unincorporated Area), 1916–1929 Inclusive.[11]

	Infant mortality rate	
Year	*White*	*Mexican*
1916	70.0	285.0
1917	67.4	255.1
1918	71.3	348.1
1919	61.9	170.0
1920	60.2	186.7
1921	57.6	179.0
1922	78.4	243.4
1923	80.5	250.6
1924	61.3	163.2
1925	58.5	166.1
1926	41.9	124.6
1927	45.4	96.9
1928	51.7	116.8
1929	39.6	104.5

[9] United States Department of Labor, Children's Bureau. "Causal Factors in Infant Mortality" (1925).

[10] The infant mortality rate is the number of deaths, exclusive of stillbirths, under one year of age per 1000 live births.

[11] Figures from Los Angeles County Health Department, 1930.

Comparison of the white and Mexican infant mortality rates indicates sharply the poverty and unintelligent mode of living of the Mexican group. In 1916 over one-fourth of all Mexican babies born died within their first year of life, an extraordinarily high rate, and while the rate showed improvements in 1919, 1920, and 1921, it still stood at 250.6 in 1923. At that time the county established an intensive program of maternal and infant hygiene, which has served to reduce the death rate among Mexican infants to 104.5 in 1929, but this rate still remains over two and a half times as high as among the white population.

Comparison of the white and Mexican infant mortality by causes brings out the contrast still more sharply. In his analysis of the causes of infant deaths, Dr. John L. Pomeroy, director, Los Angeles County Health Department, states: "Premature birth is a general cause not related to mode of living, and for this cause little difference is to be noted between the white and Mexican rates. For the other causes, gastrointestinal, communicable, and respiratory diseases, are all controlled mainly by intelligent type[s] of living habits and precaution measures. For these causes the Mexican rate is from two to eight times higher than the white rate."[12]

.   .   .   .

Communicable Disease

A study of communicable disease, the number of cases, number of deaths, and particularly the case fatality rate, serves as a general index of the mode of living, the care received, and the physical resistance of the individual.[13] From 1921 the Los Angeles County Health Department has made a racial segregation in its records. This separation of figures as to the white and the Mexican population brings out the fact that one-sixth of all communicable cases and one-fourth of all such deaths are of Mexicans. Without accurate population statistics, which are not obtainable, the percentage of Mexicans in the population can not be computed but according to estimates of population, the number of cases and

[12]"The Mexican as a Health Problem," Los Angeles County Health Department, 1928.

[13]Figures, statements and analysis by Dr. John L. Pomeroy, Director, Los Angeles County Health Department.

deaths among the Mexicans is disproportionately high. The case fatality rate—the number of deaths per hundred cases—can, however, be computed and this serves as an index of care and resistance. In 1921, among the Mexican population, nearly one-fourth of all cases of communicable disease (which includes all diseases reportable by law) terminated fatally. This rate was nearly twice as high as the fatality [rate] among the white population. Under an expanded service inaugurated by the County Health Department in 1921, the communicable diseases have been given care and treatment far more intensively than in former years; the general case fatality rate nearly cut in two, and the Mexican rate still more sharply reduced. The "white" rate was cut from 13.4 to 7.4 and the Mexican rate from 22.9 to 9.6. The greater decrease in the Mexican rate is credited to the fact that it was so much higher when the situation was taken in hand by the County Health Department, and for this reason the county had to assume a more complete measure of authority. But in spite of all their efforts the Mexican rate remains nearly a third higher than the white rate, and is considered by the health authorities as indicative of a fundamentally less sturdy stock.[!]

Tuberculosis

The prevalence of tuberculosis among the Mexican population of California is one of the outstanding problems of health and relief agencies wherever Mexicans are found in large numbers. Statistics from the Los Angeles County Health Department for the unincorporated area of the county indicate this condition. In 1921 all deaths of Mexicans (211) represented 11.5 percent of the total deaths (1835) in that area, while ... Mexican deaths from tuberculosis amounted to 14.8 percent of the total due to that cause. In 1927 all deaths of Mexicans (459) represented 13.9 percent of the total deaths (3303), while among the deaths due to tuberculosis Mexican deaths represented 19.6 percent, while in 1925 it will be noted that Mexican deaths from tuberculosis were almost one-fourth (24.0 percent) of all deaths from that disease. The increasing proportion of all Mexican deaths in that area is probably due to the increasing proportion of Mexicans in the population; but the Mexican proportion of deaths from tuberculosis has increased much more rapidly than their proportion of all deaths.

Segregated statistics of deaths from tuberculosis disclose the fact that in 1929 Mexicans constituted over one-fifth of all deaths from tuberculosis, where eight years earlier they had represented only one-seventh. Undoubtedly the increase is due in part to the increasing proportion of Mexicans in the population, but the addition to the population of tubercular whites largely offsets this factor.

.   .   .   .

Comparable figures regarding the prevalence of tuberculosis among Mexicans in other sections of the state are not available, but the seriousness of the situation is borne out by a census taken of all cases under observation in the tuberculosis clinic maintained by the Los Angeles City Health Department, on June 1, 1928. Out of 1516 patients, which included diagnosed cases, pretubercular cases, patients under observation and contact cases, 413 or 27 percent of the total, were Mexican. As Mexicans are estimated to constitute about 10 percent of the city's population, the fact that he totals [sic] over one-fourth of the clientele of the tuberculosis clinics is probably due in part to poverty and the necessity of seeking free treatment, but undoubtedly reflects also a high general tuberculosis rate among the Mexican population.*

For further information upon the prevalence and seriousness of tuberculosis among the Mexicans a detailed study was made by the Los Angeles County Charities Department on May 1, 1926, of the cases on aid at that date in which tuberculosis was involved. From that study certain significant facts and comparisons may be drawn.

.   .   .   .

From these figures it will be noted that nearly two-fifths of all tuberculosis cases in which county relief was granted were Mexican, and nearly a fourth of all Mexican relief cases involved tuberculosis, while only one-tenth of all non-Mexican cases involved tuberculosis.

Seven-eighths of the heads of the Mexican families having tuberculosis were born in Mexico, but nearly four-fifths had been in the United States over five years. The dates of arrival in the

---

*Such conclusions are indicative of the conclusions which public officials consistently tried to draw about not only Mexican-Americans, but members of other minority groups as well. To blame "fundamentally less sturdy stock" (p. 115) or a "high general tuberculosis rate among the Mexican population" was to discount the effects of squalid living conditions and to absolve the dominant society of blame for those conditions and of responsibility for rectifying them.

United States of these families were checked very carefully. If accurate, the large number developing tuberculosis after being in the country five years or more would indicate living conditions in this country tending towards the development of the disease, and probably, a fundamentally susceptible stock.*

. . . .

As a further index of sickness and the need of health service, a compilation was made of the number of cases active in the nursing division of the Los Angeles City Health Department on January 30th of each year since 1920, which indicates that Mexicans constituted from one-third to nearly one-half of the persons served by the nursing division. The increase in service rendered to American families in the last few years is due to the establishment of well-baby clinics in certain nonimmigrant districts, an educational service not reflecting either sickness or poverty. The other groups served by the nursing division reflect directly the measures taken by the City Health Department to meet the pressing problems of poverty, sickness, and ignorance.

. . . .

Mexicans in the State Hospitals

The care of the insane and feeble-minded is one of the increasing burdens of public charity. At the present time all of the state institutions are overcrowded and only the cases most urgently in need of institutional care can be given treatment. Under these conditions, fewer admissions have been made in recent years than would have been made if facilities had permitted the admission of all cases where state care is desirable. The factor of deportation also affects analysis of these figures, since an alien who becomes insane within five years after entry may be deported. In the biennium, 1927–1928, 218 Mexican patients were admitted to state hospitals, of which number 88 (40 percent) were deported by federal authorities. The policy of deportation accounts for the fact ... that the proportion of Mexican inmates is much less than the proportion of Mexicans admitted to the hospitals. The possibility of deportation undoubtedly serves also as a deterrent to the reporting of milder cases.

. . . .

For the year 1922–1923 Mexicans constituted 3 percent of the total admissions to hospitals for the insane and 2.7 percent of admissions to institutions for the feeble-minded. In 1927–1928 Mexicans admitted to the hospitals for the insane had increased to 4.3 percent of the total, an increase of nearly 50 percent in five years, and in the institutions for the feeble-minded the number of Mexicans increased in the same period of five years from 2.7 percent to 6.9 percent of all persons admitted.

The Dependence of Mexicans Upon Charity

Mexican Families Receiving State Aid

State aid is granted in California to orphans, half orphans and certain classes of children whose fathers are tubercular or completely incapacitated. On January 1, 1928, aid was paid to 5,288 families, representing a total of 13,105 children. Of this total 515 families were Mexican, which represents 9.7 percent of the total number of families. Family groups among the Mexicans being larger than among the general population brought the total number of Mexican children receiving aid slightly above one-tenth of the total.

Among the conditions of eligibility for aid is that of legal residence within the state for at least two years. Largely on account of this requirement the eight counties of southern California, because of the recent arrival of a large part of their population, received in 1928 only 30.8 percent of the total amount of the state aid, although their estimated population was about half that of the entire state. This residence condition renders many needy Mexican families ineligible to aid from the state, since many have resided in the state less than two years. Also, state aid may not be paid to a family which entered [the] state in a dependent condition, and this condition also renders many Mexican families ineligible. From the fact that one-tenth of all state aid to children is now paid to Mexican families and that residence qualifications render many other needy Mexican families ineligible to aid, it becomes evident that poverty and need are proportionately more common among Mexicans than among the general population of the state. In Los Angeles County Mexicans represented one-fourth of the families receiving state aid. As they are estimated to comprise about 11 percent of the population, their greater general poverty and need is indicated.

Dependent Children in Institutions

Information concerning the racial background of all children in all orphanages and other institutions for dependent children was secured by the Department of Social Welfare as of April 1, 1928. These institutions were caring for a total of 5,357 children, of which number 416, or 7.8 percent, were Mexican. Among the institutions in northern California only 85 Mexican children were being cared for out of a total of 3,019, but in the southern counties Mexican children numbered 331 out of 2,338, or 14.1 percent, and in the institutions in Los Angeles County practically one-sixth (16.4 percent) of all the children were Mexican. As a number of the institutions accept no Mexicans, the proportion in the rest of the institutions becomes conspicuously high.

.   .   .   .

County Relief in Los Angeles County

Financial relief to the needy in Los Angeles County is administered almost entirely by the Outdoor Relief Division of the County Charities Department, the Community Chest and other private charities devoting their efforts and resources to family welfare, clinics and other health services, and other community projects. A statement of the funds given by the county charities in total and to Mexicans, therefore, covers the bulk of financial relief given in that area.

In the following table [which is omitted] is given the total number of cases and the number of Mexican cases on county relief for the five years, 1923–1924 to 1927–1928. In 1924–1925 Mexican cases ran over one-third of the total, but for the other years they have represented approximately one-fourth. The total amount of money given in relief has risen from $938,167 in 1923–1924 to $1,509,780 in 1927–1928. The amounts paid to the Mexican families have not been segregated so that it is not possible to state whether the amounts given to them are greater or less than their proportion of the total number of cases.

.   .   .   .

In addition to relief given through the County Charities Department, the only agency administering a considerable relief budget is the Catholic Welfare Bureau. In the accompanying table [which is not included] are given the number of children cared for during 1924, 1926, 1927, and six months of 1928. Nearly half of all the children cared for are Mexican, but less than half of the funds expended were for their care. In family relief the bureau has cared for a far smaller proportion of Mexican families.

· · · · · · · · · · · · · · · · · ·

Service to Mexicans by Los Angeles Chest Agencies

To supplement the statistics of financial relief in Los Angeles County the Los Angeles Community Chest was asked by the Department of Social Welfare to have all chest agencies serving any Mexicans in their clientele make a segregation in their records so that the proportion of service to Mexicans could be shown. Segregated records were kept from June 1 to November 1, 1928, by seventeen agencies. As there are over a hundred agencies in the chest, it will be noted that about five-sixths of the agencies serve no Mexicans, but among those serving Mexicans are several of the largest charitable agencies of the city.

Hospital and clinic service and family welfare are the chief fields of service of these agencies. Practically no relief was given except through the Catholic Welfare Bureau.

· · · · · · · · · · · · · · · · · ·

Public Care of Indigents at Los Angeles County Farm

For the care of the indigent aged the Los Angeles County Charities conducts a county farm at which institution the cost of care and treatment of inmates total $913,156 in 1926–1927. Comparatively few Mexicans are sent to the farm, their standard of living, racial clannishness, and national food habits making assistance to them in their own group a happier solution of their needs.

· · · · · · · · · · · · · · · · · ·

Hospital Care of Mexicans, Los Angeles County Hospital

Aid in the form of free medical and hospital service has come to be a most important item of public charity. A survey made by the State Department of Public Health covering the service rendered to Mexicans by the Los Angeles General (County) Hospital for two years July 1, 1922, to June 30, 1924,[14] disclosed the fact that the care and treatment given to Mexicans during that period cost the county $2,358,088 or well over a million dollars a year. Since that time the number of Mexicans cared for in the hospital has increased over a third.

In 1919–1920 the number of Mexican patients totaled 11.3 percent of the total, and this percentage increased irregularly to 18.4 in 1926–1927, but dropped to 15.4 in 1927–1928.

Crime and Delinquency among the Mexican Population

Statistics of crime and delinquency of the Mexican element in the state in comparison with corresponding figures for the general population serve as an index of racial or national characteristics and also as an index of the adjustment or lack of adjustment of the Mexicans to American customs and standards.

. . . .

From this table [which is not included] it will be noted that on June 30, 1909, there were 87 Mexicans in San Quentin out of a total prison population of 1,814, or 4.8 percent, and during that year the Mexicans committed to San Quentin represented 5 percent of the total. From 1909 the number and proportion of Mexicans increased fairly steadily until 1918; and since that time they have remained approximately one-eighth of the total prisoners and the same proportion as to yearly commitments.

. . . .

A comparison of the figures concerning the prisoners at Folsom indicates a much smaller percentage of Mexicans at that prison than among the first offenders at San Quentin—6.6 percent at Folsom, September 30, 1929, as against 12.7 percent at San Quentin, June 30, 1929. The fact that a large part of the Mexicans in California have been in the state only a few years probably explains at least in part the smaller percentage of recidivists.[!]

A comparison of the Mexicans with the total as to the nature of their crimes indicates that the offenses which proportionately they are most inclined to commit are violations of the State Poison Act, which relates to narcotics, and the carrying [of] and assault

---

[14]"Statistical Study of Sickness among the Mexicans in the Los Angeles County Hospital, 1922-1924" (Sacramento: State Department of Health, 1924).

with deadly weapons. The crimes which they rarely commit are forgery, which is to be expected among a people having a high rate of illiteracy and little familiarity with banking, and violations of the Motor Vehicle Act. The crime for which the largest number of Mexicans are sent to Folsom is burglary, which is true of the total prison population also, but the Mexicans represent more than their proportion of persons committed for burglary; and at the same time they have a comparatively low rate of commitment for robbery. In other figures relating to crime among the Mexicans this tendency towards a high incidence of burglary as against a lower incidence of robbery, which latter crime includes personal encounter, is interesting to note.

. . . .

The 1910 census gives the population of California as 2,377,549, of which number 51,037 or 2.1 percent were native-born Mexicans. The 1920 census records 3,426,861 as the total population of the state, of which number 86,610 or 2.5 percent were native-born Mexicans. In the absence of a recent census, it is not possible to draw any close comparison with the general population. It [the Mexican crime rate] would appear to be very high but the comparison is affected by the fact that more men than women have entered the country, and the age distribution gives a larger proportion of Mexicans in the age groups most commonly found in prison. Police officials generally state a greater tendency among arrested Mexicans to plead guilty to charges and the common financial inability to extended defense and appeal of cases, both of which causes undoubtedly increase the apparent crime among the Mexicans.

Repatriation and Readjustment*

Emory S. Bogardus

While there has been an extensive movement back and forth across the border for many years, the Depression in the fall of

---

*From Emory S. Bogardus, *The Mexican in the United States* (Los Angeles: University of Southern California Press, 1934).

1929 inaugurated a homeward trek of Mexican immigrants larger than had ever been known before. Such a movement is nothing new in the history of immigration. During the past century waves of immigration to the United States from Europe came in times of prosperity, and were uniformly followed by waves of emigration. In recent decades, the Italians led the homeward procession so often that they became known as "birds of passage."

The Mexicans who have "gone back" include: (1) those who have voluntarily packed up their belongings and returned by car or train; (2) those who have returned under polite coercion; and (3) those who have been deported.[1] The second group is composed of many Mexicans who have been told by county or other public welfare agencies that if they would depart their transportation expenses to the border would be paid, but if they did not accept this proposition they would be denied further welfare aid.

In Mexico a *repatriado* is defined as person who, having left his country to live a number of years in another country, returns to his own country to reside and to assume the duties of citizenship. According to a leading Mexican official, *repatriados* are regarded in Mexico as Mexicans who have lived in a foreign country and have returned to the Republic "for the purpose of settling down, regardless of whether they came back of their own accord or were deported by foreign authorities."

From the Office of Social Statistics in Mexico City and through the courtesy of Lic. [lawyer] Ramon Beteta, the author secured the figures given in Table IX concerning repatriates. Table IX gives the data for four years, from January 1, 1930, to December 31, 1933, inclusive. The high month was November, 1931, flanked strongly by October and December of the same year. The total number of repatriates for the four years was 311,712, which means that by the present writing the total number of Mexican *repatriados* since January 1, 1930 is approaching the third-of-a-million mark. This is a large number of persons to be reabsorbed into Mexico in a depression period. Most of these repatriates, approximately 90 percent, have come from the United States.[2]

---

[1] The materials of this chapter represent a revision of the article by the writer on "Mexican Repatriates," *Sociology and Social Research* 18 (November–December, 1933).

[2] According to Mexican government figures obtained by James C. Gilbert.

Table IX. Mexican Repatriados

	1930 Nos.	1931 Nos.	1932 Nos.	1933 Nos.
January	3762	6627	9394	3216
February	3446	6216	6501	3291
March	3367	7719	6151	3278
April	3817	7448	6229	5058
May	3719	7616	8594	3120
June	5102	9959	7927	3175
July	5662	8465	8266	2042
August	5522	8624	6291	2550
September	6957	9398	4302	1944
October	8610	17092	5368	2552
November	9679	21055	5686	2816
December	9927	14742	5939	3466
Totals:	69,570	124,991	80,648	36,508

Where do the *repatriados* go in Mexico? They have returned to their native villages and towns, to the large cities, and to the repatriation colonies established by the government. While it is evident that by far the largest percentage have gone back to their native communities and that only a small percentage have gone to the large cities and to the repatriation colonies, the extent of these percentages is not clear.[3] Perhaps we may estimate that about eighty percent have returned to the villages; fifteen percent to the large cities; and five percent to the repatriation and colonization centers.

Those who have returned to the villages have been received into their respective family groups freely, according to the Mexican custom. Shelter and food have been shared with the returning relatives even though no work or additional food was immediately available.

Others have struck out for the larger cities and sought work under metropolitan conditions. A *repatriado* who had lived fourteen years in the United States and who during the summer of 1933 was working temporarily as a painter on the National Theater in Mexico City, said to the writer: "I have made a terrible mistake. I should have stayed in the United States. Opportunities here

---

[3]According to interview materials secured from a Mexican official early in 1933 by Marion Flad, University of Southern California, approximately eighty-five percent of the repatriates return to the villages and repatriation centers, and fifteen percent to the large cities.

[Mexico City] are fewer than in the United States." Only the most resourceful are able to get readjusted in the large cities within a reasonable length of time.

Still other *repatriados* have gone to the large government centers (a total of about 5,000 was reported to be in the two largest centers in July, 1933). Preliminary reports indicate that these centers have not yet succeeded. They involve many changes in ways of living that the repatriate can make only with the greatest difficulty. Large-scale collective establishments call for habits and culture patterns different from those of the small-scale camps to which Mexicans have become accustomed in the United States.[4]

Why do some repatriates succeed in Mexico and others fail? Is adjustment purely a matter of luck, or can some principle or rule be discovered? What effect does advancement of the economic and cultural scale in the United States have upon the returned repatriate? Do education and cultural advancement hinder or help adjustment in Mexico?

Although the repatriates are welcomed by their village relatives, yet the more advanced quickly grow restless. Not being able to transform their native villages, they fall back into the old ways, or else they grow disappointed and scornful. If they be small in number, the falling back process occurs without much delay; but if their numbers be large, they form a kind of recalcitrant minority. A conflict ensues with the result that the repatriated minority are called "gringos" because of their superior airs and American ways.[5]

> For this reason there arises at times a natural antagonism which is often even unconscious between the characters, automatic attitudes, and tendencies of the reactionary majority and the progressive minority of those who are being repatriated, who are charged with being "Yankified" innovators, Masons or pagans, destroyers of the old customs, freakish, intruders, etc.[6]

The conflict continues until the minority succumbs or some of its leaders go to the large cities, only to find themselves strangers there, although some are able, by their wits, to get ahead.

---

[4]Manuel Gamio points out a number of factors which explains the failure of the early repatriation enterprises in Mexico. See his *Mexican Immigration to the United States*, pp. 235 ff.

[5]Emma R. Stevenson, "The Emigrant Comes Home," *Survey*, 41:176.

[6]Gamio, *Immigration*, p. 236.

The picture of the returned Mexican immigrant operating a big tractor in his home community is largely buncombe. Here and there he is able in a minor way to bring about changes in the culture traits of his fellow townsmen or villagers. The blue overall is slowly superseding the more picturesque white cotton suit, but more fundamental changes are coming very slowly. Sometimes the blue denim is worn over "the regulation Mexican white shirt and pajama trousers."[7]

In Arandas, Jalisco, Dr. Paul S. Taylor was impressed more "by the relatively small degree of change in the attitudes and ways of living of the returned emigrants than by the material change which experience in the United States sometimes produced in the economic conditions of individuals."[8] The repatriates easily "slip back into the old ways" after the clothes and money they have brought with them are worn out. However, they find it hard to work for small wages after having received larger ones in the United States. The natives are unwilling to admit the superiority of the repatriates.[9]

Do the various members of a returned emigrant's family adjust themselves with similar ease or difficulty in Mexico? Clearly, no. The father seems to have less difficulty than does the mother or the children, and the younger children less than the older ones. The father has been more accustomed to migration and less attached to any particular spot in the United States. The younger children have not yet become "American" in any sense. The older children, however, have learned English, acquired "American" ways made "American" friends; many protest against returning to Mexico. They are more "American" than Mexican. Although their hopes and ambitions may have been dimmed in the United States still this country is home. Despite the Depression and the lack of opportunities to work, the culture level here is higher than in the Mexican village to which they return. Their difficulties are twofold they do not want to leave their friends in the United States, and they do not feel at home on the culture level of the village life in Mexico.

The mother is in a dilemma. She wants to go back with her husband to Mexico but does not want to desert her older children.

---

[7] Osgood Hardy, "Los Repatriados," *Pomona College Magazine*, 21:73.

[8] *A Spanish-Mexican Peasant Community, Arandas in Jalisco, Mexic* (Berkeley: University of California Press, 1933), p. 55.

[9] *Ibid.*, p. 60.

who beg to remain in the United States. She faces a divided family. She is pulled strongly in two different ways at the same time.

The repatriation movement presumes that extensive agrarian progress has been made in Mexico and that land with water is available. To be sure, there is plenty of land but not with water to a great extent. Developments of importance, however, are taking place; for example, the National Irrigation System, No. 4, located north and west of Monterrey, Mexico, where the impounded waters provide irrigation for seventy-five thousand acres and where perhaps in two years water will be provided for one hundred and fifty thousand acres. The national government owns the land and rents it or will sell it on a twenty-eight year installment plan. According to James C. Gilbert, repatriates who returned to Mexico with tools and some money are doing fairly well raising cotton and corn although they had previously "gone broke" in Texas raising cotton.[10] Pending the development of agrarian opportunities the outlook for the *repatriados* is limited.

Many Mexican immigrants are returning to Mexico under a sense of pressure. They fear that all welfare aid will be withdrawn if they do not accept the offer to help them out of our country. In fact, some of them report that they are told by public officials that if they do not accept the offer to take them to the border no further welfare aid will be given them, and that their record will be closed with the notation, "Failed to cooperate." Rumor becomes exaggerated as it passes from mouth to mouth. It takes only an insinuation from an official in the United States to create widespread fear among Mexican immigrants.

The plan of shipping Mexican immigrants to the border instead of giving them welfare aid has an important financial aspect. Figures secured by James C. Gilbert show that the cost of returning nine thousand Mexicans to the border from Los Angeles was about $155,000, whereas the welfare cost of taking care of the same number for one year was approximately $800,000.[11]

Questions are being raised concerning the justice of our Mexican immigration procedure. In times of prosperity Mexican immigrants have been "invited" by large-scale employing concerns to come to the United States. They have come, furnishing an alleged

[10]From a letter by James C. Gilbert.

[11]From data being gathered for a Master of Arts thesis by James C. Gilbert, of the University of Southern California, who spent several months in Mexico in 1933 and 1934, studying the problem in a first-hand way.

"cheap labor" supply. In times of depression when they are no longer an economic asset but a liability, they are sent back to their native communities "penniless — a burden on those already poor." It is not surprising, therefore, that thinking Mexican leaders are inquiring about the justice of such a procedure. Are Mexican immigrants to be sent for again when prosperous times return, to be treated as "cheap labor," and then again to be returned penniless to poverty-laden relatives? Are industry and agriculture under any obligations to neighbors whom they bring into our country under promises of work, when the latter are stranded here in a time of depression? If these people, by virtue of seasonal labor situations, of migratory labor conditions, of special urges by high-pressure "American" salesmen to buy on the installment plan, are unable to save, is anything due them by way of protection in the form of insurance? Is the obligation to them met simply by paying their transportation expenses to the border or home, especially when that home is one with which they have lost touch and which may already be overburdened with poverty? These are a few of the questions raised by those who wish to see justice done in the relations between Mexico and the United States.

Difficulties for the Mexicans who remain in the United States face them on every hand. Conflicts in customs and traditions are perplexing. Old ways are precious and new ways forbidden, and yet changes must be made. Lack of knowledge increases the difficulty in bridging the culture chasms.

> I do not speak English; my people are slow to learn English, because we live in Mexican camps or villages where [we] do not need to speak English. I read and write Spanish, but now I shall try to learn English after all these years. I have lived in Los Angeles twenty years. My children all speak English. When Ruth, my first daughter, was ten years old she asked me to give up wearing my *rebozo* [shawl]. I thought I never could do that. It seemed a part of my old life in Mexico, and I thought of how new and strange everything here seemed when I first came wearing my *rebozo*.[12]

Mexican immigrants are often shocked by the strange and apparently loose relationships between the sexes in the United States. Not only do young women meet young men on grounds of

---

[12]From interview materials submitted by H.W.W.

freedom but they often act with misleading frankness and freedom
toward Mexican young men.

> When we first came here the bathing girls were the most
> shocking thing to the family. My brother took me to W——. How
> I loved to go to W——! I was not shocked, but mama said, "The
> day I see you in those bathing suits, I don't know what I will do."
> Later on, though, we went to the beach and bathed — it is just the
> custom you know. Mama thought there was too much liberty in
> this country, and still believes so.[13]
>
> There is one way in which they think American young women
> should be more careful: they should know Latins before they
> become intimate with them, not because they may not themselves
> be fine, or their men friends among Mexicans be high-minded
> youths, but because unless they know something of Latin psy-
> chology, they should not be too free with the young men who
> come north to study, and observe; for, the newly arrived Latin
> has no reason to suppose the American girl draws any barriers at
> all, when once he notices how free she is. He simply does not know
> where she puts the limit, and it is not he that is to be condemned,
> any more than the girl; they simply must know each other.[14]

Interracial conflicts are baffling. In southern California, for
example, where large numbers of Mexicans and Japanese are
thrown together, misunderstanding easily arises, for the two cultures are different at many points, and the two sets of tempera-
ments are likewise far apart.

> You know, Japanese and Mexicans generally do not mix at all.
> They are so different in ways and temperament and seem to mis-
> trust or else misunderstand one another. But these two Japanese
> women live near the Mexican colony in A——. One has a vegetable
> market and the other is the wife of a nurseryman. They were
> anxious to learn to speak English. I told them we had a night
> school but that it was Mexican. They begged to come too, and so
> we talked it over at night school and the Mexicans decided to
> invite them.
>
> At first the Mexicans thought these ladies were very funny,
> and enjoyed laughing at them a great deal. But I explained to
> the Mexicans that the Japanese have a very hard time to learn
> English because their pronunciation and even their alphabet are

---

[13]*Ibid.*

[14]From interview materials submitted by E.H.M.

so very different from ours. And I finally got them to be more
friendly and polite.

The Mexicans have come to admire these Japanese women
very much. They are very bright and learn fast. They are devout
members of a Protestant church. On Wednesday they are never
at night school as they go to prayer meeting then. The Mexicans
tell me they think these Japanese are fine Christians, better than
most Americans, and for that reason they seem to admire them a
great deal.[15]

Mexicans and Filipinos sometimes clash. Competition for work
is the usual cause. The younger Mexicans are more overt in their
antagonism than are the older people. From V ——— , California,
comes the following account:

The Mexicans are very hostile to the Filipinos, for economic
reasons. Last fall, the Valencia crop was unusually small in size,
and the Fruit Association thought it necessary to cut wages. As
the Mexicans refused to accept the cut, the Filipinos were prom-
ised that if they would work then, they would have work when
the navel crop came on. Most of the Mexicans left V—— to pick
nuts, and when they returned for the navel season, they found
that the Filipinos had their jobs. . . . There have been some fights
between the two groups. On one occasion, Filipinos were attending the night school at the Mexican health center, and some
Mexican boys outside began calling them names. One of the
Filipinos jumped through the window and started a fight. . . .
Troubles of this kind are mostly between the younger Mexicans
and the Filipinos. The older ones resent the presence of the Filipinos but do nothing about it.[16]

Then, there is the problem created by the fact that persons of
all races condemn members of other races on the ground of a
single unfortunate experience with a member of that race.[17] Quick
generalization on limited experience is a serious evil.

One American will do something bad, then some Mexicans
think all Americans are like that, and just the same way. One
Mexican is drunk, or one Mexican steals, or one Mexican does

---

[15]From interview materials submitted by H.W.W.

[16]From interview materials submitted by E.H.

[17]E.S. Bogardus, *Immigration and Race Attitudes* (Boston: D.C. Heath and
Company, 1928), p. 243.

something else bad, and then Americans think all Mexicans are bad. Just the same, some Americans think all Mexicans are dirty. They are not. S—— down here is very dirty, but you know too, Mrs. Y—— is very clean. All Mexicans are not clean, all Mexicans are not dirty; all Mexicans are not bad, all Mexicans are not good. We have to know people. No? But I like to live in the neighborhood with Mexicans. I want my children to learn good Spanish; I want my children to go to good American schools to learn good English. It is better for them to know both. *Verdad?*[18]

Thus, the problem of making adjustments grows complicated. The people of the United States can help or hinder greatly in the Mexican's reorganization difficulties. Unfortunately he often shows little interest and the result is a serious loss to the Mexican.

In this struggle to make his adjustments, in this process so full of conflict of cultures, he is unfortunately losing much of the fine old grace of his people, and he is imitating much that is crude while he acquires some that is good. He has a wealth to contribute to this country: love of play, buoyancy of spirit, appreciation of the beautiful, if he is only given a chance to do so.[19]

---

[18]From interview materials submitted by H.W.W.

[19]Helen W. Walker, "Mexican Immigrants and American Citizenship," *Sociology and Social Research* 13:471.

Chapter Four

World War II and the Mexican-American

No one can deny that World War II brought death, mutilation, and extreme suffering to many persons, especially the young, in the United States. Yet not all the consequences of the war were evil. For the Mexican-American, as well as for other minorities in the United States, World War II had some very beneficial as well as some detrimental results. Among the beneficial results were that formerly closed jobs were opened, that segregated living—both voluntary and imposed—was abolished to a degree, and that the Mexican-American began realizing that he too was an American. Among the detrimental effects that resulted from the war were that the formerly strong family life was weakened, that some pre-draft-age Mexican-American youngsters became pachucos or zoot-suiters, and that the fine record of Mexican-American servicemen was therefore ignored.

Because the Zoot-Suit Riots of the pachucos received the greatest notoriety and because the other post-war effects and events are treated in the following chapter, the four selections included in this section deal only briefly with the Mexican-American draftees and volunteers, and extensively with the zoot-suiters. The short piece on the draftees and volunteers was purposely included in order to avoid misrepresentation of the wartime Mexican-American youth. This selection depicts a patriotic zeal on the part of the Mexican-American that contrasts vividly with the articles which follow. These articles, two written by Robin Scott and one by Patricia Rae Adler, present a historical view of the pachucos, the press, and the police in examining the most controversial events of Mexican-American history in the United States.

Draftees and Volunteers*

Raúl Morín

The first volunteers were those who joined the regular army before World War II. They enlisted during peacetime at military centers such as: Fort Sam Houston, Fort Bliss, Fort McArthur, and the Presidio at San Francisco, headquarters for the 4th and 5th Army Corps areas.

On October 29, 1941, Pedro Aguilar Despart of Los Angeles was the holder of number 158 in the national draft lottery, the same number pulled out by President Roosevelt; and thus became the first Angeleno to be drafted for selective service in World War II.

On December 8th of the same year, the National Guard was federalized on President Roosevelt's proclamation. Many civilian members who had signed up in the guard "just to keep in shape," or to play soldier once in a while, suddenly found themselves in the role of real soldiers in many National Guard Divisions.

After the bombing of Pearl Harbor, the draft boards set up the machinery to send a steady stream of selectees into the Armed Forces as the nation stepped up mobilization for all-out war. Even alien non-citizens living in the United States were immediately classified 1-A and drafted into the service.

Many of the Spanish-speaking aliens that Uncle Sam drafted were later given the opportunity to become naturalized American citizens by taking the oath while a member of the United States Armed Forces.

In June, 1942, Mexico also joined other Latin-American countries in declaring war on the Axis. Soon many young Mexican nationals crossed the border at such points as Monterrey, Nuevo Leon; Matamoros and Nuevo Laredo, Tamaulipas; Piedras Negras and Villa Acuña in Coahuila; Cuidad Juárez, Chihuahua; Naco and Nogales in Sonora; and Mexicali and Tijuana in Baja California to volunteer for service with the United States.

*From Raúl Morín, *Among the Valiant: Mexican-Americans in World War II and Korea.* Reprinted by permission of Borden Publishing Company, 1855 West Main Street, Alhambra, California 91801.

Other volunteers here in the States were the many young high school students who, upon reaching the age of 18 (or 17 with their parents' permission), immediately signed up before being drafted, so that they could get into the branch of their choice. Many others also volunteered in time to beat the draft call and go into the Navy, Marines or Air Force, to keep from getting stuck in the "unglamorous Army."

The draft boards in Los Angeles, Nogales, Albuquerque, San Antonio, El Paso, Corpus Christi, and the Lower Rio Grande Valley of Texas were never caught short-handed when they had a large quota to fill. These boards were loaded with Spanish names on their files; and very few were ever exempted, reclassified, or found too essential to be drafted. Local rural youths were being drafted so fast in comparison with others, that land owners of large farms and ranches, faced with manpower shortage, voiced stern protests with the local draft boards.

Where They Came From

The Army received the larger portion of the draftees. Navy quotas were easily filled by the large number of volunteers. From the draft boards, the selectees were sent to the nearest induction center. Here were all types of raw recruits. They came from farms, from large cities, from small villages, from the backwoods, and from the hills — from all parts of the United States and from some parts of Mexico.

They had been laborers, small businessmen, farmers, truck drivers, craftsmen, students, and just plain *vagos* (vagrants). While the majority of the Spanish-speaking recruits in the local camps were from the large cities of the great Southwest, the names most often-repeated, when they would get together, were those of the many small *barrios* (neighborhoods) and suburbs which many called "home" and constantly mentioned in their conversations. Such places as *Maravilla, Chiques* (Oxnard), Simons, Jimtown, *Limonera, Sespe,* San Antonio's "Westside," *Calle Ancha* in Austin, "Magnolia" in Houston, Bessemer in Pueblo, "Larrimer" in Denver, *El Pachuco, Juariles, La Smelter,* Hollywood, *La Daisy, El Dorado, El Ranchito,* Chinatown, and *El Hoyo* were well represented. They usually had endearing nicknames for their hometowns (or gang groups) with which they identified themselves. They bragged about "Sanjo" "Fernando," "Corpos," "Verdugo," "Fresno," "Recles," "El Globo," "Jerome," "Tucson," "Santa Rita," "Las Cruces," "Tucumcari," "Conejos," "Trinidad," "La Junta," *"Foré Wes,"* "Del Río," "San Marcos," "San Benito," "Los Dos Laredos," "Varelas," and such.

Besides being from the well-known neighborhoods of towns in the Southwest, many of the Mexican-Americans in the induction centers hailed from such rarely-mentioned places as North Platte, Nebraska; Garden City, Kansas; Cheyenne, Wyoming; Missoula, Montana; Ogden, Utah; Chester, Pennsylvania, and other far away places like Gary, Indiana; Detroit, Michigan; Lorain, Ohio; St. Louis, Missouri; and Oklahoma City, Oklahoma.

One could always tell where they came from by their manner of speech (when they expressed themselves). It was quite easy to distinguish the fast-English-speaking Angelenos from the slow-Spanish-speaking Texan or New Mexican. The *Caló* talk (slang words) of the border habitant from El Paso and Juárez was in contrast to the homespun Spanish of the Coloradoan or Arizonan. Those that originated from far away localities where very few of our people live stood out because their knowledge of Spanish was limited and they much preferred the English language.

The gathering of so many from different sections afforded the Spanish-speaking people living in the United States a valuable and much-needed opportunity to study and improve their social life. Here for the first time they had an opportunity to observe, compare, and personally get to know many others of our ethnic group and what they were like.

There were, of course, many Latins who were part of the large Spanish-speaking segments in the United States not closely identified with those living in the great Southwest. Many were native-born or descendents of Puerto Ricans, Cubans, Central and South Americans, and Españoles from Spain. The largest group, by far, were those living in the Southwest, mostly identified as "Mexicans" or Mexican-Americans.

A study of this particular group will give an idea of what a "crazy, mixed-up" group they were — the different kinds of "Mexicans" that were to be found in the Army.

First, we had the American-born of Mexican parents. Although born, raised, and educated in the United States, this type still clung to many of the Mexican customs and traditions. Well acquainted with American folklore, nevertheless, they enjoyed the music and songs that came from across the border. Their speech was more Spanish than English, sometimes a mixture of both.

They had a marked preference for the companionship of other Mexican-Americans.

Quite different were those born and raised in Mexico. Some had left there since early childhood, others more recently, although all had become naturalized citizens. The latter were still very "Mexicanized." Most of them had a good education, were very well versed in Mexico's history, and possessed much of the rich culture that abounds in the land of the Aztecs. They were good orators, they could quote from Amando Nervo [immortal Mexican poet], and with the same ease recognize a Diego Rivera [famous Mexican mural artist]. They acknowledged all of Mexico's national holidays and were devoted to their religion. Their favorite entertainers and idols were most likely to be stars of the screen, radio, and sports world from Latin-American countries. They felt ill at ease in the presence of others when the conversation ran mostly in English, even when they understood the language.

Undoubtedly, the largest group were those born in the United States whose parental lineage ran back to the original settlers and the early immigrants of the Southwest. In this group were the Spanish-Americans from New Mexico and Colorado, the *Tejanos* from Texas, and the *Pochos* from California. Those belonging to this group were definitely more "American." They spoke and read less Spanish. They mingled very well with either the Anglos or Latins. For companions they preferred their school chums or town-folk, regardless of their racial background. They enjoyed Spanish songs, Latin rhythms, and Mexican *mariachis,* but also were very "hep" to the latest American songs, dances, and the latest "craze" or sayings of our modern-day youths. They enjoyed eating both Mexican and American food as well as other dishes of foreign make. They engaged in sports and social activities of both ethnic groups, those boasting of being *chicano,* or *mejicano.* They had holiday festivals that were regularly celebrated all over the Southwest.

Among them were many *encartados,* or half-breeds; and to be found were Mexican-Italians, Mexican-Filipinos, Mexican-Negroes, Spanish-Mexicans, French-Mexicans, Irish-Mexicans, Mexican-Germans, and English-Mexicans. Then came the Mexican-raised Anglos who had spent most of their lives among the Mexicans. These spoke good Spanish and always associated with Mexican-Americans. They loved everything Mexican, and had become so accustomed to being around the Mexicans that when they were asked, *"Que eres tu?"* (What are you?), they would answer —

sometimes smiling, sometimes serious — *Yo soy tan mejicano como tu.* ("I am as Mexican as you are.") Many of these came from Texas and from towns along the border; even a few [from] below the border.

From the standpoint of idiom or mannerisms, the GI's of Mexican descent were not too different. The only difference, if any, was in what they called themselves, or rather, what they were accustomed to being called by the people back home.

The so-called Spanish were in many instances accused of being ashamed of the term "Mexican." Being native-born and -raised Americans, they never felt any sentiment for Mexico or its people; they had never lived there. Their Anglo friends, out of politeness or in ignorance, called them "Spanish." Not being Anglo or Mexican, the term which referred to them was pleasing, and they long since became accustomed to it.

Then came the "Spanish-Americans" or Hispanos. Most of these were from New Mexico or Southern Colorado. They had been told long ago that only the people from south of the border were Mexican. They were all native-born Hispanos and expounded the fact that history revealed the Spaniards had been the founders and settlers of Santa Fe and other points from where they had originated.

Next came the so-called Latin-Americans. Most of these lived in Texas; a few came from the northern or middle-western states. They had struggled for many years to prove to everyone that they were from this country and not Mexicans from Mexico. Then, as stated by writer and research worker Pauline Kibbe, in a move to off-set discrimination and to differentiate themselves from the immigrants of Mexico, they had popularized the hybrid term "Latin-American," because of a "growing self-consciousness on the part of the Spanish speaking and the desire on their part to escape from a subordinate status."[1]

Last were the *mejicanos* ("Mexicans"), the proudest of all our groups, those boasting of being *chicano,* or *mejicano.* They had nothing but scorn for those who denied their racial ties or pretended not to understand Spanish; although these were not necessarily from Mexico, some were. Most had been raised in predominantly "Mexican" surroundings along the border towns and in southern Texas or southern Arizona. It was hard to tell whether they were native or foreign-born.

[1]Pauline Kibbe, *Latin-Americans in Texas* (Albuquerque: New Mexico University Press, 1946).

Strangely, the so-called "Spanish" did not speak Spanish. The Spanish-Americans and Latin-Americans spoke more Spanish than English, or with a mixture of Americanized Spanish and English, which no true American or Mexican could very well manage to interpret. The *mejicanos* would feel insulted if you spoke English only [alone] when Anglos were not present.

Native Californians were known as *Pochos; New Mexicans* as *Manitos.* Others were called just plain *chicanos* or *Tejanos; del Terré* or *del otro lado,* for those from south of the border.

All the different terms to describe the Spanish-speaking people of the Southwest have stemmed from the attempts by these groups to be set apart from the aliens. The futility of it all is noted by the small impression made on the other Americans. Whenever they would bring up our group in their conversation, we would always be referred to as "those Mexicans." They have failed to notice the differences of any group.

Many of us, too, have shared that feeling with a slight dissent. We do not notice any big characteristic difference in our people, only that they cannot be called Spanish, Mexican, or Latin-American, since we are not in Spain, Mexico, or in Latin-America; and to be called Americans would not suffice because of our different cultures, language, and complexion.

For this reason we have made the term "Mexican-American" our choice. We then imply that we are proud to be Americans, and at the same time are not trying to deny our Mexican ancestry. Another widely used identification term for our group, perhaps the more proper of the two, is the long-worded term, "Americans of Mexican descent."

The Sleepy Lagoon Case and the Grand Jury Investigation*

Robin F. Scott

On August 1, 1942, on the east side of Los Angeles one member of the "38th Street Gang" was roughed up by a rival gang, the

*From Robin F. Scott, "The Urban Mexican-American in the Southwest, 1932–1955" (Ph.D. dissertation, University of Southern California, 1969).

"Downey Boys." He made a vow to get even and soon returned to the area with other members of his gang. They searched near their favorite swimming hole — a germ laden reservoir nicknamed the "Sleepy Lagoon" — but found no one there. The Sleepy Lagoon was located on the Williams Ranch near Slauson and Atlantic Boulevards. The gang continued to search the Williams Ranch area until they found a birthday party in progress in a home on the ranch. Here they discovered the rival gang. Some scuffling took place but nothing serious happened. On August 2, the body of a Downey Boy, José Díaz was found dead next to the Sleepy Lagoon. The police picked up the members of the 38th Street Gang and charged them with murder.[1] During the subsequent trial it was stated that no one saw the murder. There was no murder weapon produced by the prosecution. There was no proof that Díaz actually was murdered — he had been drunk and had repeatedly fallen to the ground.[2]

Boys' gangs, and especially Mexican-American gangs, were not popular with the police. They caused many problems for law enforcement officials. Vandalism, gang fights, burglary, and disturbing the peace were common complaints. Anytime the police had the chance to punish these gangs for being such public nuisances they took advantage of the opportunity. The arrest of the 38th Street Gang showed no exception. Carey McWilliams wrote that "in the process of 'investigating' the case, the police severely beat up two of the boys."[3] When these youths appeared before the Los Angeles County Grand Jury for indictment, they were dirty, haggard, and bruised. During the courtroom proceedings it was discovered that Clyde C. Shoemaker, the Assistant District Attorney, "had instructed the jailer that the defendants were not to be allowed haircuts or change of clothing on the ground that their 'distinctive appearance' had to be maintained for purposes of identification."[4] It took a special motion by the defense attorneys to permit the Mexican-American defendants to have haircuts and clean shirts.

---

[1]*People* v. *Zammora* (1944), 66 Cal. ap. 2d, pp. 174–177.

[2]*Ibid.*, pp. 200–201.

[3]Carey McWilliams, *North from Mexico: The Spanish-Speaking People of the United States* (Philadelphia: J. B. Lippincott Co., 1949), p. 229.

[4]Robert A. Valdez, "Incident at Sleepy Lagoon" (typewritten report in possession of author, n.d.), p. 7.

McWilliams described the trial:

> It took place before a biased and prejudiced judge (found to be
> such by an appellate court) ; it was conducted by a prosecutor who
> pointed to the clothes and style of haircut of the defendants as
> evidence of guilt; and was staged in an atmosphere of intense
> community-wide prejudice which had been whipped up and art-
> fully sustained by the entire press of Los Angeles.[5]

Prior to the trial the police had seized upon the murder of Díaz
to make a series of dragnet raids and mass arrests. Some three
hundred Mexican-American youngsters were arrested and twenty-
two (mostly minors) were placed on trial for the murder of Díaz.[6]
On January 12, 1943, nine of the defendants were convicted of
second degree murder and two counts of assault. Three were convicted of first degree murder. They were sentenced to San Quentin
Prison for varying sentences. Five defendants were convicted of
lesser offenses and some of these were committed to the Los
Angeles County Jail. Five boys were acquitted on all counts.[7]

After the jury had returned its guilty verdict against the
Mexican-American defendants, the newspapers took a softer tone.
But by January, 1943, the attacks against the Mexican-Americans
had been resumed in a slightly different way. The word "Mexican"
was avoided at the suggestion of the Office of War Information.
The newspapers substituted the words "pachuco" on "zoot-suiter"
in a manner that no explanation was needed to indicate what
ancestry was involved.[8]

In 1943 a group of concerned citizens organized the Sleepy
Lagoon Defense Committee to defend those youths imprisoned for
the murder of Díaz. Heading this committee was Carey McWilliams,
lawyer, historian, and chief of the Division of Immigration and
Housing, Department of Industrial Relations, State of California.
The committee saw the trial and imprisonment of members of the
38th Street Gang as a conspiracy against all Mexican-Americans.

---

[5]McWilliams, *North from Mexico*, p. 230. In *People* v. *Zammora*, "In a
criminal prosecution, the trial judge was guilty of prejudicial misconduct in
making undignified and intemperate remarks tending to disparage or cast
reflection on defendants' counsel . . . ," p. 168.

[6]Carey McWilliams, "The Los Angeles Archipelago," *Science and Society*
10 (Winter, 1946), p. 45.

[7]*People* v. *Zammora*, p. 173.

[8]McWilliams, "The Los Angeles Archipelago," p. 46.

The Tenney Commission, a special committee of the California Legislature to investigate un-American activities in the state, made two reports — both included references to the Sleepy Lagoon Defense Committee. Organization and purpose of this committee were questioned by the Tenney Commission. La Rue McCormick, accused by the Commission of belonging to the Communist Party, was said to have organized on October 24, 1942, the Spanish-Speaking Peoples' Congress. This organization became the Citizens' Committee for the Defense of Mexican-American Youth on the Sleepy Lagoon Defense Committee. The Tenney Commission reported that "regardless of any consideration [the Citizens' Committee] is a typical Communist front organization."[9] Chief of Police in Los Angeles, C. B. Horrall, was quoted by the Commission as believing the Defense Committee was a Communist organization.[10] Methods used in obtaining evidence heard by the Tenney Commission in 1943 and 1945 were not unlike those practiced by Joe McCarthy in the 1950's. Witnesses found it difficult yet almost unnecessary to prove their accusations. Reports were published by the Commission without due regard for innocent victims. Many innocent people and organizations were labeled as Communistic or "fellow travelers" — thus ruining their productivity and reputations. The Sleepy Lagoon Defense Committee, however, proceeded with its work.

In October, 1943, the Sleepy Lagoon Defense Committee began a nationwide campaign to try to raise twenty thousand dollars for an appeal of the court decision in the trial. Fund-raising buffets and concerts were held. Advertisements were placed in newspapers. In order to counteract the effects of much negative publicity, a significant portion of the Defense Committee's efforts "were spent on publicizing its work in Mexico and among persons of Mexican descent in the United States."[11]

On October 4, 1944, the District Court of Appeals reversed the guilty verdict. The defendants had spent nearly two years in San Quentin Prison. Hundreds of Mexican-Americans greeted the freed

---

[9]California Legislature, Senate, 55th Session, *Report: Joint Fact-Finding Committee on Un-American Activities in California to California Legislature* (Calif. State Printing Office: 1943), p. 216.

[10]California Legislature, Senate, *Excerpts from Senate Journal of April 16, 1945 Contain Report of Joint Fact-Finding Committee on Un-American Activities in California* (Published by the Senate, 1945), p. 160.

[11]Valdez, "Incident at Sleepy Lagoon," pp. 16–17.

defendants as they returned home to Los Angeles. "For the first time in the history of Los Angeles, Mexicans had won an organized victory in the courts and, on this day, bailiffs and deputy sheriffs and court attaches were looking rather embarrassed in the presence of Mexicans."[12]

The District Court substantially upheld the appellant's charges in ruling that the trial judge had erred and injured the defense by rebuking the defense counsel in the presence of the jury. The District Court did not agree with the appellant that the charge of racial prejudice was involved.[13]

On December 29, 1944, the Sleepy Lagoon Defense Committee announced plans for its dissolution. "Having accomplished the purpose for which it was established, the Sleepy Lagoon Defense Committee will be dissolved effective January 1, 1945."[14]

A very important aspect of the Sleepy Lagoon Case was an investigation by the Grand Jury of Los Angeles County in 1942. This investigation was taking place at the same time the 38th Street Gang was being tried for murder. After their mass arrest, the Grand Jury started public hearings on the problems of the Mexican youth. Federal, state, and local agencies were heard from.

> The hearings did much to counteract the disasterous effect of the high-handed police tactics and paved the way for a subsequent visit to Los Angeles of Alan Cranston of the OWI [Office of War Information], who succeeded in bringing about a noticeable change in tone and character of newspaper reporting on the Mexican problem.[15]

The Grand Jury had appointed a special committee to examine Mexican problems and it was called the Special Mexican Relations Committee.

Perhaps the most amazing piece of information given to the Grand Jury was the pseudo-biologic and sociologic findings of Lieutenant Edward Duran Ayres of the Foreign Relations Bureau of the Los Angeles County Sheriff's Department. He explained that

---

[12]McWilliams, *North from Mexico*, p. 231.

[13]*People* v. *Zammora*, p. 236.

[14]Found in papers of Sleepy Lagoon Defense Committee, 3500 pieces in 11 boxes (1942–1945), Box 5, p. 1.

[15]Carey McWilliams, "Los Angeles' Pachuco Gangs," *The New Republic*, 108 (Jan. 18, 1943), p. 77.

crimes committed by Mexican-Americans were due in part to the
economic conditions of the home and the lack of recreation facilities. He pointed out that swimming pools, parks, and theatres
were mainly restricted to whites with "Tuesdays reserved for
Negroes and Mexicans." The refusal of service in restaurants,
according to Ayres, caused resentment among the Mexicans. The
more basic causes for crime, however, were on a biological basis.
Ayres' thesis for this presentation to the Grand Jury was "that
crime is a matter of race."[16] In other words, criminal actions could
be inherited. In an allegorical manner, Ayres compared the way-
ward Mexican-American to the "wildcat." "Although a wildcat
and a domestic cat are of the same family, they have certain
characteristics so different that while one may be domesticated the
other must be caged to be kept in captivity."[17] Ayres continued
his explanation of the Mexican behavior. The Mexican was part
Aztec and the Aztecs believed in human sacrifice. "This total
disregard for human life has always been universal throughout
the Americas among the Indian population; which of course is
well known to everyone."[18] Henry Hoijer, a UCLA anthropologist
disagreed with the Ayres' statement that the Mexican-American
was criminally inclined because his ancestors practiced human
sacrifice. In a statement to the Special Relations Commission
Hoijer testified:

> Can it be that this so-called inborn desire to kill has been found
> only twice in the history of the Mexican people—once among the
> relatively pure Indians of the Aztec Empire and the second time
> among a certain element of the Mexican population of Los
> Angeles[?][19]

The significance of Ayres' pseudo-scientific statement was reported by Ruth Tuck. "The amazing statement of another member
of the sheriff's office before the County Grand Jury in October
1942 that Mexicans were biologically predisposed toward criminal
behavior — because the Aztecs had once practiced human sacrifice — was quoted and requoted."[20]

---

[16]Edward Duran Ayres, "Findings," found in papers of Sleepy Lagoon
Defense Committee, Box 5, p. 1.

[17]*Ibid.*

[18]*Ibid.*

[19]*Ibid.*, Box 3, p. 33.

[20]Ruth D. Tuck, "Behind the Zoot Suit Riots," *Survey Graphic* 32 (August,
1943), p. 315.

Ayres testified further before the Grand Jury committee that the social experiment of the Mexican Revolution failed because Mexicans were lazy — they would rather work half of a week than a full week. This was the group of Mexicans that migrated to the United States for an easier life.[21] In addition, the European fought with his fists but the Mexican used knives or other lethal weapons. The Anglo-Saxon did not understand this part of being of Latin or Indian descent.[22] Ayres reached the crescendo — the race must be punished, at least the biologically depraved part of it. "Again, let us repeat — the hoodlum element in a whole must be indicted as a whole."[23] Ayres did admit that some Mexicans were law-abiding citizens. It was true that many of them wanted to be rid of the scourge of the lawless.

In a letter to the 1942 Grand Jury, dated August 20, 1942, Los Angeles County Sheriff Eugene W. Biscailuz supported his lieutenant. "The statistics and data embodied in the report read before your body by Lieutenant Edward Duran Ayres of my Foreign Relations Bureau ... together with the statements submitted by the Los Angeles Police Department, I believe fully cover the situation."[24] In a letter to the Grand Jury, dated August 13, 1942, C. B. Horrall, Chief of Police of the City of Los Angeles, supported the position of Lieutenant Ayres. "Lieutenant Ayres of the Sheriff's Department, gave an intelligent statement of the psychology of the Mexican people, particularly, the youths."[25] Horrall added that persons in gang activities are of the second generation. In the one part of the letter Horrall wrote that the parents, due to their poor economic status and poor education, have lost control of the youth who have far surpassed them in educational achievements.[26] Instead of sympathizing with the Mexican-American because of his lack of status and his "biological weaknesses," Horrall wanted instead to crush the offending youths. In another letter to the Grand Jury, dated August 12, 1942, Horrall did not agree with Ayres' statement that the criminal tendencies of the Mexican youth were due in part to the lack of recreational facilities. "I do not feel that additional recreational facilities will

---

[21]Ayres, "Findings," p. 2.

[22]*Ibid.*, p. 2.

[23]*Ibid.*, p. 3.

[24]*Ibid.*, Box 5.

[25]*Ibid.*

[26]*Ibid.*

in any way assist in the solution of the problem which is a vicious outgrowth of a recreational system established several years ago by the juvenile authorities."[27] The Sleepy Lagoon it seemed was a proper place for the Mexican-American boys to swim. After all, Horrall complained, the Mexican youths tear up everything built for them. Juvenile offenders should be prosecuted to the fullest extent of the law — time should not be wasted in searching for reasons why the Mexican-American boys were committing so many crimes.[28]

On October 8, 1942, Carey McWilliams wrote to the Special Mexican Relations Committee of the Grand Jury:

> While California for historical and geographical reasons should be at a place where the two major cultures of the Western Hemisphere have fused, such, most emphatically, is not the case. I mention this at the outset because it seems to me that the problem of Mexican youth in Los Angeles County is in the widest sense of the term, a problem of cultural conflict.[29]

In the same letter he stated that most of the studies of the Mexican-American problems made in the 1920's and 1930's failed to deal with the second-generation problem because there was not much of a second generation of Mexican-Americans.[30] He added that most Mexican settlements were as bad in 1942 as in 1918; that little if any improvement could be noted.[31] McWilliams followed with some comments on the isolation of the Mexican-Americans:

> Court records such as the recent action over the municipal swimming plunge in Pomona clearly confirm the fact that Mexicans live in our communities, or on their outskirts, but they seldom constitute an integral functioning part of the civic and social life of these same communities.[32]

There were other court proceedings besides the Sleepy Lagoon case.

[27]*Ibid.*
[28]*Ibid.*
[29]*Ibid.*, Box 3, p. 2.
[30]*Ibid.*, p. 3.
[31]*Ibid.*, p. 5.
[32]*Ibid.*

The same Special Mexican Relations Committee of the Grand Jury received a report called "A Tabulation of Facts on Conditions Existent in Hick's Mexican Camp." The report described the extremely poor conditions in which the Mexican-Americans were forced to exist.[33]

There were other witnesses called to testify before the committee. Guy T. Nunn, Field Representative, Minority Groups Service, War Manpower Commission, testified before the group as follows: "Violations of the President's Executive Order forbidding discrimination in war industries for reasons of race, creed, color or national origin, were so frequent as applied to Mexican working men as to be the rule rather than the exception."[34] Nunn did feel that many of the working barriers had been removed by the end of 1942 but the Mexican-Americans did not realize it."[35]

Manuel Aguilar, Mexican Consul in Los Angeles, was asked to testify and he made many suggestions. Aguilar asked that all felony violators be arrested and prosecuted, especially the leaders. He stressed that mass arrests with the attendant publicity should be avoided. He pleaded for job training of the unskilled Mexican-American, and suggested providing adequate recreational facilities with the much-needed supervision.[36] Aguilar also stated that there were a hundred local unions in the Congress of Industrial Organization. Of the hundred thousand members, fifteen thousand were Mexican or Mexican-American. He added that the CIO's program of fostering minority skills was in keeping with the needs of the community.[37]

On December 22, 1942, the Report of the Special Committee of Problems of Mexican Youth was submitted and approved by the 1942 Grand Jury of Los Angeles County. In its concluding remarks the Committee asked for community tolerance of the Mexican population. "Your committee is convinced however, that young people of Mexican ancestry have been more sinned against than sinning, in the discriminations and limitations that have been

[33]*Ibid.*, p. 10.

[34]*Ibid.*, p. 18.

[35]*Ibid.*

[36]*Ibid.*, p. 30.

[37]*Ibid.*, p. 33.

placed on them and their families."[38] Seventeen recommendations were proposed. Some of these are briefly summarized as follows:

1. Help should be provided for the training of Mexicans in the schools.
2. Public playgrounds and swimming pools should be opened to the Mexican-American.
3. The Health Department should alleviate unsanitary conditions in Mexican homes and camps.
4. The Housing Authority of Los Angeles County should give immediate attention to the Mexican housing.
5. Defense industries should stop discrimination against Mexicans.
6. The police should stop brutal treatment of prisoners.
7. Specially trained police (including a knowledge of Spanish), should be placed in Mexican districts.[39]

Unfortunately the Grand Jury recommendations were ignored to a great extent by the special agencies and the general public. Students and workers in social welfare were all aware of the explosive situation in the Mexican-American communities long before the zoot-suit riots of 1943. They had unsuccessfully tried to obtain an allocation of extra Community Chest money to finance special youth projects in "blighted" areas of the county.[40] Manuel Ruiz, Jr., an attorney, working in conjunction with the Los Angeles County Probation Department, organized a coordinating council for Latin American youth. It succeeded in opening up job training and placement for Mexicans through trade schools. It was helped in its efforts by the Minorities Division of the War Manpower Commission.[41] Eduardo Quevedo, president of the Coordinating Council for Latin American Youth, tried to organize a Boys' Club before the riots. He believed that the zoot-suited Mexican-Amer-

---

[38]Los Angeles County Grand Jury, *Final Report of Los Angeles County Grand Jury for the Year 1942: Report of Special Committee on Problems of Mexican Youth of the 1942 Grand Jury of Los Angeles County*, p. 45.

[39]*Ibid.*, pp. 45–46.

[40]John A. Ford, *Thirty Explosive Years in Los Angeles County* (San Marino: Huntington Library, 1961), p. 136.

[41]Tuck, "Behind the Zoot Suit Riots," p. 313.

ican boys needed help because of their inability to find a place in the majority society.[42]

Carey McWilliams described conditions in Los Angeles on the eve of the zoot-suit riots. The pachuco gangs had been well publicized. The police were inclined to believe the Ayres report. The newspapers were determined to find a "fifth column" in the United States — having disposed of the Japanese-Americans living on the coast. The Mexican-Americans and non-Mexicans, by their polarization, were on their way to starting a small civil war. Into this tension-filled city came the men of the armed services, bored and ready for a "last fling."[43] The dress of the Mexican-American youth did little to ease the feelings of the visiting and local servicemen.

> Unfortunately, a minority of the wartime Mexican-American youths, the Pachucos or zootsuiters, reacted in a most un-Mexican-like manner. Dressed outlandishly, as they followed the styles of less acceptable minorities, they quickly undid the hard-earned reputation of the pre-war Mexican.[44]

The zoot suit was originally worn as the proper costume for the jitterbug. Wearing this outfit became a "fad" and the Mexican-American seemed to find status at least in his own youthful society in wearing it. The zoot suit attracted attention and it showed emancipation from the older generation.[45]

Beatrice Griffith in *American Me*, did not bracket the delinquent Pachuco with the zoot-suiter. She asserted that in Los Angeles County less than five percent of the Mexican youth were delinquent. On the other hand, she reported that between 1940 and 1945, two-thirds of the Mexican-American youth wore zoot suits in one form or the other.[46] The general public and the servicemen, however, believed that all zoot-suiters were pachucos and treated them accordingly.

---

[42]"California: Zoot-Suit War," *Time* (June 21, 1943), p. 18.

[43]McWilliams, *North from Mexico*, p. 238.

[44]Manuel P. Servín, "The Pre-World War II Mexican-American: An Interpretation," *California Historical Society Quarterly* 45 (December, 1966), p. 334.

[45]Emory S. Bogardus, "Gangs of Mexican-American Youth," *Sociology and Social Research* 28 (September–October, 1943), p. 56.

[46]Beatrice W. Griffith, *American Me* (Boston: Houghton Mifflin Co., 1948), p. 45.

The Zoot-Suit Riots*

Robin F. Scott

The stereotype of the zoot-suiter as an undesirable Mexican allowed the people of Los Angeles to feel relieved of any moral obligations to the Mexican-American youth and sanctioned widespread hostile crowd behavior against the zoot-suiters. The general public heard only of the attacks on the "deserving" zoot-suited pachucos while the frequent indiscriminate attacks on innocent Mexican-Americans were ignored.[1] The term "zoot-suiter" was originally used by the newspapers to circumvent the Office of War Information order to the press that the derogatory manner in which the term "Mexican" was used was an insult to the war ally, Mexico.[2] Ralph Turner and Samuel Surace in "Zoot-Suiters and Mexicans: Symbols in Crowd Behavior," discussed the result of the change of terms. "Unlike the symbol 'Mexican,' the 'zoot-suiter' symbol evokes no ambivalent sentiments but appears in exclusively unfavorable contexts."[3] "Zoot-suiter" did not bring to mind the romantic past associated with old California, the Plaza and Olvera Street, the Ramona plays, and Mexican foods. It was far easier for a crowd to become hostile toward the "zoot-suiters" than the "Mexicans."[4]

One can only speculate as to the immediate causes that precipitated the confrontation between Mexican-American youths called zoot-suiters and an Anglo-American group consisting mostly of United States servicemen which occurred in Los Angeles in June, 1943. Edward McDonagh, a sociologist, believed the symbolic

---

*From Robin F. Scott, "The Urban Mexican-American in the Southwest, 1932–1955" (Ph.D. dissertation, University of Southern California, History Department, 1969).

[1]Ralph H. Turner and Samuel J. Surace, "Zoot-Suiters and Mexicans: Symbols in Crowd Behavior," *The American Journal of Sociology* 62 (July, 1956), p. 20.

[2]Ruth D. Tuck, "Behind the Zoot Suit Riots," *Survey Graphic* 32 (August, 1943), p. 315.

[3]Turner and Surace, "Zoot Suiters and Mexicans," p. 19.

[4]*Ibid.*, p. 20.

status of the uniform versus the zoot suit might have been a factor. The Mexican-American boy wore a long suit coat with trousers pegged at the cuff, draped around the knees and deep pleats at the waist, and a low-hanging watch chain. He kept his hair long and well-greased, presenting a striking contrast to the crew-cut American sailor dressed in his "whites." "In retrospect, it is probably true that many of the Mexican boys desired the patriotic status of the military uniform and many of the sailors wanted the freedom symbolized by the zoot suit."[5]

Another immediate cause of the rioting could be traced to wives and girl friends on both sides. "The most prominent charge from each side was that the other had molested its girls."[6] The Mexican-American girls seemed to cause much of the difficulty. Many of them had also gone in for costumes and were as distinctive as the boys in their short skirts, net stockings, extra-high-heeled shoes, and elaborate hair-do's. The sailors were attracted to these girls and trouble resulted. When the sailors and soldiers dated the Mexican-American girls they invited conflict with the zoot-suited boys. The service men were usually badly beaten.[7]

Beatrice Griffith summarized various hostile attacks leading up to the Los Angeles riots. In April, 1943, some United States marines and sailors went to "clean up" two hundred Mexican and Negro zoot-suiters in Oakland, California. The same kind of activity took place in May in Venice, California.[8]

> Rumors, conflict, and incidents between the sailors and the teenage Mexican-Americans continued to increase in Los Angeles . . . Sailors were beaten and robbed in Mexican neighborhoods.[9]

In the latter part of May, 1943, a week before the rioting got under way, taxis carrying individual sailors began to "case" the Mexican-American community in East Los Angeles.[10] Griffith described the feelings of the sailors just before going overseas. "It

---

[5]Edward C. McDonagh, "Status Levels of Mexicans," *Sociology and Social Research* 33 (July, 1949), p. 451.

[6]Turner and Surace, "Zoot Suiters and Mexicans," p. 17.

[7]John A. Ford, *Thirty Explosive Years in Los Angeles County* (San Marino: Huntington Library, 1961), p. 135.

[8]Beatrice Griffith, *American Me* (Boston: Houghton Mifflin Co., 1948), p. 17.

[9]*Ibid.*, p. 19.

[10]*Ibid.*

was going to be a good weekend in a war-packed city. The riot fever and community madness had caught on."[11]

The Zoot-Suit Riots began on Thursday, June 3, 1943, in Los Angeles. Sailors left the Chávez Ravine Armory armed with rocks, sticks, clubs, and palm saps. The Georgia Street Emergency Hospital was quickly filled with riot victims.[12] A Mexican-American crime-prevention group was reportedly one of the first victims of the rioting.

> On the evening of Thursday, June 3, the Alpine Club—a group made up of youngsters of Mexican descent—held a meeting in a police substation in Los Angeles. They met in the police station, at the invitation of an officer, because of the circumstance that the nearby public school happened to be closed. With a police officer present, they met to discuss their problems, foremost of which, at this meeting, was the urgent question of how best to preserve the peace in their locality.[13]

When the meeting concluded they were taken in police patrol cars to the street corner which was closest to the neighborhood in which most of the youths lived. "The squad cars were scarcely out of sight, when the boys were assaulted. Thus began the recent weekend race riots in Los Angeles."[14]

On Saturday, June 5, the Los Angeles *Herald-Express* carried the following dispatch:

> "Task Force" Hits Los Angeles Zooters. A Petty Officer says, "We're out to do what the police have failed to do—We're going to clean up this situation to the satisfaction of ourselves and the public. . . ."[15]

In East Los Angeles and Belvedere Gardens, the police arrested nine sailors on charges of disturbing the peace. On June 7, the *Herald-Express* featured photographs which showed two servicemen in the hospital and zoot-suiters in chains being taken to jail

---

[11]*Ibid.*, p. 22.

[12]*Ibid.*, p. 20.

[13]Carey McWilliams, "The Zoot-Suit Riots," *The New Republic* 208 (June 21, 1943), p. 818.

[14]*Ibid.*

[15]Los Angeles *Herald-Express* (June 5, 1943), p. A-1.

after the "Battle of Skid Row," the "Battle of Firestone," and the "Battle of North Broadway."[16]

The *Los Angeles Times* on Tuesday, June 8 featured the riots on its front page:

> Heaviest street rioting in downtown city streets in many years. Thousands of servicemen, joined by thousands of civilians last night surged along Main Street and Broadway hunting zoot-suiters. Chief of Police Horrall declared riot alarm at 10:30 P.M. and ordered every policeman on duty. More than fifty zoot-suiters had clothing torn off as servicemen and civilians converged on bars, restaurants, penny arcades, and stores in downtown area searching for zoot-suiters. Streetcars were halted and theatres along Main Street were scrutinized for hiding zoot-suiters ... [More] clashes broke out later in the evening in various parts of the county with more than 200 servicemen gathering at a theatre at 4th Street and Brooklyn Avenue and rousting zoot-suiters out of their seats. Police were handicapped by the tremendous crowds of civilians who apparently had listened to the police riot calls on the radio and had rushed into downtown. . . . Traffic blocked as groups raced into streets after victims. [They] would disperse only after they "unpan[t]sed" the wearer of the comical clothing.[17]

On June 8, the *Herald-Express* displayed pictures showing "zooters" in "protective custody." They were being held in jail to keep them from being attacked by the angry servicemen. Another picture showed a crowd of typical men and women gathered around service men who were man-handling and stripping any zoot-suiters who approached. The crowd cheered the service men.[18]

Most of the heavy rioting took place over the week-end but the newspapers did not finish with their stories. On June 9, the *Herald-Express* carried two feature articles with large pictures of the participants.

> A Vernon police officer near death from being run down by a carload of zootsuit gangsters who set a trap for him.

> A "pachuco woman" held for assertedly being prepared to smuggle aluminum "knucks" to zoot suit hoodlums.[19]

---

[16]*Herald-Express* (June 7, 1943), p. A-3.

[17]*Los Angeles Times* (June 8, 1943), p. 1.

[18]Los Angeles *Herald-Express* (June 8, 1943), p. B-1.

[19]*Herald-Express* (June 9, 1943), p. A-1.

On June 10, the *Herald-Express* headlined the following:

Zoot Girls Stab Woman; State Probes Rioting

Grand Jury to Act in Zoot-Suit War[20]

On June 16, the *Los Angeles Times* headlined the following stories:

Zoot Cyclists Snatch Purses

Mexican Government Expects Damages for Zoot Riot Victims[21]

The editorials of the newspapers left no doubt as to which side the papers were on. The following editorial was entitled "Zoot Suiters Learn."

> It was a sad day when zoot suiters began to molest some United States Navy men and some members of their families.... They promise to rid the community of one of its newest evils—those zoot-suited miscreants who have committed many crimes and have added a very serious side to juvenile delinquency problems.[22]

The Los Angeles County Grand Jury held an investigation of the riots. This body looked into juvenile crime and delinquency. In its final report the Grand Jury acknowledged the seriousness of the situation and the failure of the 1942 Grand Jury investigations and recommendations to stimulate community interest in coping with juvenile gang violence. "When the 1943 Grand Jury came into office the problem seemed no nearer solution than it had six months before. Indeed it seemed to be in an even more aggravated condition."[23] The Grand Jury, however, refused to conclude that this condition had been brought about because of racial prejudice.

> The Jury finds that juvenile crimes do not have for their motive or reason class or racial hatred or discrimination. Ill-informed and reckless persons, by unfounded charges of racial discrimination against the Mexican people, have done little to promote harmony between this nation and our sister republic to the south.[24]

---

[20]*Herald-Express* (June 10, 1943), p. A-1.

[21]*Times* (June 16, 1943), p. 2.

[22]*Herald-Express* (June 8, 1943), p. B-2.

[23]Los Angeles County Grand Jury, *Final Report of the 1943 Los Angeles County Grand Jury: Report of the Special Committee on Racial Problems*, p. 27.

[24]Los Angeles County Grand Jury, *Findings and Recommendations of the Grand Jury of Los Angeles County (1943), Based Upon Its Inquiry into Juvenile Crime and Delinquency in that County*, p. 4.

Governor Earl Warren also initiated an investigation into the riots. The *Los Angeles Times* reported that this special committee had taken recess after learning "that the zoot suit problem was not a racial one. . . ."[25]

On June 17 and 18, 1943, the *Times* featured the opposing viewpoints of Eleanor Roosevelt and Robert Hotchkis, President of the California State Chamber of Commerce. The First Lady stated that the riots could be traced to what she called long-standing discrimination against Mexicans in that part of the country. "For a long time I've worried about the attitudes toward Mexicans in California and the States along the border."[26] Mrs. Roosevelt added that the riots were not simply youth problems but were provoked by elements which had little to do with youth. Mr. Hotchkis, filled with righteous indignation, answered Mrs. Roosevelt on the next day: "The statement that the citizens of California have discriminated against persons of Mexican-origin is untrue, unjust, and provocative of disunion among people who have lived for years in harmony."[27]

Time magazine devoted some space to zoot-suit riots and added its own opinion. It pointed out that "California's zoot-suit war was a shameful example of what happens to wartime emotions without wartime discipline."[28] *Time* criticized local publishers Hearst and Chandler for stirring the violence to higher proportions.[29] *Time* stated that young Mexican-American organized gangs had gotten out of hand. "They had robbed and used their knives on some lone sailors on dark side streets."[30] The magazine added:

"If the pachucos had asked for trouble, they got more than was coming to them last week. The military authorities were notably lax. . . . The Los Angeles Police apparently looked the other way."[31]

The Los Angeles community itself had to share the blame for escalating the riots continued *Time*. "And Los Angeles, apparently unaware that it was spawning the ugliest brand of riot action since the coolie race riots of the 1870's gave its tacit approval."[32]

---

[25]*Los Angeles Times* (June 16, 1943), p. 2.

[26]*Times* (June 17, 1943), p. 2.

[27]*Times* (June 18, 1943), p. 2.

[28]"California: Zoot-Suit War," *Time* (June 21, 1943), p. 18.

[29]*Ibid.*

[30]*Ibid.*

[31]*Ibid.*, p. 19.

[32]*Ibid.*

Beatrice Griffith also pointed the finger of blame at municipal officials for not cooling hot tempers. She accused the mayor and police of either downgrading the magnitude of the rioting or excusing the excesses of the sailors. One high official had said, "Many of us were in the First World War, and we're not going to pick up kids in the service."[33] Griffith reported that on June 7 when the civilians joined in the search for zoot-suiters, officials began to retreat from their position of indifference, and on June 8 the Los Angeles area was declared off-limits to Navy personnel.[34] Two public meetings took place in the city in an effort to calm the populace. One was composed of high officials—navy, army, police, sheriff, and city—each holding the other responsible for the rioting. One hundred and fifty civic leaders gathered for the other public meeting in which a member charged that "a complete collapse of civil authority" had taken place.[35]

In *North From Mexico,* Carey McWilliams wrote, "The riots were not an unexpected rupture in Anglo-Hispano relations but the logical end-product of a hundred years of neglect and discrimination."[36] In his assessment of the riots, McWilliams joined others in placing the immediate responsibility of the riots upon the Los Angeles press and the Los Angeles police.[37] Perhaps this view was too simplified. The newspapers aggravated a touchy situation while the police failed to understand that a situation existed. Pachuco gangs had been terrorizing certain sections of the city and this had to be curtailed. The vigilante action of the sailors, however, was not the answer. Violence of this type had a short-range effect of reducing pachuco terrorism but it damaged a total generation of Mexican-Americans for years. McWilliams listed various reasons why he blamed the newspapers and the police.

1. Zoot suit gangs are not criminal gangs. The pachucos who may be criminals are loosely organized in the neighborhoods.
2. The delinquency rate of Mexican-Americans is less than the citywide average.
3. Much of the crime reported was the work of men—not boys.

---

[33]Griffith, *American Me*, p. 23.

[34]*Ibid.*, p. 24.

[35]*Ibid.*, p. 25.

[36]Carey McWilliams, *North from Mexico: The Spanish-Speaking People of the United States* (Philadelphia: J. B. Lippincott Co., 1949), p. 257.

[37]McWilliams, "The Zoot-Suit Riots," p. 819.

4. The sailors were not driven to violence by needs of self-defense.
5. About 98% of the "Mexican" youth in Los Angeles was American-born, American-raised, and American-educated.[38]

The police department refuted the blame. In interviews with the 1943 Grand Jury various police officials accused juvenile authorities for the rise in the delinquency rate.

> The failure of the juvenile authorities to instill a proper respect for constituted authority in the minds of juvenile delinquents and their failure for the elimination of juvenile criminals from association with and dominance over the other boys in their neighborhood [promotes juvenile delinquency].[39]

Ruth Tuck wrote in "Behind the Zoot-Suit Riots" that thousands of military and civilian men beat up anyone who looked like a Mexican whether he was a gang member or merely a bystander. "The wearing of a zoot suit seems to have been entirely incidental; pictures of police lineups show less than half of the Mexican boys so attired."[40] Tuck believed that Mayor Fletcher Bowron of Los Angeles was avoiding the issue when he told the State Department that "there could not be any racial issue involved, as ninety-eight percent of the youths had been born in Los Angeles."[41] She described the fears of the Mexican Consulate who during the riots "advised all persons of Mexican origin or descent to stay in their homes after sundown for their own safety."[42]

The changing meaning of the term "zoot-suiter" reflected public resentment. First, "zoot-suiter" could mean anyone, but particularly a Mexican or Negro who was wearing a zoot suit. Later, the term meant any dark-skinned person the public did not like: "Overt hostile crowd behavior is usually preceded by a period in which the key symbol is stripped of its favorable connotations until it comes to evoke unambiguously unfavorable feelings."[43]

Turner and Surace, in their research project on zoot-suiters, read copies of the *Los Angeles Times* for ten years preceding the riots. One copy of the *Times* for each month of this period was

---

[38]*Ibid.*

[39]*Findings and Recommendations of the Grand Jury*, 1943, p. 5.

[40]Tuck, "Behind the Zoot Suit Riots," p. 313.

[41]*Ibid.*

[42]*Ibid.*

[43]Turner and Surace, "Zoot-Suiters and Mexicans," p. 16.

analyzed, and the articles written on the subject were placed in five different categories:

	Favorable Old California Mexican Culture and Religion	Neutral	Unfavorable to Mexican Delinquency Poverty	Negative Favorable Counter-Attacks	Zooter as a Badge of Delinquency
1933-36	80	11	90	0	0
1936-39	61	23	13	3	0
1939-43	25	32	5	8	30

The chart illustrated the changing position of the *Times* with respect to Mexican-Americans.[44]

The 1943 Zoot-Suit Riots:
Brief Episode in a Long Conflict*

Patricia Adler

Los Angeles during World War II was a tense, fevered place. The overcrowded city was strained and resolute, and at the same time like an unplanned carnival. Defense workers with new security badges packed into the street cars. On the waterfront, the night shifts worked in a blaze of light along the keels of Liberty ships. Downtown, near the bus station, servicemen on leave watched families from Arkansas and Oklahoma and the deep South unloading children from their used-up cars, trying to get their bearings, asking where to find a job. Sailors stood in line for the movie theaters, eyeing their reflections in the plate glass department store windows, restless, with more money than there was time to spend. Everyone was restless. The city's disquiet intensified and

---

[44]*Ibid.*, p. 11.

*From a study by Patricia Adler, prepared for a course in the History of the Mexican-American in the Southwest, at the University of Southern California.

burst out, in early June, 1943, in a sudden pageant of violence—
the Zoot-Suit Riots.

After Pearl Harbor, Los Angeles had braced itself for a sea
attack, for a strike by Japanese invaders coming onto the beach
from submarines or perhaps flying in on bombing raids out of
the undefended Pacific skies. The Japanese fishermen on Terminal
Island and the families growing vegetables on the bluffs along
the coast were immediately suspect. Military and civilian authorities came to swift agreement that not only these, but all Japanese,
must be moved inland, away from the vulnerable shoreline.

The Japanese were the most conspicuous but not the only
source of anxiety in Los Angeles. The Southern California pen-
chant for supporting outlandish political schemes gave a basis
for the suspicion that Hitler's agents might be able to raise a fifth-
column here. Communists, too, had seemed to multiply during the
depression, despite a campaign to suppress them and what non-
union Los Angeles considered their labor agitation programs.

A series of books on the question of American loyalties which
appeared in 1940 were read and discussed in Los Angeles as
relevant to the local problem—Martin Dies' *Trojan Horse in
America,* Harold Lavine's *Fifth Column,* and Lawrence Dennis'
Dynamics of War and Revolution. The America First movement gained adherents. In January, 1941, the California State
Legislature created a joint Senate-Assembly committee to investigate Communist, Fascist, Nazi, and other foreign-dominated
groups. It was to "ascertain, collate and appraise all facts causing
or constituting interference with the National Defense Program
in California or rendering the people of the State, as a part of
the Nation, less fit physically, mentally, morally, economically, or
socially."[1]

This Joint Fact-Finding Committee on Un-American Activities in California, the "Little Dies Committee" headed by State
Senator Jack B. Tenney, held its first hearing in Los Angeles
in July and October, 1941. It came primarily to investigate the
CIO strike at North American Aircraft Company which it considered the outgrowth of local Communist activity.[2] It returned
soon after Pearl Harbor to study the subversive organizations
found to be active in the Southern California Japanese community.

---

[1]*Report of the Joint Fact-Finding Committee on Un-American Activities in
California* (Sacramento: State of California, 1943), p. 5.

[2]*Ibid.,* pp. 52–53.

While the bulk of the committee's first report deals with Communism, local Nazi Bundists, and Fascist front groups, it also includes testimony on the Shinto religion and Japanese state philosophy which the committee found to be a fanatic nationalism gripping American citizens of Japanese parentage as well as immigrants from Japan. The Committee recommended strict and continuing surveillance of all Japanese, regardless of their claims of United States citizenship.

Late in 1942, alerted by newspaper accounts of violence in the Mexican community, the committee launched an investigation of the *Sinarquistas,* an anti-Communist society seeking to influence politics in Mexico and charged with subversion in the *barrios* of Los Angeles. The committee was quickly convinced that sinister forces were at work. Its hearings, continued through the war years, contributed a semi-official respectability to the city's xenophobic suspicions of the Mexican minority.

Another factor which predisposed the city to suspicions of its Mexican-Americans was a mounting obsession with juvenile delinquency which was, at the time, associated in the public imagination with the Mexican gangs of downtown and East Los Angeles. After the relocation of the Japanese was completed, in March, 1942, the old hotels and rooming houses they vacated in Little Tokyo filled with incoming war workers and their families. Rental housing had always been in short supply in Los Angeles. During the war families moved into store fronts and garages, doubled up with relatives, and poured into wartime housing projects as soon as they were built. In downtown Los Angeles, children responded to the crowded quarters and the tensions of their parents with mischief, truancy, and a wildness which appeared to authorities to be a wave of delinquency. Delinquency was measurably worse in the most urbanized areas—juvenile arrests by the Sheriff's Department declined while arrests in the metropolitan precincts of Los Angeles. The committee was quickly convinced that sinister of white boys increased at about the same rate as did arrests of non-whites, the police and the public were particularly impressed with Mexican delinquency due to the belief that violence was peculiar to Mexican gangs.

In a survey of wartime juvenile delinquency the Los Angeles District Attorney protested that, "The declaration of war in December, 1941, did not cause any abrupt change in the delinquency trend (except in regard to auto cases). There was a considerable increase in delinquency in 1941 so that the further increase which occurred in 1942 was particularly serious. However, the 1942 increase in delinquency was unduly exaggerated in the public mind due to the fact that *many incidents of violence and gang activity which actually involved adults was attributed to juveniles.*" [Emphasis appears in the report] He also pointed out that Mexican boys appearing in juvenile court made up only 26.3 percent of the total, contrary to the public's belief.[3]

A comparison of local news reports in the Los Angeles press during 1942 and 1943 with the statistics compiled by the district attorney, and later confirmed by other officials, indicates that the newspapers, especially those published by William Randolph Hearst, were presenting a highly distorted picture of delinquency. Beginning a few weeks after the Japanese relocation story had left the front pages, the war news was frequently interspersed with news about roving gangs of Los Angeles teen-agers and the crimes of violence they supposedly committed. It was not, however, an entirely new theme. The morning papers of August 17, 1941, had carried the first sensationalized story—the report of the death of two boys after a party-crashing fight in the Rose Hill section. An invading gang had rammed and overturned a car full of departing guests—allegedly members of a rival gang. Both gangs were composed of Mexicans—as the papers called them without distinction as to their individual citizenships—and some of the boys were dressed in the bizarre style favored for "jive" dancing, the "zoot-suit."

The existence of gang fighting and zoot-suit styles in the Mexican district did not come as a revelation, but rather as a confirmation, of the Los Angeles stereotype of Mexican conduct. According to the stereotype, there was always violence in the *barrios,* hidden behind the picturesque "Old California" facade which fascinated the tourists. At the same time, Mexicans were thought of as ignorant and lazy. The nature of this stereotype invited the hostility of the majority community. It also blocked all sincere efforts at understanding when the outbreak of violence made understanding of crucial importance. The majority community could see the "Mexican problem," but never the actual Mexicans.

---

[3]Fred N. Howser, District Attorney, *Report on Juvenile Delinquency in Wartime Los Angeles,* mimeographed report (Los Angeles: County of Los Angeles, 1943), p. 3.

The stereotype had developed long before. A feature writer for the *Los Angeles Times* had written as early as 1925, "We always picture Mexico as a cactus-covered desert populated exclusively by bloodthirsty natives whose chief interest in life is cutting one another's throats. . . Yet, we have in Los Angeles 100,000 Mexicans living in different sections of the city, apart from our social life, in a miniature world all their own. All along South Main Street and North Spring Street, you see them in the Mexican theaters and restaurants. . . As you watch them at play in a large group you realize the numerous bloods blended in their veins . . . and in their humble and quiet manner you read the history of a great and romantic people."[4]

This ambivalence in the "Anglo" stereotype of the Mexicans persisted into the war years, was clearly evident during the Zoot-Suit Riots of 1943, and dominated public debate in the aftermath of the riots. Social workers shared this attitude, and perpetuated it. Since the first great migrations from Mexico in 1910, they had explained the obviously substandard Mexican sections of the city in terms of the uncivilized habits transplanted from south of the border. The *barrios* were "the result of years of oppression . . . the heritage of generations who have been forced to adapt themselves to bitter poverty and insupportable tyranny," rather than a reflection of American conditions.[5] This notion continued to prevail despite the fact that Mexicans born and raised in Los Angeles had outnumbered those of Mexican upbringing since the 1930's.

Although the Mexican immigrants in Los Angeles had an inordinately high rate of crime, social workers did not consider this as evidence of inherited criminal tendencies not present in other ethnic groups. It was the police department which accepted the theory that criminal tendencies were hereditary and based on ethnic factors. The Los Angeles Police Department tabulated crimes according to race until 1950, using the categories "White," "Black," "Red" (Indian, i.e., Mexican), "Yellow," and "Brown" (Filipino). The department published in its annual reports tables of statistics on the nationality of offenders, and offenders' parents.

---

[4] Agnes Pallen, "Mexicans in Los Angeles," *Los Angeles Times*, May 3, 1925, in *Los Angeles Clippings*, Vol. 3, (compiled by staff, USC Library), items 43–44.

[5] Elizabeth Fuller, *The Mexican Housing Problem in Los Angeles*, Studies in Sociology Monograph No. 17 (Los Angeles: University of Southern California Press, 1920), p. 1.

As a prominent University of Southern California sociologist analyzed Mexican criminality, it was a cultural disability: "His crimes are usually elemental, simple, overt. Lack of self-control and of social control in a complex and perplexing environment are major explanations. Mexicans rank abnormally high in crimes of personal violence against each other. They have brought their customs with them relative to settling their disputes. These methods which are sometimes honorable in an elementary culture level, are 'crimes' in our sophisticated civilization."[6] English and American common law had long ago rejected this aspect of chivalry and interposed the mediating arm of the state. The police department could not, in the twentieth century, be governed by ancient social customs in their task of applying the statutes.

The primitive Mexican custom of socializing outside the home, in bars and on the sidewalks, appeared to social workers as another unfortunate anachronism which ought to be abandoned. Boys especially, in America, were expected to be kept off the street. Police shared this idea, and both police and social workers were backed by the firmly held conviction of the dominant class in America that idleness, under any circumstances, was morally wrong. Yet another conviction written into law and at odds with Mexican folkways was that drunkenness, at least in public, was an offense against the community. As a sympathetic commentator on the *barrios* of Los Angeles wrote, "for the adult Mexicans the trouble is 'drunkenness,' as a rule uncomplicated by any other charge. The offenders are, largely, the laborers of middle age and over. . . The *colonia* is not proud of these befuddled oldsters, but it has a certain sympathy for them. 'Those police cars are like *zopilotes* (buzzards). They circle these streets. It doesn't make any difference how quiet a man is. If he is alone on the streets at night, he is stopped. If he has had a drink or two, he is drunk.' "[7]

The police, who stood for the white Anglo-Saxon Protestant norms of conduct, at the same time represented to the Mexican community the weakness of the proclaimed American democratic principles, when it came to the application of these principles to

---

[6] Emory S. Bogardus, *The Mexicans in the United States*, School of Research Studies No. 5 (Los Angeles: University of Southern California Press, 1934), p. 53.

[7] Ruth D. Tuck, *Not with the Fist: Mexican-Americans in a Southwest City*, (New York: Harcourt Brace and Co., 1946), p. 213.

people who did not share the conduct norms. The community remembered the deportations to Mexico during the depression, when families had been herded onto railroad cars without a chance to prove their United States citizenship. The police were constant reminders of the arbitrariness of American policies, and of the background "Anglo" hostility toward the Mexican way of life. Conflict with the police was a fixed condition of existence in the *barrios*, outlasting the riots, and the investigations, and the recommended changes, and the exhortations of innumerable citizens' committees.

For their part, the police regarded the Mexican family as a prime source of anti-social behavior in the city. A sociologist noted that, "in many instances the parents are ignorant of child training methods. . . The officers spend some time in giving parents instruction. 'Mexican peon parents have no ideas about raising children.' "[8] The notion of the Mexican family as a defective "Anglo" family proved to be unshakable in the thinking of both social workers and the police.

There had long been a recognition of the fact that the second generation was rebellious. The riots seemed to be a demonstration of this, and the post-riot handling of the "Mexican problem" was predicated on the same assumptions about the causes of the rebelliousness which had become established years before. Social workers considered it typical for the families of immigrants from all countries. Mexican parents should be no more baffled by the behavior of their children than the parents of second-generation Polish- or Italian- or Irish-Americans had been.

Parents tended to accept the restlessness of youth as part of the North American environment. They, as well as the police and social workers, were aware of the conflict long before World War II. "The *pachucos* ["hoodlums"] existed long before the zoot-suits came into style," one social worker wrote. During the unrest and dislocations of the depression years, teen-agers had been sharply aware of their inability to compete for jobs with the schooled, protected, "American" youths, and had reacted with displaced and disguised hostility. They had revolted "against not one but two cultures. They neither understood nor wanted any part of either. . . Being lost, they looked for a means of expressing their group solidarity. They found it in hostility to the established order and

---

[8]Bogardus, *op. cit.*, p. 56.

in the pleasures of shocking public opinion."[9] The Mexican community was fully as shocked by *pachuquismo* as the "Anglo" community.

Between midsummer 1942 and midsummer 1943, the institutionalized Calvinist conscience of Los Angeles—the police department, the time-honored apologetics of the social workers, the scapegoating operations of the Tenney Committee, the war mood of the press, the restlessness of the crowded city, and the rebelliousness of the pachucos all came together to produce mob violence— the Zoot-Suit Riots.

As hot weather began in 1942, the press played up a series of "midnight battles" between the Belvedere gang and the Palo Verde gang in East Los Angeles. A party-crashing fight between two other gangs on August 1st, according to police accounts, preceded the slaying of a young Mexican-American, José Díaz. His death beside an East Los Angeles swimming hole, the "Sleepy Lagoon," appeared to be one more episode in an inexcusable succession of Mexican outrages.   The police rounded up 24 youngsters, all alleged to be gang members.   The Grand Jury returned indictments against nineteen, with two of these youths asking and receiving approval for a separate trial. The remaining seventeen were convicted January 13, 1943, on various charges of manslaughter and assault after a poorly conducted trial with neither the fact of murder, the murder weapon, or the presence of the accused at the scene being established. There was unrestrained prejudicial comment by the press throughout the period of the trial.

The broader "Mexican problem" was put on trial in the press at the same time. The Tenney Committee returned to Los Angeles to begin hearings on Communist Party agitation in the Mexican community, and the Los Angeles County Grand Jury called members of the police and sheriff's departments to give explanations of the underlying causes of Mexican delinquency.

In efforts to "get to the bottom of this thing," the 1942 Grand Jury provided a forum for the expounding of the police theories that crime was fundamentally a matter of race. The Mexican propensity for violence was an inherited trait, according to the well-publicized police statements. One concerned member of the Grand Jury managed to have scientific refutations of this ancient

---

[9]Beatrice Griffith, "Who Are the *Pachucos?*" *Pacific Spectator* (Summer, 1947), p. 355.

fallacy presented in open session, and the final report of the 1942 Grand Jury includes no recommendations which would implement the racist theories, but the damage to the public concept of Mexican-Americans was not undone. It was reflected the following year, in the recommendations of the 1943 Grand Jury for removing all delinquent and "pre-delinquent" Mexican youths to special facilities. It was also reflected in the proposal that juvenile court jurisdiction be denied for participants in zoot-suit gang offenses, which was advanced by the Grand Jury's Special Committee On Older Youth Gang Activity in Los Angeles and Vicinity.[10]

While the Mexican population was being tried by various committees and the press, the police department redoubled its efforts to get the gangs under control. Chief Horrall's assistant was soon able to report, "The Los Angeles Police Department in conjunction with the Sheriff, California Highway Patrol, the Monterey, Montebello, and Alhambra Police Departments, conducted a drive on Mexican gangs throughout Los Angeles County on the nights of August 10th and 11th. All persons suspected of gang activities were stopped. Approximately 600 persons were brought in. There were approximately 175 arrests for having knives, guns, chains, dirks, daggers, and any other implement that might have been used in assault cases. . . Present plans call for drastic action. . ."[11] On October 30th, 1942, seventy-two Mexican youths were arrested by the newly activated "LAPD Riot Squad," following a party-crashing fight in the Crenshaw district.

Following the conviction of the Sleepy Lagoon murder defendants, a group of Los Angeles liberals organized a committee to bring to public notice what seemed to them a miscarriage of justice, and to raise funds for an appeal. It was headed by an able magazine editor and writer, Carey McWilliams. The committee worked to good effect. It succeeded in mounting an appeal which led, in 1944, to the reversal of the convictions, the dismissal of charges, and a reprimand of the trial judge for his conduct of the court proceedings.

---

[10]"Summary of Recommendation and Progress to Date of the Special Committee on Older Gang Youth Activity in Los Angeles and Vicinity," in *Final Report of the Los Angeles County Grand Jury, 1942*, p. 48.

[11]Joseph F. Reed, Administrative Assistant, to C. B. Horrall, Chief of Police, Los Angeles, August 12, 1942, quoted in Carey McWilliams, *North from Mexico: The Spanish-Speaking People of the United States* (New York: Monthly Review Press, 1961), pp. 235–36.

Meanwhile, the "riots" which had been reported by the police and the press for months actually assumed riot proportions. The violence, when it erupted, was not between gangs but was an outburst of Anglo hostility against Mexicans identified as hoodlums by their wearing of the flamboyant zoot-suits. It began June 3, 1943, with off-duty policemen staging a hunt for zoot-suiters who had allegedly attacked 11 sailors entering the Mexican district. The police "Vengeance Squad," the papers reported, had failed to find the culprits. The following night 200 sailors hired a fleet of taxicabs and cruised through the Mexican district, stopping to beat lone zoot-suiters and rip their clothing. The police followed along and arrested the victims. With variations, the violence was repeated the 5th, 6th, 7th, and 8th of June. On the 8th, Mayor Bowron told reporters, "sooner or later it will blow over," and County Supervisor Roger Jessup said, "All that is needed to end lawlessness is more of the same action as is being exercised by the servicemen." The Los Angeles City Council passed an ordinance making the wearing of zoot-suits a misdemeanor.[12] On the 9th, military authorities placed downtown Los Angeles "Off-Limits," and the violence came to a halt.

Immediately after the riots the Tenney Committee returned to pursue the question of Communist agitation in the *barrios*. The original charges that the Los Angeles Mexican-American community harbored a Nazi-supported fifth column called the *Sinarquistas* had been made by Mrs. LaRue McCormick, an acknowledged member of the Communist Party. The committee proved to be more concerned with investigating Mrs. McCormick and her Communist ties than the *Sinarquistas*. *Sinarquista* affiliations with Nazi agents in Mexico were established by committee investigators, but the matter was dropped because of difficulties presented by Spanish-language testimony, the rudimentary nature of the local organization, and the paltry sums of money actually received from abroad.

It is difficult to understand the priorities or the logic of the Tenney Committee. It operated on a guilt-by-association principle and often lost itself in a web of its own tracing by following membership lists into other membership lists, and implicating suspected Communists who served in turn to re-implicate each other. However, its 1943 and 1945 reports suggest that the highest

---

[12]McWilliams, *op. cit.*, p. 250.

priority in the *Sinarquista* investigation was to tie the label of Communist on the entire Sleepy Lagoon Defense Committee by showing that it was contaminated not only by the presence of Mrs. McCormick, but by CIO organizers identified by the committee as Communists during its investigation of the North American Aircraft Company strike.

The committee became solicitous of the *Sinarquistas* in the process. It reported that, "The Communist press, Communist spokesmen, loud-mouthed Communist sympathizers and fellow travelers charged the *Sinarquistas* with the responsibility for the riots," but that, in fact, it had been the other way around.[13] The committee offered its proof that it had been the foes of the *Sinarquistas*, the Communists, who had started the riots, having realized that, "The *Pachuco,* or so-called 'zoot-suit' fad among Negro and Mexican youth in Los Angeles' east side was a golden opportunity for Communist racial agitation. . ."[14]

Carey McWilliams, as chairman of the Sleepy Lagoon Defense Committee, was called to testify on his activities among Mexican-American youths prior to the riots.

"While the [Sleepy Lagoon murder] case was pending on appeal," he writes, "several members of the committee, including myself, were subpoenaed by the Committee on Un-American Activities in California . . . and grilled at great length. Naturally these various grillings were reported in the press in a manner calculated to make it most difficult for us to raise money for the appeal."[15]

McWilliams deplores, but does not analyze, the innuendoes of the committee's line of attack. It wished to publicize the Communist threat to the moral as well as the military and political safety of the state. Communists, according to the committee, wanted to promote miscegenation, which was a foreign notion inimical to American moral well-being. The defenders of the zoot-suiters in Los Angeles were to be exposed as believers in miscegenation. The committee wanted the press and the public to have the benefit of its information while the causes of the riots were being discussed and analyzed.

Senator Tenney himself questioned Carey McWilliams. The committee report summarizes the testimony which Tenney con-

---

[13]Report of the Joint Fact-Finding Committee on Un-American Activities in California (Sacramento: State of California, 1945), p. 172.

[14]*Ibid.*, p. 160.

[15]McWilliams, *op. cit.*, p. 232.

sidered routine, while the exchanges he considered significant are given in full, headed: "McWilliams' views on racial intermarriage are identical with COMMUNIST PARTY ideology." The report reads, in part:

Q. (Chairman Tenney.) I would like to ask you what you think of miscegenation?

A. (McWilliams) I think miscegenation statutes are a reflection of prejudice in the community.

Q. Do you think they should be abolished?

A. I do.

Q. You think there should be free intermarriage?

A. I don't think there should be a legal prohibition against inter-marriage . . .
(Long interchange on same lines)

Q. I don't think you have answered my question . . . Do you favor intermarriage?

A. I say it is presumptuous upon me to say that 'A' should marry 'B'.

Q. I understand. I am not talking about 'A' and 'B', I am talking about negroes and whites.

A. I am not advocating. I think the prohibition should be removed.[16]

McWilliams may have been unaware of the relationship between miscegenation and Communism in the thinking of the Tenney Committee, and of at least some law enforcement officials. An example of police thinking on the subject had been read into the minutes earlier. It came from a paper on Communist tactics presented at a state conference of the California Peace Officers Association. The Communist party was seen as "trying to discard its more barbarous and loose libertinism for the attempted appearance of respectability. But within the party's ranks there existed a situation where white women openly consorted with Negro men; white, Japanese, Mexican and Filipino members had set up their own little alliances. . . 'Communist marriages,' not

---

[16]Carey McWilliams, "Testimony Before the Committee," in Report . . . Un-American Activities. . ., 1945, p. 194.

blessed by benefit of clergy, founded upon this color-and-race combination basis, abounded. . ."[17]

A sexual aspect of the zoot-suit rioting was present not only in the ties with Communist ideology as publicized by the Tenney Committee but directly, in the persons of the Mexican girl friends, the *pachuquitas*, over whom the initial clash of zoot-suiters and sailors took place. The Mexican *pachuquitas* were very appealing to American servicemen, and jealously guarded by the Mexican-American boys. They scandalized the adults of the "Anglo" and Mexican communities alike, with their short, tight skirts, sheer blouses, and built up hair-does. The pursuit and beating of zoot-suiters and the destruction of the "drapes," or costumes, by mobs of servicemen were so many defeats of Mexican manhood and symbolic conquests of at least the access to the then-undefended *pachuquitas*.

Chief of Police C. B. Horrall seemed to recognize the sexual aspects of the riots. In his opinion, they made the violence less serious. He testified before the Tenney Committee:

> These disturbances, of course, started with the Latin-American gang situation, which was among themselves up until approximately a year ago. . . . However, about a year ago we had a little difficulty down at San Pedro, wherein they got mixed up with the sailors down there. . . . The latest disturbance started in the north end up here around the 1700 block on North Main Street, as apparently the result of some sailors making advances to some Mexican girls or talking to them. I don't know whether it went any farther than that . . . reached a point where it got some publicity in the papers, and that was what caused the gangs to congregate downtown that night and brought all the crowd out. However, some people have chosen to call it riots; I don't think it should be classified as that. Quite a few of the boys had their clothes torn off, but the crowds weren't particularly hard to handle. And the feeling in general among them was one of fun and sport rather than malice."[18]

Carey McWilliams recalled the mood of the crowd quite differently in his book, *North From Mexico*. He wrote:

> Marching through the streets of downtown Los Angeles, a mob of several thousand soldiers, sailors, and civilians proceeded to

---

[17]California Peace Officers Association, "Report of the State Conference, Fresno, October, 1940," in Report...Un-American Activities..., 1945, p. 92–93.

[18]C. B. Horrall, "Testimony Before the Committee," in *Report . . . Un-American Activities . . .*, 1945, p. 161.

beat up every zoot-suiter they could find ... Street cars were
halted while Mexicans, and some Filipinos and Negroes, were
jerked out of their seats, pushed into the streets, and beaten with
sadistic frenzy. If the victims wore zoot-suits, they were stripped
of their clothing and left naked or half-naked on the streets,
bleeding and bruised ... From affidavits which I helped prepare at
the time, I should say that not more than half of the victims were
actually wearing zoot-suits. A Negro defense worker, wearing a
defense-plant identification badge on his workclothes, was taken
from a street car and one of his eyes was gouged out with a knife.
Huge half-page photographs showing Mexican boys stripped of
their clothes, cowering on the payments, often bleeding profusely,
surrounded by jeering mobs of men and women, appeared in all
the Los Angeles newspapers.[19]

According to McWilliams, overt racism was finally checked in
Los Angeles by the overturning of the convictions in the Sleepy
Lagoon murder case. He acknowledges, however, that the police
resumed their raids and the press resumed its stories after a few
months time. If racism is considered in broader terms than the
Mexican issue, it is difficult to demonstrate that the court action
produced any improvement. A survey of the Negro newspapers,
the *California Eagle* and the *Los Angeles Sentinel,* shows that
police harassment of minority groups increased, "shoving incidents" on the crowded street cars were common, and, by 1946, the
Ku Klux Klan was again burning crosses in Los Angeles.

The Negro press bears out Carey McWilliams' contention that
racial prejudice was a basic cause of the riots—an important point
to establish in view of the many statements by Los Angeles officials
and social workers to the contrary. On the other hand, the Negro
press does not equate the Los Angeles riots with those occurring
elsewhere during 1943, as McWilliams does. In his estimation,
"The week-long zoot-suit riots which began in Los Angeles . . .
touched off a chain reaction of riots across the country. Similar
disturbances were reported in San Diego on June 9; in Philadelphia on June 19; in Chicago on June 15; and in Evansville on
June 27."[20]

These outbursts were triggered in some but not all cases by
zoot-suit wearers, but lacked the Mexican gang element. They
were directed against Negroes. The major riots which McWilliams
saw as related to the Los Angeles events—the Detroit riot of

[19]McWilliams, *op. cit.,* pp. 249–250.
[20]McWilliams, *op. cit.,* p. 256.

June 20–21 and the Harlem riot of August 1–2—were very little concerned with zoot-suiters. They stemmed from fear of the Negro minority on the part of the dominant white community. No comparable fear of the attacked minority entered into the zoot-suit riots of Los Angeles.

The aftermath of the zoot-suit riots was contained in the inception of the riots. The whole thing was a continuum. The week of violent debauchery by white mobs changed nothing in the attitude of the police. It failed to shake the stereotype of the Mexican in which the social workers believed, nor did it alter the "Anglo" assumption that the problem to be handled was the minority race. The hearings and exposés of the Tenney Committee continued, and the formation of citizens' committees to study the Mexican problem went on at a rapid rate.

Ignacio L. López of Pomona College wrote a few years after the riots:

> In Los Angeles, out of the guilt of the dominant group, arose a faddism for the Mexican-American. Committees gave birth to litters of other committees. Co-ordinator battled co-ordinator. There was a new set of resolutions every morning. Still, when the emotional fever and the defensiveness subsided, few real gains had been made for or by the Mexican-American group. They were basically where they had been for twenty-five years, and the flare of faddish interest was dying."[21]

In a series of articles entitled, "Los Angeles' Answer to Bigotry," the *Los Angeles Examiner* was more optimistic. It reported:

> The wartime 'zoot-zuit' riots in Los Angeles sent such a huge counter-army of community organizations into the field to prevent further disorders that by 1946 they were stumbling all over each other. They overlapped in services, duplicated one another's work, and sapped their effectiveness by adding to the general confusion. The Welfare Planning Council, stepping in to find out how to bring order out of these well-meaning but chaotic efforts, found in a survey there were no less than 50 agencies working in the field of community relations. In 1947 the Welfare Planning Council invited these organizations ... to coordinate activities.[22]

---

[21]Ignacio L. López, introducing Ruth D. Tuck, *Not with the Fist*, p. vii.

[22]*Los Angeles Examiner*, "Let-Live Policy Wins," Feb. 22, 1960, reprinted in *Los Angeles' Answer to Bigotry* (Los Angeles: The Examiner, 1960), p. 5.

The affiliation of these organizations produced the Community Relations Conference of Southern California, which has continued to serve the Los Angeles area. Accomplishments of the Conference in the years following the Zoot-Suit Riots included the negotiated end of racial segregation in public housing projects, a part in ending racial segregation policies of the Los Angeles City Fire Department, and assisting the police department to establish a human relations course.

Among the conference's early member organizations was a Mexican political action group, the Community Service Organization, which had its beginnings in the riots in 1943. José Antonio Villarreal wrote that he joined the group when, "a touch of conscience began to work on the educated Mexican who had made the transition and joined the main-stream of his society. Lawyers and teachers and businessmen of Mexican descent began to make demands upon the authorities, to formulate plans for the emancipation of a people."[23]

Of deeper significance than the committees which came out of the riots was the beginning self-understanding of individual young people of Mexican descent. Although it has been a slow and private conceptualization which may not properly be regarded as the aftermath of any one event, it is related to the trauma of the zoot-suit years. The trauma has gone deeper than the beatings and harassments of the mobs in 1942 and 1943. It included the animosity and rejection by the Mexican community of the *pachucos* who had presented it with an irreducible dilemma. To defend the youths was to affirm the racial over the superficial causes of the violence. It meant opposing both the explanations and the remedies offered by the "Anglos" and, in fact, to contend with the whole community including the police. To sympathize with the *pachucos* required a reconciliation the older generation of Mexicans was not prepared to make. Yet, to deny them was to deny that prejudice and discrimination existed which might justify their revolt. The Mexican press attempted a middle way by rejecting *pachuquismo* and treating the mob violence as abstractly as possible.

The leading Spanish-language newspaper in Los Angeles, *La Opinión*, warned the Mexican-American community that wrong-doers would incite the mobs of servicemen to continue invasions of the *barrios*. By wrong-doers the paper meant *pachucos*. It

---

[23]José Antonio Villarreal, "Mexican-Americans in Upheaval," *West Magazine, Los Angeles Times*, Sept. 18, 1966, p. 22.

warned that few would escape the wrath of the sailors. Idlers would be beaten, "y pagaron justos por pecadores," "the just would pay for the misdeeds of the guilty."[24]

A member of the District Attorney's staff said of *La Opinión:*

> I don't think you will find any criticism in that newspaper of the prosecution or of the police or the sheriff in regard to that case [the Sleepy Lagoon trial], or any similar case. You'll find the better elements in the community, both Mexican, colored and white, all believe in law enforcement with respect to those matters. But this group of radicals . . ."[25]

The "radicals," the members of the Sleepy Lagoon Defense Committee, presented in their attempts to gain public support a picture of the *pachucos* which contrasted strikingly with the picture in the Mexican press. Guy Endore, the committee's chief propagandist, wrote:

> These were nothing more than neighborhood gangs of frolicsome kids. Their escapades were always on Saturday night, pay-day night, for they were hard workers the rest of the week. There was no leader, no membership, nothing of the sort. These boys and girls simply lived near each other, knew each other, liked each other, and hung around together.[26]

The *pachucos* themselves, in retrospect, describe still another picture. Gabe Villaseñor recalled in 1954 that:

> We were kids, anxious to be wanted but we just couldn't make the grade. We were openly discriminated against in public swimming pools. There were no recreational facilities to speak of. We could only raise hell in the streets. Gangs gave us a feeling of being tough, of not caring what the adults thought of us. I don't want to defend what we did. It was bad. But the police didn't help any. They were unnecessarily cruel with us. I think the newspaper headlines helped incite public opinion against us, too. We felt rejected and wanted revenge.[27]

---

[24]"Alarma en el Barrio Mexicano," June 6, 1943, p. 1.

[25]Clyde Shoemaker, "Testimony Before the Committee," in *Report . . . Un-American Activities . . . , 1945,* p. 181.

[26]Guy Endore, *The Sleepy Lagoon Mystery* (Los Angeles, Sleepy Lagoon Defense Committee, 1944), p. 14.

[27]Marina Mireles, "The Zoot-Suit Era: From Gangs to Respectability," *Herald-Examiner,* April 20, 1954.

The largest of the gangs on the outskirts of the East Side was the Clanton–14th Street, composed of about 80 boys. Tony Chávez, a leader of the Clantons during the riots, recalled, "I was scared all the time, but I had to keep up a front. I could not let down. When I faced myself alone at night, I felt horrible. But I liked the power I had. I couldn't let go."[28]

Mike Durán, a deputy probation officer and once a zoot-suiter, said of the riots, "I wish I could close my mind on it, the senseless fighting, the constant insecurity and guilty feelings unless I was with the gang. I had great resentment, but it was a resentment I couldn't define."[29]

The Mexican-American youths who did not become zoot-suiters also suffered deep frustrations. Raul Morín, who spent the war years in the army, wrote in his chronicle, *Among the Valiant*, of "the constant struggle to make our Anglo neighbors see and realize that we were no longer the stereotype Mexican they had always pictured us to be. . . We were placed in the categories of cheap laborers, thriftless, lazy, unorganized, lacking in leadership, unkempt, and uneducated."[30]

To Carey McWilliams, looking back over the nation-wide changes in attitudes which occurred in the 1940's, it seemed that, "within the last decade, the whole mythology of race as a determinant of culture has been demolished with interacting and far-reaching consequences. . . Even those who advocate white supremacy are today aware of the fact that they speak as poets of hatred and not as scientists."[31]

The fact that they spoke as "poets of hatred" did not, however, prevent the racists from continuing to speak in Los Angeles. They were heard from after the "Bloody Christmas" of 1951, when seven Mexican-American youths were beaten by police officers in Lincoln Heights jail. They were heard from in the *Los Angeles Times* in 1953, exactly ten years after the zoot-suit riots, in a series of articles following the killing of a businessman during a gang fight in downtown Los Angeles. The headline reads, "5000

---

[28]*loc. cit.*

[29]Mireles, *op. cit.*

[30]Raul Morín, *Among the Valiant* (Alhambra, California: Borden Publishing Co., 1966), p. 23.

[31]Carey McWilliams, *Brothers under the Skin* (Boston: Little, Brown & Co., 1964), p. 13.

L.A. Hoodlums Belong to Violence-Dealing Gangs." The writer relied on his readers to know that these gang members were all Mexicans. He doesn't state it until the 6th paragraph. The article goes on, "Anyone who has driven around Los Angeles streets at night has seen the gangs. They're the groups of laughing, joking boys who hang around the hot dog stands and street corners, just standing around. . . They don't look vicious, particularly, and they don't act vicious, particularly. But anyone who doesn't think they can become killers without batting an eye is just kidding himself. It happens all the time. . ."[32]

---

[32]Bob Will, "5000 L.A. Hoodlums Belong to Violence-Dealing Gangs," *Los Angeles Times*, December 17, 1953.

Chapter Five

The Post-War Years: Two Quiet Decades

World War II brought many benefits to the Mexican-American. He became Americanized in the armed forces or in the factories. He received the GI Bill of Rights and could at least purchase a modest home. He could also receive an education in either a college or in a vocational institution. But unfortunately the Mexican-American, despite his magnificant war record, did not take full advantage of the opportunities offered to him. In keeping with his former position and his Hispanic and Indian culture, it was hard for him to overcome his retiring and guarded social tendencies. Thus, notwithstanding his improved living conditions and better job opportunities, he did not make any great strides in achieving distinguished positions in politics, in the labor movement, or in the professions.

This lack of achievement in a period when such an accomplishment could be made has led Manuel Servín to compare the achievements of the pre–World War II generations with those of the war and post-war periods. Servín's research and findings are not exactly flattering to the post-war generation.

Kaye Briegel, who traces the development of Mexican-American organizations since the first immigration of 1900, presents a similar but more optimistic picture of this generation. But by continuing her study to the present, she also shows that the post-war generation of the years 1945–1965 is not as cohesive and as effective as the earlier and later generations. Her study, despite the fact that it covers the entire period of Mexican-American history in the United States, is placed in this section because of the many Mexican-American organizations that appeared in the post-war period.

Finally the last article, which is from *Ramparts*, was selected because of the influence that the braceros had upon the Mexican-American migrant workers and because it points up the early ineffectiveness of the Mexican-American community in improving their situation. The article also vividly demonstrates that the exploitation of the Mexican in the United States continues and is very deep-seated.

The Post–World War II Mexican-American, 1925–1965: A Non-Achieving Minority*

Manuel P. Servín

The Mexican-American resident in the United States constitutes this nation's most unique, if not mystifying, minority group. Descendant of the aboriginal American inhabitants and of the first European settlers in the New World, the Mexican-American, despite the fact that he preponderantly lives in areas that were wrested from him, has until the recent war years been considered not an American but a foreigner. This fact has been so evident that even European immigrants, whose accents patently reveal their very recent arrival in the United States, did not hesitate to regard the Mexican-American not as an American but as a Mexican, whom they considered less American than themselves.

That such an attitude should prevail is clearly understandable to those possessing a historical insight to early Anglo–Mexican relations. Incredible as it may seem, the Mexican became a minority group not when he immigrated to the North American republic, but rather when the North American migrated to Mexican Texas and California, finding a very poor class of settler. Consequently, despite his residence on his own national soil, it was the Mexican who became the backward, somewhat unassimilable foreigner.

---

*This essay was originally delivered at the Annual Conference of the Western History Association on October 15, 1965, at Helena, Montana. A slightly revised first section, "The Pre–World War II Mexican-American: An Interpretation," appeared in *California Historical Society Quarterly* 45 (December, 1966).

This attitude toward the Mexican, particularly in Texas, was further intensified by the Texas and the Mexican wars. With the few exceptions of the *ricos* who passed themselves off as Spaniards, the Mexican truly became a minority group in the worst sense of the word. Generally despised in Texas, dispossessed of his lands in California, and denying his racial heritage in New Mexico, he lacked an acknowledged Mexican aristocracy—social, economic, and clerical—which would visibly prove to him that he was capable of achieving success and status.

The plight of the Mexican in the United States, however, did not reach its lowest depth with the Texas and Mexican wars. Notwithstanding Mexican treachery at Goliad, cruelty at San Antonio, and lack of bravery at San Jacinto, Santa Fé, and Monterey, the image of the Mexican was to be even further denigrated. The discovery of gold in California attracted an even lower class of Mexican—the *Norteño* or Sonoran—than even the early settler of New Mexico, Texas, and California. Little Mexicos, called "Sonora towns," sprouted throughout the gold routes of the Southwest and California. These towns and their residents represented the least civilized and least urbane element of Mexico.[1] The towns were far from rivalling Querétaro, León, or San Miguel de Allende—that is, far from being centers of culture, virtue, art. Sonora towns were, as Los Angeles was, a home for thieves, murderers, and unappetizing *putas* (prostitutes).[2] Consequently, while some of the less puritanical gringos enjoyed the life of this somewhat depraved but enjoyable minority, such was not the case with the majority of the Americans. This was especially true after the opening, in the 1880's, of the southern transcontinental railroad lines which transported the hordes of solid, but perhaps sanctimonious and prosaic, middle westerners to California, Arizona, and Texas.

The decades that followed the North-Americanization of the Southwest and that preceded the early-twentieth-century wave of Mexican immigration are in an historical sense extremely quiet concerning North American and Mexican-American relations. Perhaps it would not be too rash to surmise that the Mexican-American of this period generally resigned himself to a fate that

---

[1]Concerning the Sonorans see J. M. Guinn, "The Sonoran Migration," *Annual Publications of the Historical Society of Southern California* 8 (1909–1910), pp. 30–36; Carey McWilliams, *Southern California Country* (New York: 1946), pp. 55–68.

[2]An interesting description of Los Angeles is found in Robert Glass Cleland, *History of California: The American Period* (New York: 1922), pp. 312–322.

previous historical events had cast upon him. He was, at least in the eyes of the North American, an inferior being, a half-breed, if not a *coyote*; he was unassimilable, especially if he was dark skinned; he was treacherous; he was cowardly; he was lazy; and thus he was not an American but a Mexican whose lot was to exist in poverty, subservience, and isolation.

That such was the fate of the Mexican after the 1880's is attested to by the treatment of the Mexican immigrant who arrived in the United States after the fall of Don Porfirio Díaz (May, 1911). Unfortunately for this new immigrant, he was neither prepared for the treatment that he would receive nor would he be able to understand the reasons for it. Because of the great changes, relative progress, and social and political stability imposed upon Mexico by the benevolent dictator Don Porfirio Díaz, the twentieth-century Mexican immigrant was a different person than his early predecessor in the Borderlands. He was far from lawless—Díaz's *rurales* had created respect for law and order. He was not the idle, lazy greaser so eloquently characterized by early American writers—he had been oppressed in peonage for much too lengthy a period. Generally speaking, he was a moral and religious man—almost without exception he had emigrated from the highly religious areas of Mexico. Finally, he was meek and submissive—Díaz's policy of *pan ó palo* had been effective.

It was this humble and meek person who arrived in great numbers beginning in 1901. His increasing immigration reflected the chaotic condition of revolutionary Mexico and the North American need of cheap labor. Thus in 1901–1910 over 93,000 Mexicans legally entered the United States; in 1911–1914, approximately 77,000; in the war years of 1915–1919, about 137,000; in 1920–1924, over 135,000; and in 1925–1930, just under 109,000.[3] By 1930 about 617,000 Mexicans had entered the United States legally, constituting almost one-half the Mexican population in the nation.[4] Actually, however, it is quite safe to state that if the illegal entrants—the predecessors of the wetbacks and fence-climbers—were taken into account, the majority of the Mexicans then residing in the United States were foreign-born.[5] And, perhaps even more significant than the number of foreign-born

---

[3]U.S. Bureau of Census, *Fifteenth Census of the United States, 1930: Population* vol. 2 (Washington: 1933), p. 498.

[4]*Ibid.*, pp. 25, 27, 405.

[5]*Ibid.*

Mexicans, is the sound evidence that they were not predominantly a rural group (as is often asserted) but were in the majority emigrants from urban and semiurban areas.

This wave of legal and illegal Mexican immigration, plus the birth rate of the early-Spanish-Borderland Mexicans, swelled the total 1930 Mexican population in the United States to just under 1.5 million.[6] Although Mexicans migrated in some numbers to such states as Michigan, Illinois, Kansas, and Indiana, it was in the Southwest, the former Mexican territory, that the overwhelming majority—some 1.25 million—settled.[7] By 1930, Texas, long reputed among Mexicans as the most racially bigoted state, had the largest Mexican population, some 683,000; California had approximately 360,000; New Mexico, at least 200,000 (although only 59,000 of these throwbacks to colonial times confessed to being Mexican to the census taker); Arizona hosted just over 110,000; and Colorado, about 57,000.[8]

Contemporary materials on the life of the early twentieth-century Mexican, particularly of the poor, ignorant, docile immigrant, are sparse. Had it not been for foresight and imagination of Professors Paul S. Taylor and Emory S. Bogardus, of the Universities of California and of Southern California respectively, little would have been written of his ignominious suffering. It is basically from their works (particularly those of Dr. Taylor), from the interviewing of immigrants of the period, and from my boyhood recollections that the following brief picture of the plight of the pre–World War II Mexican has been reconstructed.

The panoramic view of the early twentieth century Mexican is an interesting, and compared to that of the post-World War II Mexican-American, a more respectable one. Arriving in poverty, unable to speak English, and inheriting the anti-Mexican prejudice engendered decades before, the Mexican was definitely at a disadvantage and greatly in need of help. Unfortunately, such help was not given, particularly by the groups from which the Mexican expected aid. The Spanish-speaking aristocracy—old

---

[6]*Ibid.*, p. 27; Enrique Santibañez, *Ensayo acerca de la immigración Mexicana en Los Estados Unidos* (San Antonio: 1930), pp. 47–48.

[7]*1930 U.S. Census: Population* 2:ix, 35.

[8]*Ibid.*

Mexicans who disguised their heritage under such euphemisms as Californios, Spanish-Americans, and Hispanos—not only ignored but apparently despised the immigrant.[9] The Roman Catholic Church, aside from building churches and stationing refugee Mexican priests in Spanish-speaking parishes, did little to aid materially or socially.[10] Paradoxically, it was certain Protestant churches, especially the Methodist, that appeared to be most cognizant of the plight of the immigrant.[11] It is, therefore, not strange that bitterness toward the Spanish-speaking aristocracy and some antipathy toward the Church should have developed—a bitterness that characterized the "aristocracy" as *una junta de cabrones* and resulted in the conversion of many Mexicans to Protestantism.

Unaided by their own groups and unable to obtain work in their previous occupations, the Mexicans were forced to take the lowest-paying jobs as well as the hardest work. In the agricultural areas of Texas, Colorado, and California they became neglected, underpaid, exploited migratory farm workers. In the north-central areas of the nation they performed various forms of low-paid unskilled labor. In Chicago and the Calumet area, for example, they worked in the railroad sections and in the meat-packing plants. In Minnesota they worked in the sugar beet industry. And, in the area of Bethlehem, Pennsylvania, they became unskilled steel workers. Thus were the Mexicans consciously relegated to the

---

[9] Of the various older Mexican immigrants that I have interviewed, not one has had a kind word for the early Hispanic settler in California and the Southwest.

[10] The Rev. Francis J. Weber, "His Excellency of Los Angeles: The Life and Times of the Most Reverend John J. Cantwell," manuscript in Archives of the Archdiocese of Los Angeles (Los Angeles: n.d.), pp. 96–103; "Notes: Outline of Protestant Proselytism in the United States," in Archives of the Archdiocese of Los Angeles (Los Angeles: 1945), pp. 1–8, 54–55, 66–82; Kathryn Cramp et al., "A Study of the Mexican Population of Imperial Valley, California," manuscript in Bancroft Library, Berkeley, California (Berkeley: 1926), p. 23.

[11] To obtain a true insight of the zeal and efforts of the Methodists in working with Mexicans of the period it is only necessary to read the *Minutes of the Southern California Conference of the Methodist Episcopal Church, 1879–1939*. For a very limited view into Methodist Church activities see Edward Drewry Jervey, *The History of Methodism in Southern California and Arizona* (Los Angeles: 1960), pp. 90–100.

lowest working positions.[12] Perhaps the classical example of this policy was best expressed by an executive in the Chicago and Calumet area who bluntly stated the hiring policy found in the area. "We use Mexicans. We have more refined work and have not had to resort to greasers. They use them for rough work and around blast furnaces."[13]

But regardless of the demeaning nature of the work which they were assigned, the Mexicans, according to conflicting testimony, appear to have been good but not excellent workers. Preferred in California and Texas as farm laborers, the Mexicans —despite the remarks of California's brilliant Irish surname Senator [Murphy]—did not merit this preference because they were built closer to the ground and possessed a physical advantage. The preference was simply economic: they were unorganized, apparently docile, and did not demand decent wages and living conditions.[14] In the industrial areas their record, as in the farming areas, was also respectable. The reports compared them both

---

[12]For the work the Mexican performed see Paul S. Taylor, *Mexican Labor in the United States*, published in the University of California Publications in Economics. Dr. Taylor's different studies utilized in this essay and cited individually are: *Mexican Labor in the United States: Imperial Valley* (Berkeley: 1928); *Mexican Labor in the United States: Valley of the South Platte, Colorado* (Berkeley: 1929); *Mexican Labor in the United States: Dimmit County, Winter Garden, South Texas* (Berkeley: 1930); *Mexican Labor in the United States: Bethlehem, Pennsylvania* (Berkeley: 1931); *Mexican Labor in the United States: Chicago and the Calumet Region* (Berkeley: 1932). Also see Kathryn Cramp *et al.*, "A Study of the Mexican Population in Imperial Valley, California," Manuscript, 1926, Bancroft Library; Santibañez, *Ensayo acerca de la immigración Mexicana en los Estados Unidos*, especially p. 53; The Governor's Interracial Commission, *The Mexican in Minnesota* (Minneapolis: 1953); and Carey McWilliams, *North from Mexico* (Philadelphia: 1949).

[13]Taylor, *Mexican Labor ... : Chicago ...* , p. 80.

[14]For a summary of Mexican attempts to unionize agriculturally in early 1900's see Federal Writers Project, "Organization Efforts of Mexican Agricultural Workers," manuscript, Bancroft Library (Oakland: 1939). For other areas see Cramp et al., "A Study of Mexican Population in Imperial Valley," pp. 6–11; George L. Cady, *Report of Commission on International and Interracial Factors in the Problem of the Mexicans in the United States* (1926), pp. 11, 21; State of California, *Mexicans in California: Report of Governor C. C. Young's Mexican Fact-Finding Committee* (San Francisco: 1930), pp. 159–171, especially 171, and also pp. 123–150, 176–179; Sister De Prague Reilly, "The Role of the Churches in the Bracero Program in California (M.A. thesis, University of Southern California, 1969), p. 125.

favorably with the Slovaks, Wends, Negroes, and Irish.[15] Perhaps the most favorable report on the Mexicans' work occurred in Bethlehem, Pennsylvania, when Dr. Taylor interviewed a number of executives, one of whom stated that he

> rated the Mexicans as equals or possibly the superior of the two important groups of Europeans available for the same work: "The Mexicans are a good class of men as a whole; the majority are good steady workers. As a class their intelligence is above the Slavish (Slovaks) and Wendish. They are a bright, keen race, and good workers." And in response to my [Dr. Taylor's] observation that in other localities some persons regard Mexicans as possessing low intelligence, he added, 'If some people think the Mexicans are dumb, they should see some of our Irish . . .'[16]

Notwithstanding the Mexican's at least average work record, he, along with the Negro, was the lowest paid of the workers, both on the farms and in the plants. Unlike the Japanese, who was disliked by his fellow workers because of his industriousness and efficiency, the Mexican was unacceptable to his co-workers for a number of reasons. The most generally cited were that he lowered wages and weakened union organization.[17] But the racial differences, the dark skin, unhygienic appearance, and quaint dress habits appear to be, at least to me, the more basic reasons. Following a pattern that was almost identical to the well-known segregation that existed in Arizona, California, and Texas, the Mexican had difficulty renting in the Chicago area's better neighborhoods. The litany of such forced segregation makes interesting but sad reading:

> The principal colony of Mexicans near the stockyards is located on the west side. The fact that its development was checked on the east side, where the Mexicans appeared first, and subsequently stimulated on the west side was attributed by local residents chiefly to the resistance of the Irish (including the second generation) living on the east side. . . .[18]

> The movement of Mexicans west of the yards was also opposed. There they encountered violent attacks of the Poles . . . The Poles and Lithuanians . . . declined to rent to Mexicans in their well established neighborhood . . . [19]

---

[15]Taylor, *Mexican Labor: Chicago*, pp. 77–80; Taylor, *Mexican Labor: Bethlehem*, pp. 13–14.

[16]*Ibid.*, p. 13.

[17]For examples see Taylor, *Mexican Labor: Chicago*, pp. 77–80.

[18]*Ibid.*, p. 222.

[19]*Ibid.*, p. 222–223.

In South Chicago a good deal of hostility was manifested toward
Mexican neighbors, especially when they sought to move out from
the more restricted and poorer locality which they occupied,
largely among Negroes. An old resident, a German, found the
Mexicans satisfactory neighbors. . . . But others, particularly
young Poles, probably American born, expressed vigorous complaints...[20]

The low wages received by the Mexicans, regardless of area,
plus cultural and racial discrimination, of course had a very
essential influence upon their living conditions. While Texas has
always possessed among both Mexicans and dogmatic liberals
the worst reputation for oppressing Mexicans and for retaining
them in the lowest substandard living conditions, it is my judgment—as a person who was born and has travelled in Texas,
attended school in New Mexico, journeyed extensively through
Arizona, and was reared in California—that the living conditions,
with some very few exceptions in New Mexico, were equally as
poor in utopian California as in Texas, Arizona and other areas.[21]

Southern California, whose record for indiscriminate, hypo-
critical discrimination is difficult to excel, possessed perhaps the
Southwest's most blatant contrast in living conditions between
the white North American and the Indian–Spanish Mexican. Few
Mexican *barrios* could compete in poverty with that of Maravilla
Park in Los Angeles where two and sometimes three shacks
built of scrap lumber, old boxes, and other salvage were erected
in one small lot; where there were forty houses to a city block;
where the average family income in 1928 was $795; where almost
all workers were unskilled laborers; and where out of 317 houses
only 10 had cesspools connected with flush toilets.[22]

---

[20]*Ibid.*, p. 224.

[21]The information compiled by George L. Cady, *Report of Commission on
International and Interracial Factors in the Problem of the Mexicans in the
United States,* as well as Paul Taylor's studies on Mexican Labor in California,
Texas, Colorado, Chicago and Calumet, very definitely appear to bear out this
writer's evaluation.

[22]*Mexicans in California: Report of Governor C. C. Young's Mexican Fact-
Finding Committee,* pp. 177–178. For an inclusive view of the poverty of
Mexican communities in Chicago, Colorado, Texas, New Mexico, Arizona, and
California see W. Rex Crawford, "The Latin American in Wartime United
States," *The Annals of the American Academy of Political and Social Science*
223 (September, 1942): 127.

But in reality Maravilla Park was not an exception in California. Similar living conditions could be found in El Centro, San Fernando, and the outskirts of Montebello, Whittier, and El Monte—and, incidentally, in various cities of the San Joaquin Valley, even today.[23]

Actually, such poverty was not unknown to the Mexican in his home country, and would not be a great source of unhappiness. What did strike the Mexican was the irrational prejudice and disdain that he encountered. In many areas he could not eat in the same restaurants with the American, nor could he swim in the same pools. In other areas he could not attend the same theatres, or if allowed to do so, he would have to sit in a segregated area. Naturally, the Mexican generally had to attend segregated schools and churches; but this segregation, similar to his living among his own people, did not seem to bother him—perhaps he inwardly considered himself equal or even superior to the Americans in some areas.[24]

Yet despite all the disheartening and degrading conditions that he encountered, the pre–World War II Mexican not only maintained a good record but made certain remarkable achievements.

Although he inherited the poor reputation for crime from the early Mexican settlers, his crime record, basing it on random examples, was not outstandingly bad.[25] In the Chicago and Calumet area, a two-year survey—1928–1929—revealed that 1.4 percent of all persons arrested were of Mexican nativity, while the Mexican population constituted only .57 percent of the total population.[26] In Los Angeles City the 1927–1928 percentage of Mexican arrests —revealing narcotics (probably marihuana), drunkenness, and vagrancy as the raising element—amounted to 17.5, while the

---

[23]*Mexicans in California*, pp. 178–179.

[24]A fine example of almost complete segregation is contained in Cramp *et al.*, "A Study of the Mexican Population in Imperial Valley." A partial list of segregated living and school districts in California is found in *Mexicans in California*, pp. 176–177. Also see Bogardus, *The Mexican in the United States*, pp. 28–29, for an area in which the Mexican did not consider himself inferior to the North American.

[25]George L. Cady in his *Report of Commission on International and Interracial Factors* gives a fine example of pre–World War II exaggeration, p. 10.

[26]Taylor, *Mexican Labor: Chicago*, p. 144.

Mexican population of the city was slightly over 10 percent.[27] In California's Imperial Valley, an important farming area, where the Mexican in 1925 was supposed to be responsible for 75 percent of all crimes, it was authoritatively found that he was responsible for only one-fourth, while he constituted approximately one-third of the population.[28] Thus, seeing that the rural crime rate was less in proportion to that of the urban, one might conjecture (perhaps somewhat dangerously) that since the Mexican population in the United States was almost equally divided between rural and urban, its crime rate was in proportion to, or even lower than, its total population.

A similar picture is found in California regarding juvenile delinquency—a reflection of family life. In Los Angeles County in 1928, 19 percent of the Mexican boys and 28 percent of the Mexican girls were on probation—figures which were far above the Mexicans' estimated 11 percent of the total population.[29] Yet in the Imperial Valley the picture was reversed. The percentage of Mexican children involved in juvenile court was proportionately much less than the total Mexican population, and incidentally also less than that of old North American stock.[30]

Besides possessing a rather good work record and not a bad adult and juvenile crime rate, the Mexican also possessed fairly good records in marital relations and relief. Insofar as married life was concerned, there is no doubt that his divorce rate was less than either that of the Negroes or whites.[31] His public relief record, based upon statistics of California—the nation's most magnanimous, or perhaps most foolish, state—was not quite as good, but it was below his proportional maximum. Despite unfavorable relief records in Los Angeles, Orange, and Riverside counties, and despite the low and seasonal wages he was paid, it is evident from Governor C. C. Young's 1930 report that the Mexican in California was not only not a burden on the state but

---

[27]*Mexicans in California*, pp. 203, 175.

[28]Cramp, *et al.*, "A Study of the Mexican Population in Imperial Valley," p. 11.

[29]*Mexicans in California*, p. 204.

[30]Cramp, *et al.*, "A Study of the Mexican Population in Imperial Valley," pp. 10 and 25.

[31]*1930 U.S. Census: Population* 2:842.

that he did not receive a just proportion of relief funds.[32] That such a case seems to have been true throughout the nation appears most plausible from the report of the Governor's Interracial Commission in Minnesota and from the Mexicans' practice of organizing societies for helping each other financially and otherwise.[33]

Undoubtedly the Mexican's area of least success and greatest failure was in obtaining an education. Coming from a culture that did not prize mass education, finding it necessary to put even his elementary-age children to work, and perhaps feeling frustratedly that an education would not help him overcome the prejudices and disdainful treatment he received throughout the Southwest, the Mexican failed drastically to take advantage of the educational opportunities opened to him. Of all the groups listed in the U.S. census of 1930, he had the lowest percentage of school attendance —a factor of course that in the long run militated and still militates against him and his future advancement.[34]

Yet despite the pre-war Mexican's lack of educational interest, language barrier, and racial and cultural prejudice, he made some formidable breakthroughs in addition to changing gradually his portrait in the areas of work, crime, family life, and relief. Unlike some other persecuted minorities, he established a good, culturally-conscious press, as exemplified by *La Opinión*. He broke into the motion pictures and produced respectable and respected stars such as Ramón Navarro, Dolores del Río, and Gilbert Roland. In the East he yielded such distinguished professional men as Harold Medina, the jurist, and Alonso E. Escalante, American Maryknoll missionary bishop for Mexico. In crime, he at least showed some ability to "think big" as exemplified in the case of the fugitive Los Angeles police lieutenant, Peter Del Gado.[35] In music he developed popular crooners such as Andy Russell and more serious singers as José Mojica and Tito Guízar. And in higher education he came forth with such academic limelights as historian

---

[32]*Mexicans in California*, pp. 190, 195.

[33]*The Mexicans in Minnesota*, pp. 44–45; Taylor, *Mexican Labor: Bethlehem*, p. 17; Taylor, *Mexican Labor: Chicago*, pp. 124, 128–129, 132–133; Cramp et al., "A Study of the Mexican Population in Imperial Valley," pp. 13–14; interview with José M. Bravo, Los Angeles, September 11, 1965.

[34]*1930 U.S. Census: Population* 2:1094–1095; Pauline R. Kibbe, *Latin American in Texas* (Albuquerque: 1946), p. 92, a fine example of the frustration encountered by enthusiastic Mexican students.

[35]Interview with Mr. Richard Rodríguez, Los Angeles, September 29, 1965.

Carlos Eduardo Castañeda and educationist George Isidore Sánchez, both from the University of Texas.

Breakthroughs into North American life were not, however, the only achievement of the pre-war Mexican. He also made some contributions to United States culture—and I do not mean just the adding of tacos, tamales, and margaritas to the North American diet. He contributed, as Henry López's interview with Katherine Anne Porter in *Harper's Magazine* indicates, an incentive for enriching American letters.[36]

The era of the pre–World War II Mexican in the United States came to an end with opening of hostilities late in 1941 and early in 1942. The young Mexican of the post-war period who was in secondary or elementary school—that is, the young Mexican-descended person who was born after 1925 or 1926—encountered entirely different social and economic conditions than his predecessors had. He now became an American, though a hyphenated one. Jobs previously denied to his ethnic group were open to him. Positions of authority, previously unattainable, were much more within his grasp. He could also swim in the same pools and eat in the same restaurants with North Americans. Furthermore, the war made it possible, at least for the older Mexican-Americans, to obtain a college education as the result of the GI Bill of Rights.[37]

Unfortunately, a minority of the post-war Mexican-Americans, the pachucos or zoot-suiters, reacted in a most un-Mexican-like manner. Dressed outlandishly, as they followed the styles of less acceptable minorities, they quickly undid the hard-earned reputation of the pre-war Mexican. Despite the pious lamentations of social workers, the pachucos in a rat-pack manner attacked United States servicemen and, regardless of justification or guilt, gave the Mexican community—which incidentally condemned them as much as the North American—an undeserved reputation for lawlessness, cowardice, and disloyalty.[38] As a result, the heroic service

---

[36]Katherine Anne Porter, "A Country and Some People I Love: An Interview by Hank López," *Harper's Magazine* 231 (September, 1965), pp. 58–68.

[37]For examples of the World War II's resulting emancipation see Ruth D. Tuck, *Not with the Fist: Mexican-Americans in a Southwest City* (New York: 1946), p. 198; Kibbe, *Latin Americans in Texas*, pp. 100, 105.

[38]This writer has yet to find an older, pre–world War II Mexican or Mexican-American defending or offering an apology for the pachucos. The pachuco's viewpoint is cogently presented by Beatrice Griffith in *American Me* (Boston: 1948).

of the Mexican-Americans in the Philippines as well as the outstanding bravery of the some seventeen Medal of Honor winners
were ignored by the North American whites and blacks.[39]

It has been over a score of years since the Zoot-Suit Riots, a
quarter of a century since opportunities somewhat opened up with
World War II, and forty years since the first of the post-war
Mexican-Americans were born. In this period—admittedly a
period too brief to make any definitive judgments, but definitely
long enough to give evidence of progress or regression—the post-
World War II Mexican-American has been a nonachieving
minority.

In education, where his legacy and language barrier have
placed him at a great disadvantage, the Mexican-American has
the poorest record of all minority groups recorded in the 1960
U.S. census. For instance, in the Southwest the median number
of years in school for Mexican-American males is 8.1, but 8.3 for
Negroes and Filipinos; and, to make the situation even worse,
the achievement rate of the Mexican youth appears, at least to
some educators, to be declining.[40] Whatever may be the reasons
for this lack of achievement, it is this writer's belief that the
Mexican-American cannot entirely blame the North American
community for his lack of achievement in this area. Certainly,
the Mexican-American, despite whatever discrimination there may
exist, does not suffer from the same extreme racial and caste disadvantages that the Negroes and the Filipinos endure.

But a more disturbing educational and professional situation
is the one that concerns the Mexican educator and professional
man. Admittedly, there are more persons of Mexican descent in
professional positions now than prior to the war, but this increase
is found mostly in the fields of less prestige, such as elementary
and secondary teaching, social work, and real estate work. In
the prestige areas, however—the fields of relatively difficult entrance such as medicine, dentistry, engineering, science and college
instruction—the numbers are indeed few, and far out of proportion to the total population. A case in point: There are only a
few more Mexican-descended college history instructors today

---

[39]Raúl Morín, *Among the Valiant: Mexican-Americans in World War II and
Korea* (Los Angeles: 1963), *passim*.

[40]U. S. Bureau of Census, *United States Census, 1960: Persons of Spanish
Surname*, p. 12; *United States Census, 1960: Nonwhite Population by Race*,
p. 9; interview with Rudolph Acuña, Los Angeles, September, 1965.

than there were in the thirties. And, if I may be honest, they are not in the same class as the older group. Much as I have searched books, records, and minds, I fail to find any post–World War II Mexican-American professor of the caliber of a Carlos Castañeda and George I. Sánchez.[41]

This lack of excellence pervades not only higher education, where many instructors waste more time in political activity than in scholarly endeavor, but also in other fields. There are for instance few Mexican-American lawyers like Raúl Magaña who merit the respect and admiration of their fellow lawyers.[42] While the medical men appear to have a sound, solid training, outstanding men with Spanish-sounding names are indeed difficult to identify. In regard to science the situation is of course greatly aggravated—a situation attributable to our nonscientific culture.

More depressing than the lack of outstanding men in the lucrative professions is the absence of outstanding personalities in fields where Mexicans in New Spain and in Mexico have had, and have, a heritage of distinguished achievement. In religion, for example, renowned Mexican-American priests are a rarity. There is, as far as I have been able to determine, not one Mexican-American Roman Catholic bishop, not even an auxiliary bishop in the United States.[43] While it is true that the Irish-Americans have unhumbly latched onto ecclesiastical offices, this is in my opinion an insufficient reason for lack of achievement in this area where Mexico is now producing scholarly and saintly priests, who, in my observation, are in many cases superior to the North American clergy.

A similar situation exists in the arts, both plastic and musical. With the exception of Joan Baez, the ballad musician, and Trini López, the teen-age idol and singer—a far cry from a Carlos Chávez or Agustín Lara—Mexican-American musicians have not risen above mediocrity. Accentuating the problems in this area

---

[41]Dorothy Hancock, ed., *Directory of American Scholars: A Biographical Directory. Volume I, History* (New York: 1963), and *Volume IV, Philosophy, Religion, and Law* (New York, 1964).

[42]Confidential Interview with a United States District Court Judge, Los Angeles, September 8, 1965; interview with Rudolph Acuña, Los Angeles, September, 1965; *Martindale-Hubbell Law Directory*, I, p. 489.

[43]*The Official Catholic Directory, Anno Domini 1963* (New York: 1963); *The American Catholic Who's Who, 1966 and 1967* (Grosse Pointe: 1966), p. 123, names Bishop Alonso Escalante, but he is stationed in Mexico.

is the fact that no Mexican-American music has developed or even appears to be developing. Perhaps a reason for this lack of development is the proximity of Mexico and authentic Mexican musicians, but it should be noted that this propinquity has not inhibited the development of a Mexican-American patois.

While it is easier to accept and to explain the lack of Mexican-American achievement in the areas of the professions and the arts, where excellence plays an important role, it is difficult to understand the political failure of the Mexicans. With a population of some 3.5 million in the Southwest, the Mexican-American outnumbers the Negro but has not capitalized on the opportunities offered in this area where mediocrity is far from a disadvantage. Presently possessing one United States Senator and two United States Congressmen, the Mexicans, outside of New Mexico, are grossly under-represented and flagrantly ignored in political appointments. In California, in 1964, they had one Congressman, one state legislator, three superior court (county) judges, two persons in the attorney-general's staff, and at least three city mayors. Curiously the most significant appointments are in the Department of Education whose director, Max Rafferty, has proved to be more understanding than the liberal Democratic administration.[44] In Texas the Mexicans are better represented. In 1961 they had four members of the House of Representatives, two superior court judges, and at least five mayors of cities—one of whom governs the important city of El Paso with a population of 276,000.[45] In Colorado, where the Mexican population is decreasing, the Mexican-Americans have virtually no representation at all.[46]

But if Mexican-American political organization and leadership has proved disillusioning, the behavior of the whole post–world war generation has been less than encouraging. It has become increasingly difficult to obtain noncomplimentary data on minority groups, but it can be logically conjectured that the crime rate of the post-war Mexican-American has increased. In California, a relatively unbiased state, his felon population in state prisons is 17.1 percent and in state camps 20.7 percent, far out of proportion

[44]Frank M. Jordan, comp., *Roster of Federal, State, County, and City Officials, 1964* (Sacramento: 1964), pp. 1–26.

[45]*Texas Almanac, 1961–1962* (Dallas: 1961), pp. 450–459, 399–403.

[46]*The Book of the States: Supplement I, February 1965: State Elective Officials and the Legislatures* (Chicago: 1965), pp. 3, 24, 25.

to his total state population percentage of approximately 9.1.[47]
A similarly disheartening but revealing datum is that about one-
half the "local Aid to Needy Children" case-load in the Los
Angeles area is among Mexican-Americans in East Los Angeles.[48]
It is quite evident from these limited data in the largest Mexican-
American population center that the Mexican-American has not
only failed to achieve but that in comparison to his predecessors
of the 1910's, 1920's, and 1930's, he has lost ground in the spiritual
and dignified aspects of life.

Perhaps this loss of personal dignity could be somewhat over-
looked had the Mexican-American made contrasting material
gains. Unfortunately, this has not been the case. Despite the large
crime record among post-war Mexicans, there are no famous
criminals, no Anastasias, Bannons, or Siegels—there is no achievement. In a more serious vein, the Mexican-American, whose unemployment record in California for males is not too bad (7.7
percent compared to 5.5 percent for North Americans), certainly
has not made a relative achievement in income; while in 1959 he
received a median income of $3,849, the white obtained one of
$5,109.[49] And according to my interpretation of the Los Angeles
County 1960 Census Map of Family Income,[50] the predominantly
Mexican neighborhood had a family income on the average $1000
less than the predominantly Negro sections, including the Watts
area.

The picture that documentation has portrayed of the Mexican-
American in the Southwest, particularly in California, is not a
happy one. Whatever the causes of the lack of achievement may
be, the basic fact of non-achievement cannot be denied. Perhaps
it has been partially due to racial prejudice, perhaps to a general

---

[47]State of California, Department of Corrections, "Characteristics of Felon
Population in California State Prisons by Institution" (Sacramento: June 30,
1963). Also see the *Los Angeles Police Department 1963 Annual Report* (Los
Angeles: 1964), pp. 18–19, for a comparison in the Negro, Mexican, and
white precincts.

[48]"Summary of Proceedings of the Southwest Conference: Social and Educational Problems of Rural and Urban Mexican American Youth," Occidental
College, April 6, 1963, p. 59.

[49]State of California, Department of Industrial Relations, *Californians of
Spanish Surname* (San Francisco: 1964), p. 17.

[50]These maps are produced by the Brewster Mapping Service, 5110 Huntington Dr. South, Los Angeles, California, 90032.

lessening of acquisitiveness among all North Americans, or to the decline in drive that is generally found among the children of immigrants. There is no doubt in my mind, however, that there was some truth in Hans Zinsser's autobiography (which I read as a twenty-year-old) when he stated, "give the Mexican a good home diet, cheaper beer, and tons of soap and flea power, and we shall have a great, tranquil, and friendly neighbor." Perhaps this is what happened to the Mexican-American. He was happy. He was isolated and insulated. But he is changing. He has seen the Negro advance and surpass him. And he is seeing his blood brothers in Mexico recognized and respected. Thus he sees that his Mexican-American culture has failed to give him the drive for such recognition and success. He is becoming aware of his status; he is developing leaders, particularly in the labor field;[51] and he is receiving help from his former tormentors—the North Americans. Perhaps the next score of years will reveal a picture of achievement similar to that of Mexico whose record for non-achievement was once much dimmer than that of the present-day Mexican-American.

The Development of Mexican-American Organizations*

Kaye Briegel

The first United States citizens to arrive on the Mexican northern frontier brought misunderstanding with them. Since that first arrival, the Spanish speaking people living in this area, which is now the southwestern United States, have had a problem —to discover a practical way to deal with these immigrants and their customs and laws. In the past, at least, they have been unsuccessful. To compensate for this failure they have clung to their own customs and traditions.

---

[51]"Mexican-American Labor Leaders — Los Angeles Area 1965," enclosed in Louis M. Bravo to Manuel P. Servín, La Puente, September 20, 1965.

*Based partially on Kaye Briegel's Master of Arts thesis "The History of Political Organizations among Mexican-Americans in Los Angeles since the Second World War" (University of Southern California, History Department, 1967).

In their attempt to deal with the customs and laws of the United States, Mexican-Americans have formed an uncountable number of organizations. These groups are as diverse as the Mexican-American community itself. Few of them, however, have proved viable. This characteristic, partially a result of the traditional status of Mexicans in the United States as migrant workers, is also influenced by the individualistic nature of Mexican culture. The large number of organizations and their fluid condition are factors in their failure to fulfill their social and political goals. Other factors are discrimination and inept leadership.

The oldest Mexican-American organizations, and those that have been the most viable, are mutual benefit societies. This type of group probably existed even before the Treaty of Guadalupe Hidalgo.† Mutual benefit societies attempt to protect members from the necessity of dealing with the larger community by providing death benefits and sometimes insurance against accident or sickness. Their clubhouses and halls are often still the center of the Mexican-American communities.

As the number of Mexicans in the United States began to increase after 1910, new kinds of organizations began to develop. A new middle class was formed by small businessmen in the expanding Mexican-American communities. They organized typically bourgeois, patriotic civic service clubs dedicated to assimilation [into Anglo culture]. The later working class immigrants, who provided the market for these small businessmen, attempted to form unions after the example of United States and Mexican industrial labor.

The Great Depression and the Second World War brought many changes to Mexican-Americans. After the war some began to believe the American ideal of social mobility might be available to them. These Mexican-Americans began to form organizations to participate in American democracy. Some sought to participate at the grass-roots level and attack local problems. Others organized sophisticated pressure groups to deal with the establishment at its own level. Still others participated in partisan politics.

These post-war organizations have succeeded in bringing the Mexican-American community closer to the larger community. They have ended overt and legal discrimination and achieved some significant social and political victories. They have not, however,

---

†Signed in 1848, this treaty arranged the cession of New Mexico and California to the United States by Mexico in return for $15 million — a resolution of the Mexican War.

devised a practical method of dealing with United States laws and customs. The majority of Mexican-Americans remain politically unrepresented, economically disadvantaged and inadequately educated.

More recently some Mexican-Americans have compared the record of their own organizations with that of the Civil Rights Movement. The contrast between these two groups has suggested to them that another method of dealing with United States laws and customs might be more effective. Reinforced by their experiences with the War on Poverty and other programs designed to fight second class citizenship, these Mexican-Americans have decided to try militancy. The goal of these militant organizations is to bring immediate and permanent change to those American institutions which, they believe, limit their freedom.

The militants promise action to enforce their demands. Their specific goals, however, retain many features from the mutual benefit societies. The continuities and changes in the development of Mexican-American organizations may be illustrated by an examination of a history of some of them. Even the most viable of these groups have changed with time.

An example of a mutual benefit society that has endured and expanded by changing with time is the Alianza Hispano Americana. It was first organized in 1894 and it now has branches throughout the United States. Its primary goal is death benefits: it offers low cost insurance policies that pay the funeral expenses of members. In addition, the Alianza has limited social goals. It is dedicated to the "social, economic and fraternal progress" of the Mexican-American people. It is also concerned with cultural programs to acquaint its members with "the use of modern techniques and procedures available to them for the betterment of their standard of living," and to "take the fine things of Mexican tradition and culture and present them to the English speaking people to change the adverse mental attitudes which the English speaking people possess, to favorable ones about Mexicans."[1]

The Alianza organization, aside from its insurance policies, centers largely around social activities. It is a lodge with a masonic-

---

[1]Quoted in Nancie L. González, "Spanish Americans of New Mexico: A Distinctive Heritage," Mexican-American Study Project, *Advance Report 9* (Graduate School of Business Administration, University of California, Los Angeles, September, 1967), pp. 64–65 and Beatrice Griffith, *American Me* (Boston: Houghton Mifflin Company, 1946), p. 39.

type ritual and ladies' and youth auxiliaries. The Alianza engages in some civic service–type projects, such as awarding scholarships and occasionally attempting to combat legal discrimination; it also operates cooperative night clubs.

The Alianza is changing, not in its mutual benefit society structure, but in its membership. This change is shown by the fact that a former Supreme President, J. Carlos McCormick, was the national organizer of the Viva Kennedy! Clubs in 1960. His subsequent service with the government as a consultant to the Volunteers in Service to America (VISTA) was ended, however, in 1965 when he was indicted for embezzling one-quarter of a million dollars from the Alianza during his presidential term.

Some members of mutual benefit societies began to gain influence as businessmen in the growing Mexican-American communities in the 1920's. These businessmen also began to turn away from the idea of death benefits toward that of civic service. The foremost example of this kind of middle class organization is the League of United Latin-American Citizens (LULAC).[2] It was formed in 1928 in Harlingen, Texas, to provide a central organization for several local Alianza-type lodges; it has since evolved into a civic service organization dedicated to assimilation. The LULACs now have chapters throughout the United States. Their center of strength, however, remains in Texas and expansion has generally followed the migration of Texas Mexican-Americans.

The goals of the expanding LULACs reflect their public image of conservatism. They are patriotic to the United States and seek to adopt its culture. They also retain some of the ideas of the self-protection groups by proclaiming their opposition to discrimination and specifically seeking to protect their members against prejudice. In addition, they want to preserve the values of Mexican culture. Some examples of LULAC rhetoric, from the Aims and Purposes in its constitution, illustrate this:

1. To develop within the members of our race the best, purest and most perfect type of a true and loyal citizen of the United States of America.

2. To eradicate from our body politic all intents and tendencies to establish discriminations among our fellow citizens on

---

[2]O. Douglas Weeks, "The League of United Latin-American Citizens: A Texas-Mexican Civic Organization," *Southwestern Political and Social Science Quarterly* 10 (December, 1929), pp. 257–278.

account of race, religion or social position as being contrary to the true spirit of Democracy, our Constitution and Laws.

. . . .

4. The acquisition of the English language, which is the official language of our country, being necessary for the enjoyment of our rights and privileges, we declare it to be the official language of this organization, and we pledge ourselves to learn and speak and teach same to our children.

. . . .

7. We solemnly declare once and for all to maintain a sincere respectful reverence for our racial origin of which we are proud.

. . . .

11. We shall create a fund for our mutual protection, for the defense of those of us who may be unjustly persecuted and for the education and culture of our people.

The LULACs implement their goals by social and civic service activities usually at the local level. They generally support conservative local government and place more emphasis on Americanizing Mexican-Americans than on fighting discrimination. This conservative inclination has been reflected even in their most recent programs.

In 1956, before the Office of Economic Opportunity funded the first Operation Headstart, the LULACs established a preschool English program to teach English to children from non-English speaking homes. It was called The Little School of the 400 and its objective was to teach four hundred basic words of oral English to its students.[3] Its results were that of 95 percent of its graduates entered public school on the same level as the English speaking students and that they were able to continue their education without being held back because of a deficiency in English. The program was so successful that in 1960 the Texas legislature appropriated funds to make such a program available to all school districts in the state. In addition, the LULACs award scholarships to encourage students to continue their education. As a result of these and their other activities the LULACs exercise some political influence.

The most noted event in LULAC history illustrates its influence. On November 21, 1963, Joe Garza, Texas State LULAC Director, was honored at a reception and ball in Houston.[4] Among those in

---

[3] "400-Word Start," *Time* (August 17, 1959), 59; and L. Alexander, "Texas Helps the Little Latins," *Saturday Evening Post* (August 5, 1961), pp. 30–31.

[4] William Manchester, *The Death of a President* (New York: Harper and Row, 1967), pp. 94–95.

attendance were several Texas congressmen, Senator Ralph Yar-borough, Governor John Connally, Vice-President Lyndon Johnson, and President and Mrs. John F. Kennedy. On this occasion President and Mrs. Kennedy became honorary LULAC members. It was the first time a United States president had attended a LULAC function.

The new middle class which joined the LULACs served new working class Mexican immigrants. These immigrants worked in the United States as railroad section hands and unskilled factory workers but the majority were farm workers. These farm workers generally enjoyed more prosperous living and working conditions than they had in Mexico. Compared to most of the United States citizens they saw around them, however, their status was inferior. Some followed the example of Mexican and United States industrial labor and tried to form unions to bargain collectively with growers for improved working conditions and higher wages. Those who organized the unions were encouraged by both Mexican and United States unions.

In 1928 the Confederación Regional Obrera Mexicana (CROM), a Mexican industrial union associated with the American Federation of Labor, encouraged two unions in California: one was centered in Los Angeles and the other in Brawley in the Imperial Valley.[5]

La Unión Trabajadores del Valle Imperial was organized to give Mexican farm workers a bargaining agent. The union tried to fight the contract system under which most crops were planted, tended and harvested in the Imperial Valley. Under this system a grower might make an agreement with a labor contractor to harvest a certain crop. The contractor would then hire Mexican laborers, retaining a fixed percentage of their earnings as his commission. He would also withhold 25 percent of their wages against the workers quitting before the harvest was completed. The workers complained that the contractors often failed to pay the 25 percent they had kept out and that the contractors also charged exorbitant commissions.

In an attempt to settle their grievances the union asked to negotiate with the Imperial Valley growers. It received no re-

---

[5]Governor C. C. Young's Fact-Finding Committee, *Mexicans in California* (San Francisco: State of California, 1930), pp. 123–150, and Paul S. Taylor, *Mexican Labor in the United States: Imperial Valley* (Berkeley: University of California Press, 1928).

sponse. At the time of the 1928 cantaloupe harvest, therefore, the union called a strike. Its demands were an improvement of the contract system, ice in the fields, free picking sacks and a higher piece rate. The growers refused to recognize the strike, and local law enforcement officials arrested union leaders who encouraged others not to work. With most of its leaders in jail, the strike was soon broken. Its leaders, given a choice of going to trial or leaving town, decided to leave. The union survived only in an altered form, as a mutual benefit society. Improved working conditions, however, were a result of the strike. It had shown the state labor agency and the growers the need for changing the contract system. Contractors, therefore, were more closely regulated and were also prevented from withholding 25 percent of a farm worker's wages until the end of the job.

The Los Angeles union encouraged by the CROM was the Confederación de Uniones Obreras Mexicanas. Like the Imperial Valley union, it was organized in 1928. The union had about twenty locals in Los Angeles, San Bernardino, Ventura, Riverside, and Orange counties. Its demands were similar to those of the Imperial Valley strikers, especially against labor contractors. There was no important strike in Los Angeles and the union lost membership and influence during the Depression. Its members, however, benefited from the new state labor policy regarding contractors established as a result of the Imperial Valley strike.

Like the CROM, United States unions tried to organize migrant farm workers. During the Great Depression the Cannery and Agricultural Workers Industrial Union worked in this area. Its organizing and strike activities, however, met resistance from local law enforcement officials. An undersheriff of Kern County (California), for example, was quoted during the strike as speaking for his department.

> We protect our farmers here in Kern County. They are our best people. They are always with us. They keep the country going. They put us in here and they can put us out again, so we serve them. But the Mexicans are trash. They have no standard of living. We herd them like pigs.[6]

---

[6]Quoted in National Advisory Committee on Farm Labor, *Farm Labor Organizing, 1905–1967: A Brief History* (New York: National Advisory Committee on Farm Labor, July, 1967), pp. 15–16.

This statement reflects the general attitude of the larger community toward Mexican-Americans before World War II. Despite the efforts of unions to gain respect like industrial labor and the attempts of the new Mexican-American middle class to assimilate into the larger community, this was the period of greatest legal and overt discrimination in United States history.

The Second World War brought significant changes to Mexican-American communities in the United States. As men returned from the war, many as heroes, they began to expect to participate to a greater extent than before in all aspects of American life. Toward this goal they began to organize themselves.

The Unity Leagues are an example of such post-war organizations. They were first formed in some of the smaller towns south and east of Los Angeles. In Chino, Ontario and Pomona, groups of Mexican-Americans worked together to realize their potential political power. The majority of the members were veterans and blue collar workers, but they were led by Ignacio López, the publisher of a bilingual Pomona newspaper. López had worked in the Office of War Information during World War II where his job had been to organize European minorities in the East into Liberty Leagues to support the war effort.

Following López' guidance, the Unity Leagues organized registration drives and supported the campaigns of Mexican-Americans for board of education offices and city council seats. House to house canvassing was necessary to persuade Mexican-Americans to register and then to vote. In addition, many meetings were needed to reinforce the enthusiasm of the campaign workers; careful guidance was required to avoid jealousy and personal conflicts. Using these methods, the Unity Leagues elected a city councilman in Chino, and their candidates received enough votes in other towns to make local officials aware of the new Mexican-American political power and more responsive to their requests for public services.

After the Unity Leagues had been organized in several towns, assistance was received from the American Council on Race Relations. The council sent a field organizer to advise them in organizing in other parts of southern California. With the organizer's help the Unity Leagues were expanded from Azusa and Cucamonga to San Diego.

Another organization through which grass-roots Mexican-Americans sought to participate in American democracy is the

Community Service Organization (CSO). It grew out of a committee formed in 1947 to elect Edward Roybal to the Los Angeles City Council. Although it failed in this first attempt, it was undoubtedly the deciding factor in Roybal's subsequent election in 1949.

The CSO, despite its role in Roybal's campaign, is not primarily interested in electing Mexican-Americans to public office. Its basic aim is to provide political representation for those who would be otherwise unrepresented. Toward this goal, it has organized and participated in many projects.

The CSO began with a voter registration program. Mexican-Americans who had never before thought of such a thing were encouraged to register. Some were even trained as deputy registrars. The names of the new registrants were collected and filed. At election time they were reminded of their responsibilities and encouraged to consider the issues and vote. CSO registration drives were so successful that in 1960 it was given financial assistance by the AFL-CIO to expand its activities.

In the registration drives through Los Angeles neighborhoods, the CSO discovered many Mexicans who had lived in the United States most of their lives but had not become citizens. To serve these people, the CSO began English language and citizenship classes. For those who were old and had given their lives to building California's contemporary prosperity, the CSO sought to have the Old Age Pension extended to resident non-citizens. It was a tedious battle that was not won until 1961. In addition the CSO offers another service to Mexican-Americans who may not fully understand United States laws and customs. It has an office which provides advice about such problems as filling out income tax forms, applying for social security or translating instructions from the English-speaking world.

Suffrage, citizenship and pensions are not, however, the only problems that affect poor or minority neighborhoods like the ones served by the CSO. Since the CSO seeks to deal with all the problems of its members and constituents on the eastside of Los Angeles, it had to deal with one that faces every social and economic lower-class area — the relationship between law enforcement agencies and the people they serve. The CSO's leaders believe that the law is not enforced in these areas as it is in those with lower crime rates and higher mean incomes. Mexican-Americans have long complained among themselves about police brutality and other violations of their civil liberties. The CSO, for these reasons, began to collect and document specific complaints so that concrete action could be taken. This action resulted in several significant victories for the CSO against the police in both the court and the newspapers.

The present activities and future plans of the CSO continue its tradition of encouraging Mexican-Americans to help themselves. After a period of relative inactivity, it is using a grant from the Office of Economic Opportunity to finance a number of new programs.

Some of the new projects concern consumer education. They began as a simple neighborhood organizing effort and have developed into a buyers' club, consumer complaint center, and credit union. The center employs several full-time organizers and VISTA volunteers who also work with a work experience program and a youth leadership project. In addition the CSO now publishes a small newspaper to keep members informed of its activities.

The CSO is a grass roots movement among blue collar workers. It is not controlled by, nor are the majority of its members, Mexican-Americans who have achieved education or position in the larger community. It emphasizes self-help and representation in government for those who have no position or power from other sources. Most of its leaders are veterans of the labor movement. Although the CSO seems to have been closely connected with the labor movement during some periods of its history, clearly it has been a successful and useful political movement in the Los Angeles Mexican-American community. Some of its achievements may seem small today for the large amount of tedious work that was needed to accomplish them. Before such activities were attempted, however, their success seemed impossible as the fate of pre-war labor organizers illustrates.

Another organization that operates in a manner similar to the CSO and the Unity Leagues is the American GI Forum of the United States. It is a Mexican-American veterans' group first organized in Corpus Christi, Texas, in 1948. Discrimination against Mexican-Americans was rather overt at that time: they were refused service in public places and generally forced to attend segregated schools. Attempts of Mexican-American veterans to join veterans' organizations were either refused or met with the suggestion that they form their own, separate chapters. Mexican-American veterans, who served in the United States

armed forces as equals, especially resented this discrimination;
but it was one specific insult that led to the formation of a
Mexican-American veterans' organization.

The situation centered around the burial of a Mexican-American war hero in Texas. When his family applied for a plot in a
local cemetery, the request was refused. Officials informed the
family that the cemetery was for white people only. Mexican-
American veterans, of course, were insulted, and some of them
brought the incident to the attention of the president of the United
States. This particular situation was resolved by arranging for
burial of the soldier in Arlington National Cemetery. The insulted
veterans, however, decided to insure against a recurrence of such
an event by organizing to end discrimination against Mexican-
Americans. Under the leadership of Dr. Hector García, they began
the Forums. Dr. García has remained active in Mexican-American
affairs as chairman of the board of the Forum.

The objectives of the Forum reflect the circumstances of its
founding.

1. Uphold and maintain loyalty to the Constitution and Flag
of the United States.

2. Preserve and defend the United States of America from all
enemies.

3. Develop leadership by creating interest in the Mexican-
American people to participate intelligently and wholeheartedly
in community, civic and political affairs.

4. Preserve and advance the basic principles of democracy,
i.e., the religious and political freedom of the individual and equal
social and economic opportunities for all citizens.

5. Secure and protect for all Veterans and their families, regardless of race, creed or color, the privileges vested on them by
the Constitution and laws of our country.

6. Combat juvenile delinquency through the Junior GI Forum
program which teaches respect for law and order, discipline,
good sportsmanship and the value of teamwork.

7. Award scholarships to deserving students of Mexican
ancestry.

Dr. García was instrumental in expanding the organization
of the American GI Forum throughout Texas. In less than a year
he had organized one hundred chapters. Organizing them began
in New Mexico and now has expanded to almost every part of

the United States. Local Forum chapters have autonomy to determine how actively they wish to participate in civic affairs. Some chapters are politically active in programs like those of the CSO while others are largely social clubs. National leaders have not been shy about issuing strong statements for membership consumption, but only lately have they begun to engage in the active support of their words. That the Forum now maintains a full time lobbyist in Washington, D.C., is an illustration of this. To add cohesiveness, it also publishes a monthly, four-page newspaper called the *Forumeer*. It prints social notices, news of all Mexican-American civic and political activities, and encourages Mexican-Americans to be more active in their communities.

Those Mexican-Americans who used the GI Bill and went back to college after the Second World War generally rejected the grass roots groups. They sought to form sophisticated, professional organizations that could participate in the larger community as a typical pressure group. An example of this kind of organization in Los Angeles is the Council of Mexican-American Affairs (CMAA).

The CMAA was organized in 1954 to prosecute Mexican-American claims to full citizenship and influence in government. It would like to change the image of the Mexican-American from blue collar to white. The members are happy to participate in conferences, discussions and meetings of all kinds concerning any issue affecting the Mexican-American community. They want to persuade the larger community that bilingual and bicultural citizens do not suffer a disadvantage: they can choose the best of both United States and Mexican cultures, and their experiences can enrich the entire community. For example, Mexican-Americans are uniquely qualified for diplomatic assignments in Latin America. Mexican-American children can also make a special contribution in the classroom and can help the entire class understand the implications of cultural differences.

The CMAA has not always been able to work effectively to implement its goals. The early part of its history was occupied by internal and organizational problems. Its founders began with a great vision of how to accomplish their goals; unfortunately their vision was not too clear at first. The CMAA's organizers saw their group as a formal council of all Mexican-American organizations in Los Angeles. Each organization would have weighted voting power in a House of Delegates. The success of this and other CMAA plans is accurately described by Dr. Paul Sheldon of Occidental College. The CMAA, he wrote,

> maintained an office, a full-time executive director, and a secretary. A fund-raising campaign with a goal of $50,000 ($20,000 for educational scholarships) was under way. The campaign fell short of its quota, and the Council went heavily into debt.
>
> Other problems had contributed to the crisis. At meetings of the Board it was apparent that member organizations were not paying their dues and that the CMAA could not raise a quorum of qualified delegates to elect officers or transact business. At one meeting attended by 25 or so people, only three of the 44 organizations they represented had paid the $25 membership fee necessary before their delegate could be allowed to vote.
>
> There was considerable bitterness and discouragement. One officer said that "too many Mexican-American organizations are dedicated to the destruction of each other." During this period there was a high turnover of board members and officers. Disagreements about the plan of organization, lack of funds, and personal problems resulted in the subsequent closing of the office and dismissal of the staff.[7]

One successful project, however, was begun soon after the CMAA was organized. The Education Committee was initiated in 1958 by some young Mexican-American professional educators. Through all the internal conflicts and organizational difficulties the Education Committee continued to press for improved opportunities for Mexican-American students and educators.

Among the issues emphasized by the Education Committee has been the concept of compensatory education. The committee members point out that most curricula are aimed at middle class, white Protestants. Mexican-American students, and those of other social and economic minority groups, need special compensation to help them understand these curricula or to adjust them to their needs. The committee also argued that there is need of special programs for students who have had a poor start in school. Another issue important to the Education Committee has been increased opportunities for Mexican-American educators.

---

[7]Paul M. Sheldon, "Community Participation and the Emerging Middle Class," in Julian Samora (ed.), *La Raza: Forgotten Americans* (Notre Dame: University of Notre Dame Press, 1966), p. 140.

Although the Education Committee survived the CMAA's internal conflicts, only a few of its functions have survived. An increased emphasis on the education of economically disadvantaged children has accompanied the War on Poverty and has created more activities in this area. To deal with these increased activities the Association of Mexican-American Educators was formed in 1965 and has since performed most of the active functions of the CMAA's Education Committee. The Committee, therefore, has retired from actively seeking changes in public policy to administer several Operation Headstart Centers in Mexican-American neighborhoods throughout Los Angeles County.

Despite its organizational problems, the CMAA has helped to change the public image of Mexican-Americans by presenting themselves to the larger community as educated, professional, sophisticated men. By appearing at conferences, hearings, and other functions, they have also made the larger community more aware of the situation of the Mexican-American.

The Association of Mexican-American Educators (AMAE) is another polite, sophisticated pressure group. It has gone farther than the CMAA, however, in actively presenting its case to the larger community. It was organized largely out of the CMAA Education Committee as a result of the 1965 Los Angeles Board of Education election. In that year the first serious Mexican-American candidate ran for a board office. Although the candidate lost in the primary, his campaign stirred new interest in the Mexican-American community. One reaction to this new interest was the formation of an organization of Mexican-American educators: the AMAE.

The objectives of the AMAE are to encourage boards of education and school administrators to understand and deal with Mexican-American children more effectively. They also propose to help the Mexican-American community appreciate the importance of education in United States society. They plan to encourage the advancement of Mexican-American teachers and administrators as well as the higher education of Mexican-American students. And in addition, they propose to serve as a clearinghouse for current research concerning Mexican-American education.

The AMAE has been active in making the larger community aware of the problems of Mexican-American students and educators. It was also influential in the appointment in California of a Mexican-American Deputy Superintendent of Public Instruction and a Mexican-American member of the State Board of Education. In 1967 it helped to elect a Mexican-American to the Los Angeles Board of Education and has pressed for the advancement of Mexican-Americans into administrative positions in other districts.

Although the professional, sophisticated organizations and the grass roots groups have a record of political achievement, they have avoided participation in partisan politics. The first Mexican-American group openly to proclaim itself political was the Mexican-American Political Association (MAPA). It was organized in 1959 to be the active, "hell-raising" arm of the Mexican-American community. The purposes set for it were to seek "the social, economic, cultural and civic betterment of Mexican-Americans and all other Spanish-speaking Americans through political action." Political action includes working for "The election and appointment to public office of Mexican-Americans and other persons sympathetic to our aims." MAPA also aimed to involve itself in the most basic kind of democratic political action: "To take stands on political issues, to present and endorse candidates for public office; to launch a voter registration drive throughout the state of California; and to carry on a program of political education."

To implement all these aims, MAPA's organizers sought to create a strong MAPA chapter in every assembly district where Mexican-Americans live. These local chapters were to be organized with the help of Mexican-Americans who held government offices. The Democratic victories of 1958 had given Mexican-Americans a few state positions. Other appointments were obtained at other levels of government as a result of the changing attitudes of the larger community toward all minority groups.

Almost all of MAPA's organizational plans have still to be realized. It did not benefit from the great interest among Mexican-Americans in the 1960 presidential campaign. The interest was mostly centered around the Viva Kennedy! Clubs. This interest was partially a result of Mexican-American traditional support of the Democratic Party; it was also influenced by a special relationship that Mexican-Americans felt with John F. Kennedy. Many of them shared his religion and also his persecution on its account. Interest in the Kennedy campaign distracted from the local campaigns MAPA put on to try to elect Mexican-Americans to the California legislature in 1960; none was successful.

In 1962, however, MAPA endorsed three successful candidates. Edward Roybal was elected to the United States House of Representatives; he was the first Mexican-American ever elected to the federal legislature from California. Two Mexican-Americans, Phillip Soto and John Moreno, were also elected to the lower house of the California legislature from Los Angeles.

These 1962 victories marked MAPA's apogee. Like the California Democratic Party, which gave Mexican-Americans the opportunity to organize MAPA, after the 1962 elections it began to be split by factionalism. By the time of the 1963 Los Angeles city elections, Mexican-Americans on the eastside were not even united enough to elect a Mexican-American to fill Congressman Roybal's former seat on the city council.

Since 1963 MAPA has had two major changes in leadership. Each new group proclaims itself truly bipartisan and determined to turn MAPA into an effective, well organized association. Concrete achievements await fulfillment of these goals. Meanwhile Assemblyman Soto was re-elected once, in 1964, but Assemblyman Moreno failed in his first bid for re-election. Congressman Roybal continues to serve and in 1968 another Mexican-American, Alex García, was elected to the California State Assembly.

Mexican-Americans in other parts of the Southwest also sought to organize political associations to elect Mexican-Americans to public office. Accepting a name (like MAPA) with Mexican-American in it violated the traditions of such places as Texas (where they are usually called "Latins") and New Mexico (where they generally call themselves "Hispanos"). In parts of the country other than California, therefore, another political association was formed and called the Political Association of Spanish-Speaking Organizations (PASO, also abbreviated PASSO).[8] Its organizers intended for it to include MAPA.

PASO has engaged in activities similar to those of MAPA. Its outstanding success was achieved in Crystal City, Texas, in 1963. Crystal City was a town of about 10,000 people; about 7,500

---

[8]Ronnie Dugger, "Ballot-Box Revolution: The Political Awakening of Mexican-Americans in Texas," *Frontier* (September, 1963), 7–9; Thomas B. Morgan, "The Texas Giant Awakens," *Look* (October 8, 1963), 71–75; and Ralph Guzmán, "Politics and Policies of the Mexican-American Community," in Eugene P. Dvorin and Arthur J. Misner (eds.), *California Politics and Policies* (Reading, Mass.: Addison-Wesley Publishing Company, 1966), p. 381.

of them were Mexican-Americans although they exercised little voice in city government. In the 1963 election campaign PASO, supported by the Teamsters Union, organized Mexican-Americans to pay their poll tax and vote for a slate of Mexican-American candidates. The slate was headed by Juan Cornejo, the Teamsters' business agent, and it won the election. Its main campaign theme had been that Mexican-Americans must get together and realize their potential political power.

Like MAPA, PASO has seemed unable to use its successes to spread its political organization and activities to other places. Its leaders continue to issue militant statements and demand recognition in national politics, but without notable effect.

These participation organizations—where they are openly political, professional and sophisticated, or grass roots—have failed to end discrimination against Mexican-Americans or to convince them that they must do more to help themselves if they are to succeed in United States society. The 1960 census, for example, showed Mexican-Americans to be the least educated group in California despite the fact that almost every Mexican-American organization proclaims the importance of education and many even award scholarships. More recently it has been in the field of education that there has been the most publicity; yet in one largely Mexican-American high school in Los Angeles, for example, the drop-out rate remains around fifty percent. The 1960 census also showed Mexican-American per capita family income the lowest in California and more recent figures indicate no change. These facts, compared with the standard of living of the larger community and the success of the Civil Rights Movement with militant activities, have convinced some Mexican-Americans to adopt similar techniques.

Militancy in the rural Mexican-American community began formally on September 17, 1965, when the National Farm Workers Association called a strike against grape growers in Delano, California.[9] Urban Mexican-Americans took their first militant action on March 28, 1966, with the Albuquerque Walkout. That was the time and place set for a meeting between national Mexican-

[9]Eugene Nelson, *Huelga: The First Hundred Days of the Great Delano Grape Strike* (Delano: Farm Worker Press, 1966), and John Gregory Dunn, *Delano: the Story of the California Grape Strike* (New York: Farrar, Straus and Giroux, 1967).

American leaders and the federal Equal Employment Opportunities Commission. When the leaders arrived, they found only one commissioner present and none of their previous complaints had even been acknowledged; so they walked out. A press release explaining this action sounded a new tone. "The nation's five million Mexican-Americans will begin marching and demonstrating on a national scale unless the government takes immediate steps to provide them with equal educational and employment opportunities."

Urban Mexican-Americans began implementing this statement by their support of the National Farm Workers Organizing Committee. It was organized by César Chávez who approached it from a background of organizing for the Community Service Organization. He combined CSO ideas with traditional labor union tactics. All his union wants is decent working conditions, a living wage, and to be recognized as the bargaining agent for its members. The Grape Boycott, organized by the union in support of its strike, has no significant opposition in the Mexican-American community.

The urban leaders have given less unquestioning support to another Mexican-American militant, Reies López Tijerina.[10] He has organized the Alianza Federal de Pueblos Libres in New Mexico. Its goal is to regain land lost by the people who lived there before it belonged to the United States. To support his cause, Tijerina has even engaged in guerilla warfare. As a result, the New Mexico National Guard with tanks and other heavy equipment were sent out to search the mountains for him; front page pictures of the search appeared in newspapers all across the United States in June, 1967. Tijerina was subsequently, however, at liberty and traveling around the country trying to organize support for a communal farming project his group has planned for the summer of 1969 in Tierra Amarilla, New Mexico.

Los Angeles urban leaders participated in the Albuquerque Walkout and support the NFWOC and Tijerina's goals, if not all of his activities. Militant action, however, began with the "blow-out," a student strike at a largely Mexican-American Los Angeles high school. As a result of the strike, thirteen Mexican-Americans, including a teacher at the school, were arrested and charged with conspiracy to interrupt the educational process. Because of the charge against him, the teacher was suspended from

---

[10]Michael Jenkinson, *Tijerina* (Albuquerque: Paisano Press, 1968).

working in the classroom. A sit-in at the Los Angeles Board of Education, organized to protest his suspension, ended when the teacher was allowed to return to his teaching duties. The apparent success of this strike seems to have set a pattern later followed in Denver and other Southwestern cities.

The demands of the leaders of the "blow-out" include a mixture of New Left educational reforms and specific proposals to deal with Mexican-American educational problems. The general demands included smaller classes, more relevant vocational courses, a pass–fail grading system, and more student influence in the choosing of teachers, administrators, books and curriculum. More specifically they demanded classes about the contribution of Mexicans and Mexican-Americans and a program to take advantage of the students' bilingual and bicultural heritage. There were also specific demands relative to district policies such as a swimming pool for an eastside high school.

An organization called the Educational Issues Coordinating Committee (EICC) arose to speak for those involved in the "blowouts." This committee has waged a campaign of publicity and action to try to press the need for reform revealed in the strike. It has also sought to raise money for legal fees for those prosecuted for their involvement in these activities.

Student organizations have also been organized to press for the same kinds of demands presented in the "blow-out." Perhaps the best known of these groups are the United Mexican-American Students (UMAS) and the Mexican-American Student Organization (MASO). UMAS is a confederation of clubs in which each has individual autonomy to determine its degree of militancy. They have been active in pressing for Mexican-American studies programs in individual high schools and colleges. UMAS has also sought more opportunities for Mexican-Americans in higher education.

Although the militants have yet to make a noticeable contribution to the economic or social situation of the Mexican-American community, they have increased awareness of their problems in the larger community. The militants have created the greatest potential for change of any group of Mexican-American organizations. It is still true, however, that most Mexican-Americans who belong to any organization belong to one dedicated to self-protection, death benefits and insurance, and social activities.

Bracero Politics: a Special Report*

Ramparts

In the early twenties, at San Francisco's Lowell High School, Edmund G. "Pat" Brown, now in his second term as governor of the Golden State, was a member of "The Nocturnes," a group of crapshooting schoolboys. One of his brother Nocturnes was Norton Simon, now a widely known art connoisseur (he recently bought a Rembrandt for over $2 million) and head of Hunt Foods and Industries, the nation's largest tomato processor. Over the years Brown has continued his affinity for powerful friends in the food production business. He has long been on intimate terms with Joseph and Robert Di Giorgio, of the Di Giorgio Fruit Corporation empire. Palmer C. Mendelson, a ubiquitous grower-spokesman, and Lionel Steinberg and Jim Camp, millionaire growers, are close confidants. These men are part of the nucleus of "agribusiness," the California agriculturist complex that last year rang up $3.6 billion in receipts by supplying some 40 percent of the nation's table food—and dissuaded Brown from exercising his best human instincts to kill once and for all the Mexican bracero program that has displaced and demoralized the American farm laborer.

The issue of the bracero versus the domestic worker is a hot one in a state where the political pot is always simmering. The temperature approached the boiling point last fall when Congress refused another reprieve for Public Law 78, the Korean War emergency measure that had been extended a number of times for the convenience of agribusiness. Theoretically, P.L. 78 permitted the importation of braceros only if sufficient numbers of Americans were not available to bring in the harvest. But in practice it didn't work out that way. Braceros formed the hard core of the labor force, forcing indigenous workers to compete for jobs which were offered on the basis of substandard bracero norms.

---

*This unsigned report appeared in the September 1965 issue of *Ramparts* magazine. Copyright © 1965 Ramparts Magazine, Inc. By permission of the Editors.

At the height of the program a seasonal tide of a hundred thousand braceros swept into California, disrupting any hope of the domestics for a semblance of job stability. To the single-minded interests of agribusiness braceroism was a cheap labor windfall—it drove wages and working conditions below rock bottom and kept them there. And equally important, braceros were for all practical purposes a captive labor force that could be shuttled wherever needed, thus effectively preventing American workers from organizing.

Special license never dies easily, and agribusiness, faced with the prospect of losing the braceros, girded for an all-out fight. The strategy involved a two-pronged offensive—one directed at public sympathy, and the other at political support. When California crops began to ripen this spring—as inevitably they would —growers complained of a crippling labor shortage and predicted crops would rot in the fields, never a pretty picture, even in a land of abundance. To dramatize the claim, plow-unders were staged for the benefit of the press. Freshman Senator George Murphy, far more versed in theatrics than farm labor problems, showed up in the fields to act as master of ceremonies. In one instance he drove past mile after mile of parked automobiles belonging to domestic workers busy in the fields, to preside while an Orange County farmer plowed under a single row of berries. "Every day they wait to bring back braceros adds to the tragedy here," he said. Then he hopped a northbound plane for Salinas, the heart of Steinbeck country, to carry out a similar performance on behalf of the lettuce growers.

On the political front, the big guns of agribusiness were leveled at Pat Brown, then wavering between fence-straddling and open endorsement of the growers' cause. For Brown, a former painters' union attorney and a nominal liberal, the problem was racking. There was an inescapable parallel between wanton abandonment of the farm worker and civil rights—a field in which he had achieved a fair enough record. Dr. Paul O'Rourke, his own anti-poverty director, had flatly told him that any anti-poverty program in California was meaningless until the bracero was eliminated and the plight of domestic farm worker alleviated. (O'Rourke calls Highway 99, which stretches from the Sacramento Valley in the north to the Imperial Valley in the south, "the longest slum in the world," referring to the farm laborers' shanties that border it.)

When he first moved into the governor's mansion in January,

1959, Brown gave every indication that he was not only aware of the sad consequences of braceroism, but intended to do something about it. Acknowledging the bleat of agribusiness that California was in competition with other agricultural states, he nonetheless insisted that the farm laborer be included in the proposed $1.25 minimum wage for the state (at the time farm wages were hovering around 90 cents an hour). "If a person is worth hiring," said Brown, "he is worth paying a decent, living wage. The special interest group which denies that, imperils its own future as well as California's."

The probity of Brown's remark—and its simple logic—was lost on agribusiness, which saw its prosperity as based solely on maintaining the leanest possible payrolls. And in the end it was not agribusiness which capitulated, but Brown. Within two years he yielded to the growers he once had been "ready to battle" and reneged on his pledges to give farm workers a minimum wage. He found the tug of the big power alignment irresistible.

The Anatomy of Agribusiness

The shape and form of the agribusiness lobby in California is awesome to behold. California Packing (Cal Pak), the world's largest canner of fruits and vegetables, operates at every level, from the field to the supermarket, where its familiar Del Monte label appears; sales are well over $400 million annually. Hunt Foods and Industries, producers of Hunt's catsup and tomato paste and Wesson salad and cooking oil, has diversified into steel, matches, and glass containers; it generates some $400 million a year with profits climbing. Di Giorgio Fruit, one of the largest fresh fruit grower-distributors in the world, is a $75-million-a-year enterprise. Allied with these and other less conspicuous growers are the peripheral interests, e.g., Bank of America, the world's largest bank, which has a stake in a huge slice of the state's farmlands; Southern Pacific railroad, shipper to the industry, and owner of vast acreage in the fertile San Joaquin Valley; and Kern County Land Company, which for all practical purposes *is* Kern County.

The reticular pattern of interest is shown by the interlocking directorships of the corporations. Robert Di Giorgio is a Bank of America director, while Carl F. Wente, a Bank of America vice-president, is a Di Giorgio director. Insurance–realty executive

A. E. Scarboro sits on both boards, as does influential Southern California merchandiser Prentis Hale. Edward W. Carter, a director of Hale's department store chain, is also a trustee of the Irvine Corporation, which owns a major segment of Orange County fruitlands and Imperial Valley lettuce acreage. Four Cal Pak directors sit simultaneously on the board of the Wells Fargo Bank, second largest farm financer in the state.

The corporate viewpoint has not suffered for want of spokesmen. For example, Jesse W. Tapp, an agricultural economist is board chairman of the Bank of America and president of the State Board of Agriculture. He has consistently plugged for more braceros on the ground that domestic labor just won't fill the bill. "Most of our unemployed have work habits which make farm labor unattractive to them," he told the San Francisco Chamber of Commerce, in predicting another banner year for California agribusiness. And this version has been repeatedly echoed by Earl Coke, a retiring vice-president of the Bank of America and former right-hand man to Ezra Benson, Eisenhower's ultra-conservative secretary of agriculture. Coke asserted: "Just what effect the unwillingness of the (Federal) Government to provide the usual numbers of seasonal labor would be to California is yet difficult to determine. Earlier this year we announced that we would not finance growers unless there was some assurance of labor supplies." Assured by Labor Secretary Wirtz that workers would be available, however, the Bank of America went ahead with loans to growers.

Parenthetically, University of California agriculture economist, Dr. Varden Fuller, has outlined what may underlie the interest of a bank in keeping farm wages depressed. He points out that if strawberries sell for $1 a unit and can be picked for 5 cents a unit, business is likely to be quite profitable. "At this structure of prices pickers could command much higher wages if they had the power to do so. But if pickers continue to be available at 5 cents per unit, the strawberry acreage will expand." Expansion, of course, keeps the price of farm land high, which is all to the banks' advantage.

No less interested in braceroism are the state's large independent growers. Banded together in local associations and cooperatives and represented at the state level by the Council of California Growers, they form a unified propaganda front. These associations earmark a portion of receipts for a so-called "promotional fund," actually one of the more potent political slush funds in California. Foremost among the big growers is Lionel Steinberg, a wealthy Coachella Valley grape grower and Democratic Party stalwart. Appointed by Brown as vice-president of the State Board of Agriculture, Steinberg has little difficulty catching the Governor's ear on agribusiness problems.

The dice are loaded on the State Board of Agriculture. Bank of America's Jesse Tapp, a Democrat, is president. Milton Natapoff [was a] registered lobbyist in Sacramento for a dairy farmers' association before his appointment. Ten of the thirteen-member Board are growers. All members are Brown appointees.

Thus there is little mystery behind Brown's vacillation and eventual abandonment of the farm worker's cause. Adding to its deliberateness is the fact that the liberal wing of the Democratic Party—represented by California Democratic Council and the State Democratic Central Committee—has expressed itself as resolutely opposed to further extension of the bracero system.

With the cost of field labor only two to five cents on the dollar, depending on the crop, even a substantial wage hike—passed on entirely to the housewife—would not appreciably affect prices. Increased payrolls, in themselves, are not the primary concern of the agribusiness people. What looms most ominous in their thinking is that *any* concession in the area of wages would be the beginning of the end of their privileged "Blue-Sky Sweatshop," the process of systematic exclusion of the farm laborer from the benefits of collective bargaining, accident and health insurance, unemployment compensation insurance, and other fringe benefits now standard fare in all other United States industries.

But time in mid-twentieth-century America has a habit of not standing still, and the comfortable status quo of agribusiness was once again interrupted by a renewal of the bracero issue. Agribusiness has all along contended that the bacero is absolutely essential to insure the timely harvesting of crops. That California's number one industry, $3.6 billion strong last year and described by Bank of America agricultural economist Earl Coke as "the most efficient agriculture in the world," should have to lean so decisively on an ancient tradition of captive labor seems patently incongruous.

More to the quick is the realization by agribusiness that once the bracero passes forever from the California scene, unionization of farm labor will become a reality. Until now the omnipresence of the bracero—the fact that he could be shuttled from place to place when disputes with domestic labor arose (sporadic as they were)—effectively throttled any semblance of labor–management dialogue. Once unionization is an accomplished fact, agribusiness will have to abide by the same touchstones of decency and equity as any other industry. This would entail quite an adjustment from callous indifference to the worker—one that growers are not uniformly prepared to make. As one Salinas Valley grower expressed it: "The handwriting may be on the wall, but we'll do everything possible to slow down unionization."

A Tradition of California Captive Labor

California has a history of imported labor that dates back to the mid-nineteenth-century Chinese railroad gangs: Public Law 78 merely certified what had long been a de facto method of operation. In earlier times immigrants from Mexico and the Orient were dumped into labor "pools" to be tapped at the growers' pleasure under gentlemen's agreements governing wages and conditions. When, toward the turn of the century, the Chinese Exclusion Act tended to dry up the pool, growers fixed their eyes south of the border for what George Santayana termed one of the most important raw materials of industry: man.

The history of the migration of Mexican manual labor to the United States is one of gradual drift, pushed on the one side by chaotic conditions within Mexico itself and pulled on the other by the lure of the gringo dollar, which outweighed the peso two to one. What the Mexican found, however, was an equally barren existence. He was paid what amounted to more of a dole than a wage; it was kept that way by a steady infusion into the labor market of border-jumping Wetbacks. Dragged down by a bare-subsistence income, insulated from the mainstream of American life by language and cultural barriers, he gravitated into ghettos, thus setting a standard of impoverishment upon which agribusiness grew to rely.

During World War II agribusiness found itself confronted by its first great manpower crisis. The drain caused by the military draft was serious enough, but it was compounded by an exodus of farm workers to better jobs in California's mushrooming defense industries. Holding the line on wages with one hand, agribusiness tugged on the government's sleeve for help with the other. A bracero recruitment agreement was worked out with the Mexican government, and like another wartime measure, it has never really ended.

After the war the manpower shortage (and the bracero program) continued: understandably, the workers who had tasted a better life in the manufacturing industries were not about to return to the abysmal conditions of farm labor, nor did the growers anticipate with pleasure the return of prodigals tainted with ideas of unionism.

But the codification of the bracero program under P.L. 78 in 1951 was due as much to the insistence of the Mexican government as to the clamor of American growers. Mexico had become increasingly sensitive to the wanton abuses that had crept into braceroism, and pressed for regulation. More often than not the shelter provided was squalid. Braceros were herded from place to place in dilapidated trucks, often driven by drunk drivers, with no regard for even minimal safety standards. Labor contractors often siphoned off exorbitant percentages of payrolls that were watery to begin with. And though the bracero was indentured, he had no guarantee of steady work.

Consequently, articles were written into P.L. 78 that gave the bracero at least a modicum of relief. An element of uniformity was introduced to pay formulas; sanitary housing and adequate transportation were theoretically guaranteed (enforcement was largely perfunctory), and payment for at least three-quarters of the life of the contract was agreed upon. The scheme was at once humanitarian and cynical, for the little that it gave to the foreign farm laborer had never been considered for the American.

Agribusiness was hooked on braceroism, and began to move political mountains to secure extension after extension of P.L. 78. As time went on, the artificiality of the situation became transparent; even some growers realized braceroism—dependent as it was upon the attitudes of a foreign government—was neither a permanent nor an ideal solution to the problem of stabilizing the labor market. Opposition from church groups, labor organizations, and political liberals mounted. Finally, by 1963, Congress had had enough, its mood reflected by the statement of Representative B. F. Sisk of California: "Many of us are coming to the conclusion that the time has come to serve notice on the American farmer that he and we combined must come up with an alternative program. . . . This will be the last time I shall enter the well to ask for an extension. . . . We have come to the end of the line. . . . "

Simultaneously, Governor Brown urged the United States Congress to extend P.L. 78 for one year only, arguing that the time was needed to gradually "phase-out" the bracero system. But the stall could not go on forever, so he needed a solid peg on which to hang his sombrero. He found one, and it wore the stately mantle of academic wisdom. It was popularly called the Giannini Report.

The Giannini Foundation of Agricultural Economics, a department of the University of California at Berkeley, was endowed by the late Joseph Giannini, founder of the Bank of America. A viable tie remains in the form of Bank of America trustees of the Foundation, and the University itself has several agribusinessmen —most prominently, Norton Simon and Edward Carter—on its Board of Regents. At Brown's behest, a study of the farm labor problem was undertaken and summarized in the Giannini Report, issued in September, 1964. It evoked a storm of controversy over its conclusion that the loss of bracero would put a severe crimp in agricultural production. Indeed, it hardly seemed the report was compiled with requisite academic detachment: its principal author, Dr. Eric Thor, was an open protagonist of the agribusiness viewpoint, who had stumped the state speaking at gatherings of growers and businessmen. (Reportedly Thor is in line for the job of Earl Coke, retiring vice-president for agriculture of the Bank of America and himself a former University agri-economist.) In 1963, Thor had prepared a report of similar thrust which proposed, as an alternative solution, the importation of Negro laborers from the Mississippi delta and implied that resultant racial tensions would be the price California would have to pay for abandoning the bracero system.

In a speech delivered to San Joaquin County orchardists last January, Thor openly counselled them against being pressured by "do gooders, and non-agricultural groups" into raising wage levels for domestic workers. He pointed out that under then-existing regulations handed down by Secretary of Labor Wirtz they would be compelled to raise only the bracero's pay—not the "local labor." So it was that the University-based Giannini Foundation's eminent agri-economist, in the year 1965, endorsed the policy of paying heads of families approximately $1 an hour (no fringe benefits) for what the growers themselves described as "backbreaking work"—in an undeniably flourishing major American industry.

In a recent interview, Dr. Thor, using the rhetoric of laissez faire economics, deplored "political interference" in "what is essentially an economic problem . . . one that would solve itself if let alone." He added, "You have to understand that the growers are real businessmen, real swingers with the banks."

By November, 1964, time was running out for Pat Brown to speak his mind on braccroism. P.L. 78 was virtually moribund, and agribusiness, which had made only token efforts at mobilizing a domestic labor force since the extension of the previous year, began to project an image of desperation. Actually, California's six hundred thousand farm laborers were guardedly optimistic, since Brown had told a delegation led by César Chávez—editor of *El Malcriado: Voice of the Farm Worker* and organizer of a grass-roots labor movement—that the bracero system was bad and he would not tolerate it. But on Friday the thirteenth, Brown seized upon the Giannini Report as the basis for a proposal for a new five-year "phase-out plan."

As proposed to Secretary of Labor Willard Wirtz, the plan called for "a two-part program to provide foreign farm labor for California's immediate needs while the state builds a paramount domestic work force for long-range needs." The scheme provided for an extension of the bracero system until 1969, with the stipulation that the University "undertake a study of conditions in agriculture for the specific purpose of determining what changes need to be made to motivate more people to accept agricultural employment." This area, it was noted, "has not been examined in detail."

Interestingly enough, at the time the Giannini Report was released another less-publicized report emanated from the University of California at Los Angeles. It was prepared by Fred H. Schmidt, who grew up in the cotton fields of Texas and of late had been administrative assistant to Congressman Henry Gonzales of San Antonio. It concluded that only two things were needed to fill the fields with domestic workers: decent wages and decent working conditions. UCLA researchers had found that one-half of the unemployed interviewed in metropolitan Los Angeles were originally from farms and small towns, and one-third had done hard agricultural labor. Significantly, 31 percent of the males interviewed stated they could be attracted back to the farm if basic standards of decency were introduced. Although such responses ordinarily might be viewed skeptically, their accuracy was demonstrated in the early months of 1965 when the State

Department of Employment actually placed 34 percent of those approached to do farm work.

Schmidt, who entitled his report "After the Bracero," proceeded on the premise that agribusiness is going to have to face up to the reality of cultivating its own labor force. "So long as there is any assurance that a reservoir of foreign labor can readily be tapped to meet what appear to be shortages of labor supply, there will be continuing postponements in reckoning with the basic problems associated with farm labor." Schmidt stressed that the present concept of "casualization" of the work force is outmoded, and that the exclusion of farm workers from unemployment benefits will have to cease if any permanent force is to be assured.

Curiously, a seventeen-page section of the Giannini report was deleted between the time it left the University for Brown's office and the time it was released by Brown. This deletion was discovered by Ruben Salazar of the *Los Angeles Times* in mid-December after the UCLA report was released. With the seventeen pages included, the Giannini report reaches substantially the same conclusions as the UCLA report.

When the deletion was exposed, Dr. Maurice Peterson, head of the University of California Department of Agriculture, contended that these conclusions "could not be fully documented from University research."

Secretary Thomas L. Pitts of the California Labor Federation (AFL-CIO) blamed the deletion on "an apparent veto" by powerful farm interests.

"Farm Work: That's Pretty Low"

All of this is logical enough, but it is anathema to the intractable majority of big growers who regard the bracero as a form of mechanization—efficient, in good condition, economical to operate, and readily returnable with no strings attached. Palmer Mendelson of the Mendelson-Zeller Co. in San Francisco, a large strawberry–asparagus shipper (Mendelson likes to make it known that he has flown strawberries to Europe for Princess Margaret's breakfast and Charles de Gaulle's state dinners), says that "the bracero is a professional—others are amateurs. You have to have a hard core of professionals who can be shifted with crop conditions." Besides, he adds, "no one wants to do this work and who blames them."

Hardly anyone contests the fact that the bracero, under the whip of what Dr. Paul O'Rourke terms the "sadistic field boss," works like a dog, and willingly and well. One citrus grower describes it as an "awesome sight" to watch braceros "attack" a tree. (Paid mostly on a piecework basis, they are pitted against each other to determine who makes the most.) But in a free economy a labor force of chattels is unnatural, and tends to generate a variety of unnatural—and undesirable—consequences.

Except for a tiny trickle spent for immediate necessities, the entire earnings of a bracero return to Mexico with him, creating an outflow of currency against which President Johnson has counseled. Since braceros do not spend for goods and services in the United States, American merchants in bracero-dominated areas have been hard hit. And the small grower is up against unfair competition—every time he climbs on his own tractor, for instance, he is matching his valuable time against that of a bracero driving a big grower's tractor.

Back home in Mexico, the bracero is regarded as something of a hero. He is one of the select few that have ever torn loose from their enclaves and traveled to the great country *del Norte,* and he has come back well-heeled, even rich in the relative terms of poverty. The American farm worker, on the other hand, is an outcast in his own society, a pariah in the midst of plenty. A priest tells the story of two Mexicans he had known as braceros. He chanced to run into them at a Spanish-speaking social, dressed to the hilt, and they explained their new found prosperity. A friend from their home village had found work with a builder of tract homes in San Jose. The builder told the friend he could use more Mexicans like him, and he had relayed the word on to them. They had returned to Mexico and re-entered the United States, with the promise of jobs from the builder, under the immigration code. They had joined the hod carrier's union, and were making around $2.50 an hour, with fringe benefits. The tract homes were up, and they were waiting for another project to start. Meanwhile, they were bringing their families up from Mexico. The priest tossed them a rhetorical question: "Think you might ever go back to farm work?" "Farm work!" they laughed. "That's pretty low."

Perhaps this attitude, more than anything else, is at the heart of the matter. A stigma attaches to farm labor. In maintaining the bracero as the core of farm labor there also has been imported the syndromes of his impoverished lot—deprecation, despair, dispirit. Would it make any difference if the farm worker's status was raised to compare with other American workers who form an integral—and indispensable—part of the production process? Most growers hold that it would not; that the domestic is by nature indolent (or he would find himself a better job), incapable of "stoop-labor," and more disposed toward state largesse than a hard day's work. However, the experience of Gilroy farmer Les Grube and his Community Recruitment of Personnel (CROP) effort has disabused many skeptics of that notion.

Convinced there was an adequate labor reserve ready to step in if the price was right, Grube enlisted the help of Father Ronald A. Burke and his associates of the Interfaith Migrant Committee to conduct an intensive recruiting drive. This was in the spring of 1965, as the strawberries started to ripen and large growers, including giant Salinas Strawberries, Inc., bemoaned the lack of braceros. Grube's lure was a $1.40-an-hour wage which Secretary of Labor Willard Wirtz had pegged as the minimum that had to be offered domestic help before braceros could be considered. (The domestic worker scale had previously fluctuated around the $1 mark.)

CROP's drive was aimed at the shantytowns on the periphery of Gilroy and San Jose. At first it was disheartening; only twenty showed up for the first bus to Salinas. "I began to have some doubts myself," Grube remembers. But gradually word spread and the buses filled. "Anyone who is willing to make that one-and-a-half-hour ride down and back each day really wants to work," said Grube, disdaining use of phrase "day-haul" which he associates with the Department of Employment's mid-city loading of buses with derelicts and winos. One grower was so impressed ("I've seen a different type of person—a sober family man.") that he added a bonus of 15 cents a crate on top of the $1.40 wage. But the same grower was later allotted some braceros, and asked CROP to waive his labor commitment.

The CROP experiment worked out so well that the California Department of Employment has subsidized it and given the green light for expansion of its scope. Perhaps the most salient fact is that CROP has demonstrated the existence of a sizeable supply of people who consider themselves essentially farm workers, but who drifted away because they weren't really wanted. And one of the most dramatic side-effects was the sharp reduction in welfare payments in the area. Salinas County Welfare Commissioner William Leach announced that in April, 1964, when the bracero was still the mainstay of strawberry labor, 313 families were on welfare rolls; by April, 1965, the number had dropped to 77.

C. Al Green, director of the AFL-CIO Agricultural Workers Organizing Committee (AWOC) in Stockton, believes that the farm labor "shortage" is more manufactured than real. On December 7, 1964, Green told a United States Department of Labor Panel in San Francisco, "The fact is, there have been few real efforts made to attract United States farm workers. The wages offered are low and the working conditions miserable. When real efforts have been made to attract United States farm workers, the workers have responded with enthusiasm." Green cited several "crises" he was able to alleviate with more than enough workers.

Green, a veteran building trades union official (he knew Pat Brown when Brown was a painters' union attorney; thinks of him now as a man on the spot) who shifted to AWOC in 1962, calls the supposed labor shortage a sham that ill-conceals the growers' desire for braceros exclusively. "The existence of the reservoir of cheap, captive labor effectively exempts the growers from having to bid for workers," he says. "They do not have to compete for laborers. They do not have to raise wages and improve working conditions to attract a sufficient number of workers."

Green feels the theme that domestics will not do hard stoop-labor is only a smokescreen. "American workers are not afraid of hard work," he claims. "Why do Americans work cleaning out the city sewers? Why do Americans work as cement masons when seventy-five percent of that work is done on their knees? Why do Americans work as garbage collectors, as roofers, handling hot tar all day? What is more hazardous than being a structural steel worker?"

So far AWOC has been able to sign up several labor contractors but no growers. Last May, in the Coachella Valley, AWOC succeeded in organizing sufficient workers to strike Lionel Steinberg's operation. An AWOC official, Benjamin C. Gines, was arrested under an obscure local ordinance prohibiting "intimidating to keep employees from working." (Charges were later dropped.) "It's a tough nut to crack," remarks Green, recalling the time in 1962 when he tried to negotiate a contract at a California Packing labor compound on Union Island, in the Sacramento River delta, and was rebuffed by a locked gate and guards bristling with weapons.

The modest headway that AWOC has been able to make is rather revolutionary in a state where agricultural unionism has always been decisively—and sometimes violently—beaten down. The National Farm Workers Union of the late forties and early fifties found its attempts at strikes going up in smoke when growers rushed in complements of braceros and wetbacks. At present the only labor movement of consequences, other than AWOC, is the Spanish-speaking César Chávez group in Delano. It is founded on the gentle exhortation of Pope John: "We for that matter express our satisfaction with those sons of ours throughout the whole world who actively are engaged in the movement of agricultural workers with the intention of elevating the economic and social level of the communities of agricultural workers." Yet concessions have been few and grudging. Perhaps one of the most distressing angles has been the failure of big labor in other industries to rally solidly behind farm labor. In some respects, it has been the other way around. The Teamsters Union, for example, with a hand in the hauling of farm products (it has a "sweetheart" contract with one of the major growers), has come out in favor of lingering braceroism.

Water: The Golden State's Golden Commodity

Behind the fight against braceroism is a collection of civic groups and church bodies. On the national level, Father James L. Vizzard, the Jesuit who heads the Washington Office of the National Catholic Rural Life Conference, has been unequivocal. At a labor hearing on November 30, 1964, he declared:

> I have no tears to waste on those who have been crying disaster at the prospect of losing the previously readily available agricultural workers from Mexico under P.L. 78 but who in the meantime have taken no realistic steps to secure an adequate and dependable United States labor force.... I can only deplore those politicians who feel they must cooperate with the growers in their continued refusal to face the demands of individual justice and the common good.... Since these growers show no signs of self-reform, they need to be told emphatically and with finality that the approximation of slave-labor conditions which they have perpetuated will no longer be tolerated by this nation. They need to be made to understand in what century and in what kind of economy and society they are living and operating. They must be forced to realize that to exploit the poverty of other nations in order to beat down and crush the poor of our own country is the grossest kind of immorality.

Father Vizzard's scathing indictment has been seconded in principle by many churchmen, including Msgr. George Higgins of the National Catholic Welfare Council and Reverend Wayne C. Hartmire, Jr., of the California Migrant Ministry of the National Council of Churches. A noteworthy dissenter is Episcopalian Bishop James A. Pike, who favors a stretched-out transition from braceroism. The Bishop's stand, glaringly anomalous to his usual liberalism, rankled the Rev. Hartmire, who paraphrased the reaction of the farm worker in a letter to Bishop Pike: "You Christians speak brave words about Alabama but when the money changers are in your temples then you stand for gradualism— gradualism which means justice can wait for those of us who don't pay our way in those temples." The Rev. Hartmire observed that growers are a potent force in the church—"highly visible in a way that slum realtors, for example, are not."

Perhaps the most sustained and vibrant voice the California worker has had is Citizens for Farm Labor, organized by Henry P. Anderson, a California public health official. Its fifty-six-man advisory board is composed of attorneys, legislators, professors, clerics, and concerned citizens; it includes United States Representative Phillip Burton and Father Thomas McCullough, the boyish-looking Catholic priest who several years ago was silenced by the bishop of San Diego following grower complaints that he had participated in a field workers' rally in El Centro.

Anderson himself has investigated the farm labor problem at close range—in the fields. In the late fifties, as a research assistant attached to the school of public health at the University of California, he ranged the state probing the impact of braceroism on sanitation, housing, and other aspects of farm labor. In 1958, he was ordered to stop interviewing braceros at the El Centro staging compound, under pain of arrest, because, he claims, the Department of Labor frowned on criticism of its program. Later, his report was suppressed, particularly a section on the power structure behind braceroism. "I was told it was suppressed because of pressures from the Department of Labor and the Farm Bureau Federation [a growers' lobby]," says Anderson.

Anderson has written that "the bracero system is a hall of mirrors. It is filled with one illusion after another." One of the most illusory, he thinks, is the idea that there is a dearth of domestic farm workers. "I agree they'll never find them culling the skid rows, as does the Department of Employment. But if they bothered to go out to the fringes of the agricultural centers, they'd find experienced hands living marginally on whatever else they can pick up . . . and only too willing to go back under decent conditions."

One of the dynamos keeping Citizens for Farm Labor humming is Mrs. Anne Draper, union label representative for the garment workers in San Francisco. Mrs. Draper, who sees braceroism as one of the last remaining vestiges of labor exploitation in mid-twentieth-century America, locked horns with Palmer Mendelson on a television panel discussion of the subject ("That union woman is a good talker," concedes Mendelson). "There's more to it than wages," she says. "They want self-expression, satisfaction in a job, like anyone else. Canning and packing is seasonal, too, but those workers are organized—and have job rights, holidays, unemployment compensation and other benefits that attach them to the job."

Indeed, the paradox of bracero feudalism in space age California—of one industry concerned with importing men in bondage, of another concerned with sending men to the moon—is one of the most striking contrasts in a state that traditionally abounds in contrast. Yet there are signs that the old order changeth. In a recent *Time* magazine interview, Hunt's Foods' Norton Simon, in giving his concept of the function of a corporation, remarked: "We are beyond the day and age of the need of capitalism for survival. We need it for only one thing—the betterment of the human being. Certainly we have a lot more than we can eat, haven't we?" Asked for elaboration, a Hunt's spokesman replied, "Although we are aware of the issues on both sides, we can't make an overt statement. After all, we don't grow our own. . . we have to rely on the growers to supply us, and we can't very well come out against them, no matter what we think."

Bud Antle, self-styled "lettuce king of the world," has looked beyond the bracero for some time now. "Give me a market and I'll get the lettuce," is the sort of remark that has gotten Antle drummed out of the growers' club—which might be, in Melvin Belli's words, "like being kicked out of the Book of the Month Club." Antle, who started as a lettuce trimmer in Salinas in 1931 and now ships ten thousand carloads a year, believes the crops can be harvested without braceros. "It's easier to complain than to get the job done," he says with reference to his intransigent fellow growers. There is little mystery as to how Antle gets the job done: he attracts workers by higher wages and such amenities as air conditioned buses. Luis Scurich, Antle's production manager, comments on the domestic worker: "These people are getting better all the time. We'll harvest the lettuce."

These sentiments are echoed by a Ventura County citrus grower whose area previously had been wholly dependent on braceros. "Domestic crews have improved since the first of the year," he declares. "The first ones they (the California Department of Employment Farm Placement Service) sent us were dregs, but now the growers are paying higher and getting good men." Uppermost in the minds of the growers, he says, is the threat of unionism. "The Growers Association sends out letters on how to handle the union organizer. They try to make him appear as almost a criminal. Now they're spending six thousand dollars on a recreation hall for workers to keep them satisfied so they won't listen to the blandishments of the union."

Water is the life-blood of agriculture—"worth its weight in gold." Cheap, subsidized water is a commodity California agribusiness has been after as resolutely as it has been after cheap labor. Obviously, it needed a water boy and Pat Brown turned out to be its Gunga Din.

Canal water—captured, pumped, stored and diverted by tax-financed irrigation projects—is the wellspring of wealth and power. Without it, interior California would be just another sparsely settled Wyoming—deserts, swamps, and soaring mountains. There would be no fruits, vegetables, or row crops—only vast expanses of cattle range, winter wheat fields, and rice swamps.

Back in 1958, two weeks before Brown was elected to his first term as governor, the late J. E. O'Neill, whose companies held over a hundred thousand acres of fertile land, introduced Brown's Republican opponent, William Knowland, at a huge campaign rally. O'Neill was Knowland's northern California chairman. But in the world of politics, expediency is the balm that swiftly heals old wounds: shortly after Brown took office he appointed O'Neill to a District Fair Board and flew with him to Washington to testify for a water project which would irrigate O'Neill's holdings.

Back in Sacramento, Brown preened himself for favorable glances from two disparate groups. With one hand he pushed through the legislature several civil rights bills. With the other he wheeled a huge state-sponsored giveaway of natural resources. His nearly $2-billion water program, still a record for state bond issues, will start the water flowing to the arid west side of the San Joaquin Valley dominated by Jolly Green Giant–size landholders: Southern Pacific (201,000 acres), Standard Oil (218,000), O'Neill interests (100,000), Kern County Land Company (450,000), Los Angeles Times Corporation (268,000), J. G. Boswell (100,000), Anderson-Clayton (28,000).

The Brown program was billed as a source of more water for Los Angeles, but observers who noticed that southern California support was being whipped up by Norman Chandler's *Los Angeles Times* also noticed that the proposed route of the canal was smack through the middle of the Chandler family's 268,000-acre Tejon Ranch. Skeptics with long memories recalled that some sixty years earlier, when Los Angeles tapped Owens Valley, 250 miles north of the city, for a water supply, the *Times* stood squarely behind the "civic project." And they also recalled that Harry Chandler was a member of the syndicate that bought up, at bargain prices, over a hundred thousand San Fernando Valley acres at the nozzle end of the Owens Valley supply. The purchase was made before the publically financed project was announced to the public—hardly a very speculative venture.

But despite cries of a sellout, Brown's water plan squeaked through the 1959 legislature after a bitter six-month battle. The Governor muscled the State Senate while the *Times'* appeal to civic progress neutralized Los Angeles liberals in the State Assembly.

Opponents argued that much of the Brown plan was already incorporated in Federal Bureau of Reclamation plans and that bringing the state into the picture was nothing more than a ploy to enable landholders to skirt the federal land reform law, an anti-profiteering measure. They claimed that the state, recently short of cash, was in no financial shape to shoulder the unnecessary burden and that, as a matter of principle, the state legislature should not allow itself to be pushed around by big landholders. Jesse Unruh, the heavy-handed Democratic assembly leader who had been instrumental in excluding farm workers from state minimum wage legislation, advised his colleagues that there are times they must rise above principle.

All along, the federal land reform law had been interpreted with a latitude that permitted considerable abuse. Technically, irrigation water can be delivered to only 160 acres under any one ownership. Listing a man and wife ownership doubled the allotment. Then it was stipulated that large landholders could obtain subsidized water on unlimited acreage for ten years by agreeing to sell the land at the end of that period. As California's land values soar with the outward press of its megopolis, the risk element under this concession is nil. But this is not the point: the ominous threat is that eventual divestment would brake the trend towards large corporate farming in California.

While Pat Brown was making hay in Sacramento, Senators Tom Kuchel and the late Clair Engle were pitching in Washington for a federal water project that would mesh with the Brown plan. Under its terms, certain properties would be exempted from the land reform law. Their bill hurdled committee by a unanimous vote. Then, before it could come to a full Senate vote, a map pinpointing the land ownership in the project area was shown to Senators Wayne Morse and the late Richard Neuberger of neighboring Oregon and Paul Douglas of Illinois. Neuberger, who had gone along with the project when it was in committee, reversed himself and co-sponsored an amendment to kill the exemption clause. Morse and Douglas filibustered for the amendment for four days. Finally, out of sheer exasperation, Majority Leader Lyndon Johnson agreed to the amendment. The House went along and federal land reform, undiluted, was retained.

Two years later, President Kennedy's secretary of the interior, Stewart Udall, administratively overrode Congress' decision and granted the exemptions. For Udall, whose home state of Arizona abuts southern California, it was probably a political trade. But whatever the reason, the landholder–agribusiness combine stood to reap the benefits. And high-rolling Pat Brown had made his point.

Calling the "Shortage" Bluff

When P.L. 78 expired on December 31, 1964, Pat Brown faced the new year as a man clearly on the spot. Although Congress had expressed its will that the bracero system not continue, Brown was besieged by agribusiness interests looking for ways to bring in the bracero—regardless. (A Brown aide who has been outspokenly anti-bracero recalls that when he accidentally barged in on a Brown–grower conference that included Joseph Di Giorgio and Lionel Steinberg, Brown quipped: "Here, gentlemen, is your opposition.") At this point Brown passed the buck to his affable director of employment, Albert B. Tieburg.

Tieburg was charged, if he could, to round up enough workers to harvest the crops (curiously, agribusiness has the unique attitude that it is the duty of government to provide it with a labor force). Presumably, his assignment was foredoomed. If Tieburg was determined, he was also misled by his predominantly pro-grower staff. His approach was makeshift: he attempted to throw into the breach college students, housewives, persons on relief, Sioux Indians, drifters—and even devised a plan for early parole of prisoners on the proviso they work in the fields. Obviously, such a solution was born of desperation and hardly held long-range promise.

As the harvest season impended, grower demands for braceros grew. The threat of rotting crops was widely propagated, although Michael Peevey, AFL-CIO research director, called it a "rigged" crisis. "A deliberately deceptive publicity campaign," he scoffed, "possibly in collusion with the State's other major agribusiness interests . . . to try to force the government to acquiescence to the growers' demand for cheap labor."

But if it was manufactured emergency, Tieburg fell for it. Although in one instance he called the bluff of a San Joaquin asparagus grower who claimed to have plowed under seventy-five acres because of a shortage of help ("We could have supplied any number of qualified workers," he said), Tieburg in the end adopted the growers' line. Traveling in a grower's private airplane to Salinas, he bemoaned the shortage of workers that threatened the harvest.

When the din reached Washington, Secretary of Labor Wirtz flew out to California on a personal inspection trip. One of his first reactions was repugnance at finding no field toilets on the farms he visited, and in the case of one of the largest labor camps in the state, filthy conditions that "made me ashamed anything of this kind exists in this country." Wirtz indicated he would consider limited importation of braceros only if growers were unable to recruit sufficient domestic help with at least the inducement offered to braceros, including a semblance of tenure. (Growers had long been accustomed to placing orders for more workers than they actually needed, which resulted in many being turned away after traveling all the way to the fields, or only getting in a half-day's work.) But, said Wirtz, it would be "the worst possible affront" to Congress to accede to mass importation of braceros.

Wirtz' stand brought immediate howls from the growers and their spokesmen. Speaking on the floor of the House, Orange County's ultra-conservative James B. Utt blamed Wirtz for "a man-made catastrophe" in California. And two state senators, one an acknowledged member of the John Birch Society, called for the impeachment of Brown for "criminal waste and neglect" resulting in a farm labor shortage—a somewhat ironic twist.

In the wake of Wirtz' visit a three-man panel was appointed to check into the labor supply in individual areas. At first it went along with the growers and recommended the admission of braceros in reduced numbers. But gradually it formed the opinion that the growers were getting along all right without the foreign workers and turned down additional requests. "The most significant fact," said Wirtz, "is that all crops are being harvested despite all this talk." Brown, however, disagreed. "I think he's wrong," said the Governor, thumping for more braceros to ease what he termed the "desperate" farm labor situation.

What Brown and agribusiness apparently are after—now that Public Law 78 is dead and gone—is a de facto extension of braceroism under the McCarren–Walter Immigration Act. In the early fifties, silver-maned Pat McCarran, in order to replenish his Nevada ranch cronies' supply of Basque sheepherders, pushed through the law that permits importation of foreign help if "capable" domestics are unavailable. It is the fear of Father Vizzard and others that this law will now be used to perpetuate the influx of thousands of low-wage workers, and in effect create what might be called "domestic braceroism."

But for Pat Brown, heading into fight for a third term, the outlook is not so bleak. Brown already has California's farm workers in his hip pocket, since they obviously would not swing over to a Republican of the Ronald Reagan stripe. And having danced to agribusiness' tune, he bids well to embark on the campaign with brimming coffers. [Brown nevertheless lost the election to Reagan.]

Chapter Six

The Mexican-American Awakens

The Mexican-American, after two post-war decades of slow and quiet progress, has finally awakened. Not only has he formed militant organizations such as those described in the article by Kaye Briegel, but these groups possess a serious following regardless of changes in leaderhip and tactics.

Among the various successful militant organizations are those led by Reies Tijerina of New Mexico and César Cháves of California. Despite what reservations social scientists may have concerning Tijerina's leadership and program, his success, his militancy, and his nationalism demand that the historian of the Mexican-American understand the movement. While Tijerina's success demands study, so does the lack of political progress among the Mexican-American Texans. It is for this reason that the article on the activities of the Texas Rangers is reprinted before César Chávez' biographical sketch. It is with the Chávez piece—the sketch of a mystic, respected labor leader, and crusader—that this compilation ends on an optimistic tone.

Alianza Federal de Mercedes*

Nancie L. González

During the past three years an organization known as the *Alianza Federal de Mercedes* (Federal Alliance of Land Grants) has been gaining members and, recently, much publicity. Although not generally so recognized by the public, this organization and its activities exhibit many of the characteristics of a revitalization or nativistic cult movement. Wallace (1956: 265) defined *revitalization movements* as ". . . deliberate, organized, conscientious efforts by members of a society to construct a more satisfying culture." Nativistic movements are, to Wallace, ". . . revitalization movements characterized by strong emphasis on the elimination of alien persons, customs, values, and/or material. . . ." (*Ibid.*: 267). It is generally accepted that such movements must be analyzed in relation to culture change, but as Smith (1959: 12) has pointed out, ". . . cult movements should be distinguished from other phenomena of culture change because they are deliberate, conscious and organized and are responses to social and economic dissatisfaction." This characterization purposely says nothing about the contextual features of the movement, which may include messianic, millennial revivalistic, militant, or reformative features, or various combinations of these.

The Alianza Federal de Mercedes (hereafter referred to merely as the Alianza) may be seen to include all of these features. In spite of the fact that the Spanish-Americans have undergone extreme social and economic deprivation during the past century, there appear to have arisen no true nativistic cult movements among them until now. It seems worthwhile to describe and analyze the social and cultural aspects of this organization as

---

*From Nancie L. González, *The Spanish Americans of New Mexico: A Distinctive Heritage*, Mexican-American Study Project, Advance Report no. 9 (Los Angeles: University of California at Los Angeles, 1967). An extended and revised version of this study has been published by the University of New Mexico Press under the title of *A Heritage of Pride: The Spanish Americans of New Mexico* (1969).

part of the total New Mexican pattern on the one hand, and as an example of a nativistic cult on the other.

The Alianza was founded and is led by a dynamic young Spanish-speaking man in his forties. Born in Texas, and one of eight children, he claims to have New Mexican ancestors, and within the past three years married a young Spanish-American woman from the latter state. Throughout his childhood he lived in poverty, moving with his family as a migrant laborer from the cotton plantations of Texas to the beet fields of Colorado. He had little formal schooling, especially after his mother died when he was still a young boy. He recalls intermittent periods, however, when he was able to go to school, and tells of going through garbage cans in order to find something to take with him for lunch.

At some point he joined a Protestant fundamentalist religious sect, and after a period of training in a Bible school in Texas, went to California, where he engaged in preaching. He dates the beginnings of his present activities to a dream he had while working in California. This dream not only gave him directions as to the course he must pursue in organizing his people, but also prophesied his success. Today he de-emphasizes his Protestant faith and background out of deference to the majority of his followers who are Catholic.

After several years of preparation, which included a period of study in Mexico of the historical events pertinent to the Hispanos in this area of the world, and after engaging in at least one unsuccessful attempt to organize a group of poverty-stricken rural Spanish-Americans in Arizona, this man came to New Mexico where he began to preach a doctrine welcome to the ears of the long-suffering conquered people.

The elements of this doctrine, which constitute the goals of the Alianza, may be summarized as follows:

1. The Laws of the Indies provided that the land grants made in the territory of New Spain should never be sold, but should be passed on to the descendants of the original settlers.

2. The Laws of the Indies explicitly recognized the legitimacy of those persons born in the Americas, whether of Spanish or of mixed Spanish-Indian descent. The Alianza today claims that its members are neither "pure-blood" Spaniards nor "pure-blood" Indians, but a mestizo race. Therefore, they cannot be held responsible for the wrongdoings of either original group. They also

claim a status more honorable than that of many other "races," in that their "birth certificate" was given them by Philip II, King of Spain, in 1573.

3. The Treaty of Guadalupe Hidalgo between Mexico and the United States provided for the inhabitants of the territory annexed in 1848, giving them the rights and privileges of U.S. citizens. The Constitution of the United States guarantees the property rights of its citizens.

4. According to the constitution of the state of New Mexico (1911), "All the rights, privileges and immunities, civil, political, and religious, guaranteed to the people of New Mexico by the Treaty of Guadalupe Hidalgo will be preserved inviolable."

5. Those Spanish-Americans who sold their land, and especially those who allied themselves with Anglo interests to purchase lands from their more unfortunate brethren, acted illegally and immorally.

6. The problems and ills of the Spanish-speaking population of the Southwest today all stems from the loss of the bulk of the original Spanish land grants, amounting to some four million acres (Burma 1954: 16).

7. The Anglo-dominated federal and state governments have also been remiss in failing to protect the Spanish-speaking citizens of New Mexico from discrimination in the schools and in employment opportunities.

8. The Spanish-Americans should band together, as have other minority groups in the United States in recent years, (Indians and Negroes) to seek redress for their wrongs in the courts of the United States, and to secure equal rights under the laws of this country.

The Alianza has taken various steps toward achieving its goals. First of all, largely through the personal charisma and dynamic speaking ability of its leader it has secured dues-paying members, whose contributions support the organization, and to an unknown extent, its leader and his helpers. It is impossible to say how many members there may be at the present time, but the organization claimed twenty thousand as of July, 1966. By June, 1967, the number was estimated by the press as three thousand. Each of these figures represents an extreme; the true membership may be near ten thousand. The members are drawn primarily from New Mexico, but represent several other states as well. The members pay $1.00 per family per month, plus a $10.00 initiation fee, which is a fairly recent innovation, not having been collected until the early part of 1966. Each family is also assessed a lump sum of $100.00, which may be paid in monthly installments, to help defray court expenses. The organization maintains an office and meeting hall, in which building also live the leader and some of his family. The Alianza has sponsored and paid for advertisements on the local Spanish-language radio and TV stations, and has also printed large numbers of posters, handbills, and other propaganda materials, which are distributed not only throughout New Mexico, but sent to other states without charge.

In addition to the personal efforts of the leader of the organization there are a number of other persons who operate in the outlying rural districts to secure more members by publicizing the Alianza's message. These persons apparently work without charge and have private means of support.

Although the Alianza has its ultimate goal the securing of all the land grants lost through the years by various means, until recently it has restricted its positive action to presenting petitions to the governor of New Mexico and to the president of the United States via New Mexico's Spanish-American senator. A "march" was made on the weekend of July 4, 1966 from Albuquerque to Santa Fe in order to dramatize the Alianza's mission and to present a petition to the governor of the state. Later, during the autumn of the same year, a small band attempted to take over portion of the National Forest lands in the north which they claimed was really theirs anyway. The group was quickly routed by authorities, and state and federal charges are still pending against the leaders on several counts, ranging from the illegal killing of a deer to assaulting two U.S. Forest Service rangers.

All these efforts were largely ignored, "deferred for future reference," or simply put down as the work of hoodlums or madmen. But in June, 1967, the Alianza burst into the national spotlight in the so-called insurrection at Tierra Amarilla, a small county seat in northern New Mexico. Again, as in the previous year, the AFDM had threatened to close off a portion of the federal lands, set up an independent "republic," and issue visas to "foreigners" who might wish to enter. The state district attorney, in order to prevent such an occurrence, forbade the holding of a proposed mass meeting and proceeded to arrest several persons allegedly on their way to take part in it. Two days later members of the Alianza staged a raid on the county courthouse where their friends were being held, and in their efforts to set them free, they wounded two lawmen.

The result of all this has been to land the prophet and several of his followers, including members of his own family, in jail, facing charges as serious as kidnapping and assault to commit murder.* At the same time, the incident has generated a tremendous amount of controversy among New Mexicans and others as to the causes of the raid, the character and purpose of the Alianza, and the plight of the lower-class rural Hispano.

So far we have merely outlined the overt aspects of the movement, most of which are already of public record, and which parallel in many respects similar civil rights movements among both Negro and Mexican-American minorities elsewhere in the United States. However, there are some other, less well-known facts which place this movement fully within the category of those described elsewhere as nativistic cult movements.

There are, for instance, several supernatural elements in the movement. In addition to the dream-revelation which provides support and sanction for the leader's actions, some of his followers contribute to the classic prophet motif by telling a legend which they claim has been current among the Spanish-speaking in the state for generations. According to this, their ancestors foretold a time when large numbers of persons would come "laughing" from the East and take their land by force, thus destroying the happy life of the Hispanos. The latter would suffer for many years, but they were urged to maintain courage and to watch for a leader who would also come out of the East to lead them against the enemy who would be forced to return "crying" to their original homes. Incidents have been told of old men who, after hearing the Alianza's leader speak at public gatherings, have gone to him on their knees to kiss his feet, proclaiming him the messiah of the legend. Although this writer has been unable to find any reference to such a legend in the literature of the past century, it is not impossible that such may have been handed down by word of mouth. In any case, it is not important whether the story is an old one or has only recently begun to circulate. Each one who hears it feels certain he must

---

*Tijerina was recently convicted and sentenced to three years on each of three counts of assaulting a federal officer and two counts of aiding and abetting in the destruction of government property. (*Albuquerque Journal*, October 11, 1969.)

have heard it before, and dutifully passes it on. It is also perhaps significant to note that prophecies of a messiah who will lead his people out of adversity back to a former and better way of life, have long been recorded among American Indian groups (Fletcher 1891: 58).

The actual militant character of the more esoteric doctrine has also not generally been recognized by the public and is usually played down by the leader when talking with the press. He has been quoted as threatening violence toward Anglos if his demands are not met, but he has consistently retracted or denied such statements in public. Privately, however, and to his followers, he definitely preaches the coming of the millenium as a violent occurrence. He tells his people that they must be prepared to sacrifice and that it may take a long time, but that in the end the Anglos will be frightened and will move out of the area willingly. In the press, he is usually quoted as saying that the Anglos won't have to move out but that they will have to pay rent for lands illegally held or purchase them at their current valuation. The constitution of the Alianza clearly states that the group expects compensation not only for the lands but for the profits earned by the "foreign violators" through the years. These profits and benefits include the fruits of agriculture, of livestock herding, of water, mineral, and timber exploitation, and gains realized through the construction of highways, railroads, cities, factories, etc. (Constitution Nacional de la AFDM, Capitulo VI, Art. VI, pagina 9).

The leader is also explicit (in private only) about how the details of the apportionment will be handled when the millenium comes. He states that no lands will be owned individually, as this would be in opposition to the original Spanish directives. Rather, the Alianza will hold all lands in trust for the people, and will hold tribunals to determine who should be allotted the use of a plot of land for life. In this he clearly provides a way of distinguishing among: (a) members of the Alianza, who will be given first preference and who will share equally, (b) those of Spanish descent, who, even though not members of the Alianza, have not opposed its operation nor have denied their Spanish heritage, and (c) those "black sheep" who have worked against the best interests of their own people or who have tried to pretend that they are Anglos rather than Hispanos. Those in the second category may be forgiven if and when they see the light and join the movement, but the last group may expect some harsh but unspecified treatment. Any funds deriving from successful negotiations with the government will be divided among the organization's estimated five million potential land-grant heirs—provided they are not classified as "traitors" to the cause.

In addition to securing redress in the matter of the land grants, the organization also stresses certain other aspects of the preconquest past. Thus, another matter upon which they are presently agitating concerns the use of Spanish as a language of instruction in the grade schools. For many years this has been a difficult problem for local educators. It is well recognized that in the past instruction in many schools of the outlying areas was conducted almost wholly in Spanish by teachers of Spanish ancestry, while in other cases English was stressed to the point that the incoming children, not familiar with the language, soon fell far behind their Anglo peers. Clearly, in any "either/or" situation the Spanish child is bound to lose out, for he must be able to use English fluently in order to compete as an adult for jobs in a life-pattern which is increasingly dependent upon wage labor or employment of some sort. Although the Alianza is correct in pointing out that there are still many children who lose valuable time and enthusiasm for school in the early years because of the fact that they have not learned English at home, it is probably unrealistic to insist, as the organization has, that *all* elementary school teachers in New Mexico be fluent in Spanish as well as English. This is clearly more in line with the general nativistic viewpoint of the organization and is not merely a matter of civil rights. In addition to the Spanish language, the group holds up as symbols of its solidarity foods such as the wheat tortilla, green chile, pinto beans, and tamales, claiming that these foods represent the mixture of the Indian and the Spanish in New Mexico, being wholly native to neither cultural tradition. It has also been pointed out to this investigator that New Mexican Spanish language itself is unique.

As might be expected, there has been considerable opposition from various quarters to the organization and to the prophet himself. Some of this has come from the better educated and more affluent Spanish-Americans who are embarrassed by the more extreme aims of the group, and who feel that total acculturation is the best road to assimilation. Many of those who would not go so far as to advocate complete acculturation, are nevertheless disinclined to associate with this group because of their extreme views on mestization, their unrealistic demands, and because of their general lower-class background and orientation. These are the Spanish-American who consider themselves to be descendants of the upper-class colonials and who most vehemently disclaim any Mexican influence on their racial and cultural heritage.

Typical of the reaction of such groups opposing the Alianza is the message on a poster found tacked to a tree on the campus of the University of New Mexico in May, 1966. It read as follows:

> We true Spanish are white, and we are Catholics. We fight communists. We don't care for foreigners, Negro or White, to come and lie about our race. The only race problem is the one brought in by dirty communists who try to pass as Spanish to get our land grants.

The prophet himself is frequently attacked, either by name or by implication, as in the above statement. To the charges of being a communist and/or a wetback (illegal entrant from Mexico) or foreigner is frequently added that of operating a confidence racket for personal gain. None of these charges has been substantiated by any concrete evidence, even though his background has been thoroughly investigated by state governmental authorities with the assistance of the Mexican government and the FBI. Most reactions such as these are irrational and are based upon purely emotional responses to the organization's efforts to change the *status quo*.

However, there is another type of opposition, just as interesting to the social scientist, which comes from the highly educated intellectual liberal individuals and groups. Individuals of this type usually become frustrated in their attempts to understand and/or assist the organization's cause because of its seeming irrationality, illogic, and lack of clear "democratic" structural principles. Thus, a prominent local historian, a champion of the Hispano population, has attacked the group because there seems to be little historical validity to many of their claims. She points out that many members of the Alianza are not descendants of any Spanish or Mexican land grantees. Many fear that there are "outside influences" which are reopening this old land-grant issue for pecuniary gain.

Some members of the local board of the Commission on Civil Rights, always eager to help any disadvantaged person or group obtain a fair hearing and due process of law, became alienated after a personal appearance before them of the prophet himself. This group apparently expected a formalized civil rights type protest movement, which, although stemming from similar causes in the over-all social milieu, does not necessarily, or even usually in the United States, have the same characteristics as the militant, nativistic, revivalistic movement we are here describing. Not being familiar with the latter, most of the board members found themselves in little sympathy with this prophet and his organization. They were prepared to listen to him and his spokesmen as representatives of a minority group fighting discrimination using by-now-well-known protest techniques, most of which are actually founded on logical principles of action leading to realizable ends. But a total lack of communication developed between the two groups, and the encounter ended with the prophet walking out of the meeting and refusing assistance of any sort. The members of the board, equally disenchanted, were relieved to see him go.

The sociological and anthropological analysis of the movement herein described is of considerable theoretical interest, since true nativistic cult movements are most often reported from non-Western, fairly primitive groups. In this case, furthermore, there have been over one hundred years of contact with concomitant domination of the Spanish-speaking group by a foreign power. With the possible exception of the Penitente groups, which might well be viewed as having nativistic overtones but which were neither messianic nor millennial, there have been, to our knowledge, no movements comparable to that here described in the entire history of contact with the United States.

The "relative deprivation" theory should have led us to expect such a movement during the 1930's, when the socioeconomic status of Spanish-Americans in New Mexico appears to have hit an all-time low. Yet none appeared. However, there are some other elements that are probably of importance in attempting to explain why such a movement has developed at this particular time and place—in New Mexico of the 1960's. First of all, even though the Spanish-Americans of the state as a whole are probably better off than ever before, both economically and in terms of their relations with Anglos, this does not hold for all persons who may be so designated. Indeed, many of the more successful and most comfortable Hispanos are those who have in large part abandoned much of their ancestral culture, including the Spanish language. Yet, the bulk of the poverty-stricken lower class in New Mexico is today, as it has been since 1846, made up of Spanish-speaking persons. There is indeed prejudice and discrimination evident against this group. Although it can very well be argued that the disapprobation is oriented along class, rather than ethnic, lines, it seems to those affected that they suffer because of their Spanish or Mexican heritage. This segment of Hispanos is perhaps even more deprived today in relation to the Hispanos who are better off. Furthermore, some feel that for the first time many elements of Spanish-American culture are in danger of disappearing—the anxiety over this eventuality among many Spanish-Americans of all classes is reflected weekly in the pages of *El Hispano,* the local Spanish-language newspaper. (The Spanish language itself is the *symbol* of the entire culture.)

At the same time, the rise of civil rights movements has undoubtedly influenced the organizational structure of the Alianza, and may also have been important in its origin. The use of techniques such as the protest march, the sit-in, the seeking of publicity, the holding of annual conventions, and so forth, seem to derive from the broader immediate surroundings in the United States as a whole. Mexican-American groups in Texas and in California also have organized in recent years along the lines of civil rights movements, and their modicum of success in manipulating the environment has been an incentive to the Alianza.

It is difficult to predict the future of the Alianza, for, though young, it now seems to be in serious trouble. It appears clear that to the extent that it continues its more excessive demands for the return of the land grants and the expulsion of Anglos, it will continue to be opposed by the established power groups— both Anglo and Hispano. But if it takes a more moderate course and at the same time aligns itself with movements now developing in Texas and California designed to better conditions of Mexican-Americans, and most especially those in the lower-class brackets, it may have some success. It has already been successful in attracting the attention of the state and federal governments to the plight of the poor rural Hispano. As Wallace has observed:

> In most instances the original doctrine is continuously modified by the prophet, who responds to various criticisms and affirmations by adding to, emphasizing, playing down, or eliminating selected elements of the original visions. This reworking makes the new doctrine more acceptable to special interest groups, may give it a better "fit" to the population's cultural and personality patterns, and may take account of the changes occurring in the general milieu (1956: 275).

Although at the present time the leader of the Alianza does not seem ready to modify his *basic* doctrine, he may well do so in the near future if he is to save the movement. There have been many criticisms in recent months—some stemming from fairly powerful interests—and these may force his hand. However, regardless of what the outcome may be, the movement's history may prove to be enlightening as further data on nativistic cults in general. It may also be that the public and its governmental representatives may be more understanding of the movement if they recognize that it is not an isolated phenomenon, but one which has occurred scores of times in history under similar circumstances of deprivation. And finally, whether the movement lives or dies, it is important to this particular discussion because it represents a new type of organization, underlaid by a different set of principles than we have seen before among the Spanish-Americans of New Mexico. It is significant that although the concept of mutual aid among members of *la raza* is an important rallying point and underlying philosophy of the AFDM, it does *not* function as the older type of society, providing benefits to individual members who undergo hardships.

The Modern Texas Rangers:
A Law-Enforcement Dilemma in the Rio Grande Valley*

Ben H. Procter

The Texas Rangers, announced Senator Joe Bernal of Bexar County, are "the Mexican Americans' Ku Klux Klan. All they need is a white hood with 'Rinches' written across it."[1] "They were formed in the old days of the Texas Republic to keep the Mexicans in line," asserted Robert Analavage, an assistant editor

---

*In *Reflections of Western Historians*, edited by John A. Carroll (Tucson: University of Arizona Press, 1969).

[1] *Texas Observer* (Austin) (June 9, 1967). *Rinches* is the phonetical pronunciation of Rangers in Spanish; otherwise, the pronunciation would be Raanhares.

of *The Southern Patriot.* "They merged with the Confederate army . . . to fight to preserve slavery, and in the Twentieth Century they have been used repeatedly as strikebreakers."[2] "Abolish the Rangers," demanded the delegates at the Tenth Annual Texas AFL-CIO Convention at Fort Worth.[3] "One Riot, No Rangers—One Strike, Many Rangers," read a picket sign protesting a speaking engagement of Governor John Connally at Laredo.[4] Mexican-Americans "today are under siege at Rio Grande City by the Connally pistoleros and the [Homer] Garrison gunslingers who subject them" charged Albert Pena, a San Antonio county commissioner, "to harassment, fear, intimidation, a little head cracking and jailing on nebulous charges."[5] And so the barrage of abusive statements and damaging allegations continued ad infinitum throughout the "long, hot summer" of 1967 as Texas Rangers, world famous as fearless peace officers, were sharply reprimanded by labor leaders, state and national politicos, liberal Democratic organizations, church groups, and even university professors.[6] Not since 1934, just prior to their reorganization as a modern investigating and law enforcement body, had the Rangers received such unfavorable publicity—and to a man they did not like it.

Yet on several previous occasions the Rangers had weathered severe criticism and profited from the ordeal. Each time political involvement had been their Achilles' heel and almost their undoing. In World War I, for example, Governors Oscar B. Colquitt and James E. "Pa" Ferguson had enlarged the force to 1,000 men, ostensibly to deal with troubles along the Rio Grande. But actually the Rangers were used at times as currency to pay political debts, as a cheap method of elevating aspiring Texans to state peerage, as a kind of exclusive club for political hacks and cronies of the governor. While the force included some outstanding lawmen like Captains Frank Hamer, Will Wright, and Tom Hickman, sometimes a Ranger commission became a license to rob or kill.

[2] *The Southern Patriot* (Louisville) (August 1967).

[3] *Fort Worth Star-Telegram* (August 5, 1967); see also *ibid.* (August 14, 1967).

[4] *Austin Statesman* (June 10, 1967).

[5] *Houston Chronicle* (June 5, 1967).

[6] In Legislative Branch of the Texas State Library at Austin, see file entitled Texas Rangers, especially those newspaper articles dated April–July, 1967.

On January 31, 1919, state Representative J. T. Canales of Brownsville initiated a legislative inquiry regarding Ranger activities on the border. To fellow committee members he presented eighteen charges including drunkenness, disorderly conduct, and brutal physical assault, torture, and murder of numerous prisoners. Two months later, as a direct result of these hearings, the legislature reorganized the Rangers by limiting the force to five companies and seventy-five men. Because committee witnesses had charged that from 1914 to 1918 the Rangers had killed possibly 5,000 people (almost exclusively of Mexican descent), the act provided that any citizen could file a complaint against an offending officer and an investigation would ensue.[7]

In 1932 the force again became embroiled in politics, openly backing Governor Ross Sterling for re-election against Miriam A. "Ma" Ferguson. When "Ma" and "Pa" moved to Austin in January, 1933, the Rangers went the way of all political appointees who had crossed their boss and lost. Three days after taking office, Governor Ferguson discharged the entire force of forty-four men—those who had not already resigned—and once again the Texas Rangers were a source of patronage, corruption, and ridicule.[8] The effect upon state law enforcement was, of course, catastrophic. During the next two years crime and violence became widespread, bank holdups and murder commonplace. Few states had a more vicious assortment of gangsters or provided a safer sanctuary for the criminal element. For instance, residents in the Dallas–Fort Worth area alone included George "Machine Gun" Kelly, Raymond Hamilton, and the "mad-dog killers" Clyde Barrow and Bonnie Parker. And who besides "Ma" Ferguson was responsible for this breakdown in the public defense? To most Texans the answer was obvious. As one newspaper sarcasti-

---

[7]As discussed by Walter Prescott Webb in his 1935 book, *The Texas Rangers: A Century of Frontier Defense*, 2nd ed. (Austin: University of Texas Press, 1965), pp. 513–516; and Stephen W. Schuster IV, "The Modernization of the Texas Rangers, 1930–1936" (Master's thesis, Texas Christian University, Fort Worth, Texas, 1965), pp. 6–9. For the complete testimony of the Ranger activities on the border, see *Proceedings of the Joint Committee of the Senate and the House in the Investigation of the Texas State Ranger Force*, Texas State Archives, Austin.

[8]Schuster, "Modernization of the Texas Rangers," pp. 17–21; Seth Shepard McKay, *Texas Politics, 1906-1944: With Special Reference to the German Counties* (Lubbock: Texas Tech Press, 1952), pp. 237–240; William Warren Sterling, *Trails and Trials of the Texas Rangers* (Houston: 1959), p. 276. Rangers," pp. 25–33; Webb, *Texas Rangers*, pp. 519–544.

cally remarked, "A Ranger commission and a nickel can get . . . a cup of coffee anywhere in Texas."[9] In January, 1935, however, Governor James V. Allred soon obviated the causes of such derision. Having campaigned the previous year to "overhaul" the state law enforcement machinery, he pushed through the legislature an act creating the Department of Public Safety (DPS). To supervise administrative policies and procedures he appointed a three-man Public Safety Commission, which in turn selected a director and an assistant director. The DPS had three basic units—the Texas Rangers, the Highway Patrol, and a newly created Headquarters Division at Austin which was to be a modern scientific crime laboratory and detection center.[10]

As for the Rangers, reforms were definitely in order—so much so that Walter Prescott Webb, in his centennial history, sadly predicted their demise as a separate law enforcement entity. They would become, he feared, merely a segment of the much larger Highway Patrol, that group which the Rangers contemptuously referred to as a "bunch of motorcycle jockeys."[11] But Webb was wrong; Governor Allred and his Public Safety Commissioners made sure of that. On October 7, 1935, when they met in Austin to formulate Ranger policies, the modernization of the force began. The state was divided into five, then later into six, districts wherein a Ranger company had specific responsibility and jurisdiction. Each group usually had a captain, a sergeant, and a number of privates who resided at different towns in the area. For several years the number of appointments remained flexible until the commissioners finally decided upon a fixed complement of sixty-two men: six captains, six sergeants, and fifty privates.[12]

Allred's commissioners set higher standards for individual Rangers. For appointment examinations and recommendations, not

---

[9]Sterling, *Trails and Trials*, p. 519; Schuster, "Modernization of the Texas Rangers," pp. 25–33; Webb, *Texas Rangers*, pp. 519–544.

[10]William E. Atkinson, "The Texas Gubernatorial Campaign of 1934" (Master's thesis, Texas Christian University, Fort Worth, Texas, 1965), pp. 52ff; Schuster, "Modernization of the Texas Rangers," pp. 34–45.

[11]Webb, *Texas Rangers*, p. 567; Schuster, "Modernization of the Texas Rangers," p. 53.

[12]Schuster, "Modernization of the Texas Rangers," pp. 53, 56; interview with Sergeant Jim Riddles and Private Bill Wilson, Austin, Texas, September 10, 1966; Ranger Rosters, 1935–1939, manuscripts, Department of Public Safety files, Austin.

political pull, were important; for promotion, seniority and performance were the determining factors. To be considered for the force, an applicant had to be thirty to forty-five years of age, at least five feet eight inches tall, and "perfectly sound" in mind and body. Each man received instruction in the latest techniques of fingerprinting, communications, ballistics, and records. And he had to be a crack shot. Lack of higher education or formal schooling did not penalize an applicant, except possibly on the written exam, because the extent of his literary efforts would be the writing of an "intelligent" report. For most Rangers, this task was neither difficult nor time-consuming. Captain Frank Hamer, for instance, explained the laborious tracking and the carefully planned ambush of Clyde Barrow and Bonnie Parker in this manner: "We've done the job."[13]

Today the Texas Rangers are experienced peace officers, trained in the latest methods of crime detection and armed with modern technological equipment. Unlike those Rangers of the Republic and frontier days, or even of the 1920's, they usually ride in high-powered automobiles instead of on horses, are armed with advanced and deadly weapons, and have developed sophisticated techniques of interrogation. The men have retained, however, the traits and qualities of character that in 1935 Webb lamented were being lost; indeed, in many ways they appear to be cut from the same rough mold as their predecessors. Basically they are uncomplicated men—direct, straightforward, and not especially concerned about social amenities. They use the English language simply as a tool for direct communication, not as a device to trick or deceive (hence their difficulty at times with newsmen or reporters who tend toward sensationalism). Grammatically they are an English teacher's nightmare; yet they clearly express themselves, ςometimes punctuating their sentences with colorful if not downright earthy expressions. Although outwardly friendly and easygoing, they are suspicious of strangers and hesitant to talk ("you might have been one of those damn New York magazine writers"); but once a person wins their trust, they will go out of their way to be helpful.[14]

---

[13]Schuster, "Modernization of the Texas Rangers," pp. 54–55; C. L. Douglas, *The Gentlemen in the White Hats: Dramatic Episodes in the History of the Texas Rangers* (Dallas: 1934), p. 201.

[14]The author has arrived at these judgments after having interviewed many of the Rangers in 1966–1967.

But make no mistake about these men. They have been, and are, the scourge of those outside the law, obviously feared, sometimes hated, always respected. They are proud men—proud of their traditions and their fellow officers' accomplishments, proud of holding a job that all other Texas lawmen desire. They have an intangible, almost unexplainable quality of toughness about them. Possibly it is the way they handle themselves. Some are no longer lean and trim, a few are wrinkled and graying, one is even potbellied. Yet all exude a poise, a composure of confidence. Or perhaps it is the realization that these men have confronted the toughest criminals in the state, that their tradition of "One Riot, One Ranger" has steeled them toward danger and death. As one Ranger rather graphically put it (and with obvious pride), "Hell, Ben, whenever there's a mean ass, then they call on us."[15] But whatever the reason, these men do have the reputation of being the elite of Texas lawmen. Their esprit de corps is almost unbelievable; they will admit, in fact, that becoming a Texas Ranger has completely transformed their lives. "You feel lucky to get the Ranger badge. So many want it," Ranger Sergeant Jim Riddles candidly stated. "So you take an internal vow that whatever happens you won't break your oath to uphold the law."[16]

In 1967, however, no matter how respected or feared they had become, no matter how outstanding their record of law enforcement, the Texas Rangers found themselves in an impossible situation. It all began on June 1, 1966, in what appeared to be a routine dispute between management and labor. At the 1,600-acre, well-irrigated La Casita Farms near the small Starr County community of Rio Grande City, a strike occurred among the stoop farm laborers. Eugene Nelson, a thirty-six-year-old labor organizer who had participated in the California grape pickers' strike earlier in the year, arrived in the Valley and immediately organized some of the workers into a union which was affiliated with the California-based National Farm Workers Association.* Then he demanded that La Casita, and other growers engaged in fruit and vegetable production, raise wages to the federal minimum standard of $1.25 per hour. For workers to

---

[15]Closed manuscript in possession of Ben Procter, Texas Christian University, Fort Worth, Texas.

[16]Interview with Riddles and Wilson; interview with Captain Robert A. Crowder, Company B, Dallas, Texas, September 11, 1967.

*Note that Nelson is the author of the next selection in this book.

receive only forty to eighty cents an hour was "ridiculous," he asserted, and charged that such wages were responsible for much of the widespread poverty in the Rio Grande Valley.[17]

When the growers ignored union demands, Nelson knew that for the moment the battle had been lost, that the local economic and political power structure was in no way shaken, and that it never would be unless his small union could receive equally powerful outside support. He therefore hit upon a dramatic plan: a 387-mile march from the Rio Grande Valley to Austin which would emphasize the pathetic plight of the Mexican-American migrant workers—indeed all of the underprivileged and underpaid throughout the state. On Labor Day he and "50,000 to 100,000 laborers" would meet on the steps of the state capitol and demand of Governor John Connally that justice be done and that a special session of the legislature be called specifically to enact an adequate minimum wage law.[18]

On July 10, according to plan, forty-three members of "La Marcha," led by Father Antonio "Tomec" Gonzales and Reverend James L. Navarro, a Baptist minister, set out from San Juan, Texas, probably unaware of the far-reaching consequences their actions would have upon the state. Through fairly extensive newspaper coverage of the movement, Texans were able to follow the progress of the footsore marchers, at first rather amused by the novelty of the idea and the people involved.

What a strange sight the caravan was as it passed along the highway! In front were the Reverend Navarro, exhibiting for all to see both an American and a Christian flag, and Father "Tomec" Gonzales, wearing a cowboy hat, a Star of David, and a sign entitled "Migrant Priest"; straggling behind was a strange assortment of tired humanity in all shapes, ages, and sizes; bringing up the rear was an old bus filled with food, personal belongings, and a large canvas tent-shelter. Each night the weary group would camp outside a community, sometimes receive food from the neighboring townspeople, listen to the encouragement and prayers of their leaders, and then rest up for the next blistering day on the road.[19]

Yet by late August, as "La Marcha" was in its final phase, Texans began to realize that this expedition was no longer a

[17]*Houston Chronicle* (June 12, July 11, 17, 1966).

[18]*Ibid.* (July 11, 1966) ; *Dallas Morning News* (July 10, 1966).

[19]*Houston Chronicle* (July 11, 17, 1966).

laughing matter. These people were deadly serious; they were demanding reforms. Gradually a kind of emotional furor—disruptive, upsetting, and perhaps even terrifying to some—seemed to tinge everything concerning the march. It was increasingly apparent in the statements of church leaders, liberal politicians, and state AFL-CIO officials. Appalled by the poverty of the migrant workers, they called upon the "power structure" to "listen and analyze what the Valley marchers" were trying to say.[20] In reply, the growers and the Texas Farm Bureau argued that, even though such conditions were regrettable, the union demands were economically unrealistic and, if accepted, would drive the growers from the Rio Grande Valley. Besides, who were these so-called strikers? "We don't exactly know," exclaimed Gordon Morrow, a San Benito farmer. "They certainly are not representative of the Valley farm workers."[21] Soon reports began to appear, intimating that "La Marcha" was Communist-inspired and that the peaceful demonstrators, who at times asserted that a "social revolution" was at hand in the Valley, might become violent.

To calm the public temper and to investigate these rumors, Governor Connally, Attorney General Waggoner Carr, and House Speaker Ben Barnes on August 30 drove to New Braunfels, some fifty miles south of Austin, to confer with the marchers. Immediately after Father Gonzales and Connally embraced each other amidst shouts of "Viva Connally," the governor announced: "I will not be at the Capitol Monday, but if I had been there I don't think I would have met with you because my door ... has been open to you since the march began." Now the cries changed to "Viva la huelga" (long live the strike). Then Attorney General Carr, who at that time was also the Democratic nominee for the United States Senate, warned the marchers against the infiltration of "agitators and extremists" who might try to disrupt their peaceful protest. Again there were cries of "Viva la huelga."[22]

So with both Connally and Carr apparently trying to win a prize for the political faux pas of the year, liberal politicians

---

[20]*Austin Statesman* (August 31, 1966); *Austin American* (July 14, 1966).

[21]*Dallas Morning News* (August 31, 1966); *Austin American* (August 31, 1966).

[22]*Austin Statesman* (August 31, 1966); *Dallas Morning News* (September 1, 1966); *Houston Chronicle* (September 1, 1966); *Houston Post* (September 2, 1966); *Austin American-Statesman* (September 4, 1966).

across the state rushed to Austin to join the Labor Day finale. The situation was ideal. Before state-wide press coverage they would be able to embrace the cause of the poor and downtrodden, of the helpless underdog who was merely asking for a living wage, while damning the callousness of the "power structure." In a surprise move Senator Ralph Yarborough, an inveterate enemy of Connally, flew from Washington to march the last four blocks to the capitol and address the huge crowd. Then other liberal dignitaries and honored guests also spoke, including Representative Henry B. Gonzales of San Antonio, state president Hank Brown of the AFL-CIO, five state senators, a dozen representatives, and the leaders of the march. Even Robert Kennedy got into the act by sending a telegram of "regret." Yarborough—obviously enjoying the derisive shouts of "Where's John?"—climaxed the emotion-filled rally. "I see a storm coming," he dramatically exclaimed. "I know there is a God. If He has a place for me, I am ready . . . [for] I see the real heroes of Texas."[23]

After this rousing finale the Valley farm workers returned home, greatly encouraged by promises of support and confident that they would soon realize their goals. During the next nine months, however, their every effort met with defeat. Their political alliance was not powerful enough. In helpless frustration they watched the legislature, which convened on January 10, 1967, haggle over, delay and bottle up in committee their minimum-wage bill. And there was nothing they could do about it. The posting of two "wage sentinels" constantly outside the governor's office, as "a symbol of olden times when a chief ignored payment of debt," had not persuaded Connally to their cause. Nor did their organized efforts of packing the galleries at committee hearings affect conservative legislators from other districts. Now there seemed to be only one recourse left to them—la huelga.[24]

Early in May, 1967, the growers at Rio Grande City began anticipating a record-breaking melon crop. Since this produce was highly perishable, it was imperative that the harvest season not run more than four to six weeks. But Gilbert Padilla, vice-president of the farm workers' union, had other plans. To La

---

[23]*Houston Post* (September 4, 1966); *Dallas Morning News* (September 5, 6, 1966); *Austin American* (September 6, 1966).

[24]*Houston Chronicle* (September 6, 9, 1966); *Dallas Morning News* (September 7, December 4, 1966; March 16, 26, 1967); *Houston Chronicle* (January 24, February 17, March 16, 17, 1967).

Casita Farms he issued this ultimatum: "Negotiate or let them rot." When Ray Rochester, vice-president and manager of La Casita, refused and began hiring "green carders"—Mexican nationals who sought work on the Texas side during the day— a desperate test of strength between the growers and the migrant laborers was inevitable. Anticipating the strike, Padilla had already decided what actions the union must take. With success hinging on the fate of the melon harvest, his men would prevent the "green carders" from working. If, however, the "foreign strike breakers" could not be dissuaded and the gathering proceeded, then every "means of transportation," he publicly announced, must be "closed down."[25]

With violence imminent, Starr County officials called upon the Texas Rangers to help their small police force keep order, especially since several destructive fires and acts of sabotage during the preceding six months had gone unsolved.[26] Ranger Captain A. Y. Allee of Company D, with seven of his men, quickly responded—and then the trouble began. For la huelga was no longer just a strike by poor migrant workers seeking a living wage and a chance to escape poverty; now it had become multi-faceted, explosive, in many ways symbolic. For both the liberals and the conservatives of Texas it had become a political football, for Star County officials a "hot potato" which might affect local political careers, and for Yarborough a club to swing at Connally. Possibly labor believed that it would help strengthen the cause of unionism in Texas; perhaps socially and politically sensitive university students and church leaders thought of it as a fight for civil rights and human dignity; a number of Mexican-Americans may have hoped that it was the beginning of a social revolution which would topple the feudal economic and political systems in the Rio Grande Valley. But for the Rangers la huelga was a bewildering, angering, unpleasant assignment. It had become too complicated; old methods of law enforcement were no longer effective. Captain Allee, a crusty veteran of thirty-five years on the border, soon realized this. As he later told state Senator Don Kennard of Fort Worth: "Son, this is the goddamndest thing I've ever been in."[27]

---

[25]*Dallas Morning News* (May 7, 1967).

[26]*Ibid.* (March 26, 1967).

[27]Interview with state Senator Don Kennard, Fort Worth, Texas, September 14, 1967; closed manuscript in the possession of Ben Procter; *San Antonio Express* (May 11, 12, 1967).

For three weeks (May 11–June 1) the strike grew in intensity, each incident aggravating the public temper, each arrest increasing the animosity between the strikers and the Rangers. Soon charges arose of Ranger brutality, of violation of civil rights, of favoritism toward the growers, of strikebreaking. And just as quickly these were denied. After each clash widely divergent accounts of events circulated, all of them, however, containing a small area of agreement. But since the participants quite naturally magnified the importance of certain happenings, they therefore interpreted them in the light of their own experience.

On May 11 the first in a series of confrontations occurred. Early that morning, after Mexican police had dispersed sympathizing Mexican pickets and had allowed "green carders" to cross the international bridge at Roma, the Rangers cleared the way on the Texas side. They roughly shoved the closely-bunched *huelguistas* aside, while explaining, several union pickets angrily recollected, that it was their duty to get the workers to the fields without interruption. In reply, Captain Allee denied that his men were "taking sides"; they were merely upholding Texas law which forbade secondary strikes, picketing, and boycotts.[28] A few hours later Rangers also stopped a carload of strikers just outside of Roma and arrested the driver for having no license. Rev. Ed Krueger, a member of a special "team ministry" of the Texas Council of Churches, accused Ranger Jack Van Cleve of "throwing his weight around" and verbally scaring him, then became especially incensed when the driver was held in jail for five hours. To Krueger and other huelguistas, this was just another method of ranger strike-breaking.[29]

"Quite perturbed" over these episodes, union leader Eugene Nelson went "looking" for Captain Allee the next morning to lodge a strong protest. When he arrived at the courthouse at Rio Grande City and Allee could not be found, he reportedly lost his temper. Constable Manuel Benavides claimed that he said: "You tell that s.o.b. he had better lay off or there will be some dead Rangers." By late afternoon County Attorney Randall Nye, who was also an attorney for the strike-bound Starr Produce Company, had charged him with threatening the lives of law enforcement officers. Nelson claimed that he had been misunderstood—that he had told the constable "if the Texas Rangers don't stop, there are going

---

[28]*Vernon's Annotated Civil Statutes of the State of Texas*, Art. 5154f.

[29]*Texas Observer* (June 9, 1967); *San Antonio Express* (May 13, 1967).

to be some red-faced Rangers around here when the Senate investigators arrive." Nevertheless he spent the night in "a relic from the dark ages," the cockroach-infested Starr County jail.[30]

Beginning on May 18, as union activity increased and the strikers became more militant and hostile, the Rangers tried to keep the peace through mass arrests. Within two weeks they had jailed fifty-seven men and women either for secondary boycotting or for mass picketing. . . . Texas law prohibited more than two strikers to be "within fifty feet of the premises being picketed, or within fifty feet of any other picket."[31] As a result of these actions, the Rangers received bitter, galling criticism as well as state-wide demands for an investigation of their law enforcement methods and techniques. By June there were a number of court suits, with accompanying affidavits, charging them with unnecessary brutality and unlawful confiscation or destruction of private property.[32] Such allegations arose, of course, because there were numerous individual confrontations where the Rangers enforced the law by physical persuasion.

The night of May 26, however, was by far the most explosive —and, in the divergent stories, most confusing. At a railroad bridge near Mission, Texas, the Reverend Krueger, his wife, and eighteen huelguistas picketed a train carrying melons from the Valley. Rangers soon arrived and arrested them for mass picketing. In the ensuing roundup, so the strikers claimed, the Rangers slapped several of them (including a former state heavyweight boxing champion) "with tremendous force," and kicked Krueger, then slammed a car door on his leg while threatening to "knock . . . his head off." At that moment Mrs. Krueger tried to take pictures of the fracas whereupon, she asserted, Captain Allee grabbed her arm and twisted it, then took her camera and exposed the film.

To these allegations Allee replied that he was "a strong believer in enforcing the law and enforcing it as it is written." Then he added: "I don't think we've been wrong in what we've done." In fact, he claimed that he had not planned to arrest Krueger until the minister begged him repeatedly to do so. "I told him," Allee later explained to Jimmy Banks of the *Dallas Morning News*, "if

---

[30]*Texas Observer* (June 9, 1967) ; *San Antonio Express* (May 13, 14, 1967).

[31]*Vernon's Texas Statutes*, Art. 5154d; *Texas Observer* (June 9, 1967).

[32]*San Antonio Express* (May 26, 31, June 13, 1967) ; *Fort Worth Star-Telegram* (May 30, June 13, 1967).

that's the way he felt about it, I'd sure as hell accommodate him." Then the tough Ranger captain grabbed him by the belt and the seat of his trousers and unceremoniously escorted him to a nearby car. As for the tussle with Mrs. Krueger, Allee stated that it was "customary, when you arrest somebody and they cause a commotion, to take whatever articles they're carrying away from them. She put the camera behind her back, so I grabbed it." But at no time, he adamantly asserted, did a Ranger "expose any film."[33]

For the next few nights, as mass arrests continued, Captain Allee and his men, increasingly harried and perturbed by newsmen and cameramen flocking about them as they were trying to do their job, added more fuel to the growing furor. On several occasions they unwisely threatened to confiscate or destroy cameras, all of which seemed to substantiate Mrs. Krueger's charges.[34] Yet of all publicity unfavorable to the Rangers the "Dimas Affair" received the widest circulation. On June 1 Jim Rochester, a foreman at La Casita, claimed that on the previous night Magdaleno Dimas, a Mexican-born convicted murderer who had threatened his life several times, and Benito Rodríguez, who also had a criminal record, had driven up a loading ramp at one of the La Casita sheds yelling "Viva la huelga." Since Dimas was brandishing a rifle, Rochester fired at them, trying to puncture a tire as they sped away. Upon complaint, a Starr County deputy sheriff and Captain Allee tried to find the two men. After inquiring at the union office at Rio Grande City where Bill Chandler, an administrative assistant, denied any knowledge of their whereabouts, the two peace officers left, then waited nearby in their car. When Chandler and another man hurriedly left a few minutes later, they trailed them to a house from which Dimas emerged with a rifle. Immediately Allee took over, flashing a spotlight on the men and ordering them to surrender. Taken aback, Dimas dropped the rifle and ran back into the house as Chandler yelled: "Don't shoot, don't shoot, he isn't armed."

During the next thirty minutes Allee followed what he considered to be routine procedure in apprehending someone resisting arrest. From a justice of the peace he obtained a warrant to enter the premises, then moved in. Armed with a double-barrelled shot-

---

[33]*Texas Observer* (June 9, 1967); *Dallas Morning News* (July 9, 1967).

[34]*Texas Observer* (June 9, 1967); *Dallas Times Herald* (May 28, 1967); *Fort Worth Star-Telegram* (May 30, 1967); *San Antonio Express* (June 22, 1967).

gun, his favorite weapon, he kicked down the door—and there before him was Dimas and Rodríguez "sitting behind a table with their hands under it." In that split second Allee had to decide whether the subjects had guns hidden and, if so, whether to blast them. Instead of shooting, he ordered them to get up. When they would not, he suddenly "tilted the table back against them," rearranged Dimas' head with the barrel of his shotgun, and physically subdued him. As he later explained, "I used only the force that I deemed necessary to effect their arrest."[35]

Dimas, however, gave a much different version of what happened. Badly beaten, possibly suffering a concussion, he stated that when Allee burst into the house he and Rodríguez quickly raised their arms, lest they be killed. Then several Rangers ordered them to lower their hands and, when they would not, Allee hit him with the shotgun. Other Rangers continued the beating when he tried to protect himself against further blows.

After the "Dimas Affair" the tension between the huelguistas and the Rangers quickly subsided—melon season was almost over. By June 17 only three Rangers remained in Rio Grande City.[36] But in the aftermath of this conflict, investigating bodies, both state and national, moved into the Valley to question the participants, evaluate the evidence, and pronounce judgment. In the main the investigators were highly critical of the Rangers, especially reprimanding them for appearing "on the side of the employers," for being "completely out of line" in their dealings with the press, and for violating the civil rights of the strikers. Yet they did not challenge the contention that the Rangers were justified in being at Rio Grande City and that their presence probably prevented bloodshed. In turn, Colonel Homer Garrison, director of the Department of Public Safety, conducting his own investigation, categorically denied *any* wrongdoing on the part of the Rangers.[37]

So throughout the state Texans have questioned the actions of the Rangers and have demanded an explanation of what really happened. Possibly the forthcoming court cases will clarify certain issues. Regardless of the outcome of those legal decisions, however, there are certain problems emanating from the Valley dispute to

---

[35]*Texas Observer* (June 9, 1967) ; *Dallas Morning News* (July 9, 1967).

[36]*San Antonio Express* (May 31, 1967) ; *Houston Post* (June 17, 18, 1967).

[37]*San Antonio Express* (June 2, 18, 22, 28, 1967) ; *Dallas Morning News* (June 22, 30, July 1, 5, 6, 1967) ; *Texas Observer* (June 9, July 21, 1967).

which state officials and the people themselves must find answers. For make no mistake about it; la huelga has been much more than a controversy between management and labor, between picketers and Rangers. Unquestionably the economic upgrading of a minority group and certain political realities have been involved. But possibly not so obvious has been the interjection of civil rights into a labor dispute.

Surely Captain Allee and his men did not grasp that la huelga was anything more than just another local disturbance, at least not by their actions. At Rio Grande City they tried to enforce the law by time-tested and previously reliable methods. Toward those huelguistas who claimed that the state mass-picketing statute violated their rights and was unconstitutional, they were unsympathetic and unmoved. Toward those who infringed upon others' rights, they were stern and, if need be, violent. Their solution was "to go by the book"—and therein lay their difficulty. Never had they been confronted with problems involving that gray area, that "twilight zone" between civil and criminal actions. The cry, "I have a right to carry a picket sign," had no effect on them; only what the law said. And they were angered as well as dismayed by the criticism and abuse directed toward them. After all, they had kept the peace, protected property, upheld the law —and no one had been killed. What more was expected?

In past decades the answer to that question would have been rhetorical, but not in the 1960's. To a generation facing a Detroit or a Newark, the Rangers had proven ineffective; they had tried "to cope with current problems by using yesterday's tools."[38]

So from the Valley experience the Rangers should profit, for their administrators now have a clear responsibility to establish certain guidelines by which the force can serve more effectively. Of utmost importance is that the Rangers maintain, indeed project, a proper public image. If possible, they should not at times be ordered into quasi-civil conflicts in which they might appear to be "taking sides" or in which economic, social, or political considerations might take precedent over an unqualified enforcement of the law. As public servants they should also exert more patience and self-control in dealing with the news media, ignoring whenever possible the irritating activities of certain individuals. But of far greater concern to state administrators should be the

---

[38]Closed manuscript in possession of Ben Procter.

training of Rangers. There is no question that men of the force are experienced law enforcement officers, that they know their job, that they are top-flight in investigating crimes and apprehending criminals. Yet the developments in the Valley have indicated certain weaknesses in current methodology. In some manner the Department of Public Safety must keep these men abreast of current problems as well as possible solutions. And thus for the Rangers would be the legacy of la huelga from denunciation and scorn to rejuvenation and reform.

Who Is César Chávez?*

Eugene Nelson

It is the year 1943 in the city of Delano. A young man in his late teens is home visiting his family after working in a distant part of the state, and he decides to take in a show. He walks to a local movie house, buys his ticket, and enters the crowded theatre. As he stands at the rear of the aisle and his eyes become accustomed to the dark he observes that the people on one side of the aisle are almost all dark-skinned, Mexican-Americans like himself, while all the people on the other side of the aisle are white, Anglos.

He starts down the aisle. Of course he had known before he went away from home that the theatre was segregated, but now after being out in the broad world it hits him as never before. Why? he wonders, walking down the aisle, looking for a seat. Was he not an American citizen like these Anglos? Was he not as intelligent and as well-mannered as most Anglos? Was he not living in a country where all men were supposed to be equal? Had he not paid the same price to enter the theatre as Anglos paid? Why then should he be told he could not sit in a certain part of the theatre where others were allowed to sit?

*From Eugene Nelson, *Huelga: The First Hundred Days of the Great Delano Grape Strike* (Delano, California: Farm Worker Press, 1966). By permission of the author and publisher.

He finds a seat and sits down.

It is only a minute before an usherette taps his arm. "I'm sorry, but you'll have to sit on the other side of the aisle."

"Why? What's wrong?" the young man asks.

"I'm sorry, but Mexican people have to sit on the other side of the aisle."

"Why?"

"I'm sorry, but that's the rules."

"I'm not bothering anybody, why can't I sit where I want to sit?"

Several people are turning to look now at this young Mexican-American who apparently thinks he is as good as white people.

"Look, if you don't move, I'll have to call the manager."

The young man says nothing, and continues to look at the movie.

The manager comes; his pleadings are of no avail. He in turn goes for the police.

The young man feels a rough hand on his shoulder. He looks up to see two burly policemen standing over him in the darkness.

"All right, buddy, let's get going."

"What's wrong? I didn't do anything wrong, I didn't break any law."

"You broke the law of this theatre, now let's get moving."

"But I didn't —— ——"

"Look, are you coming with us, or do I have to use a little persuasion?"

The young man suddenly finds himself yanked up out of his seat, pushed toward the entrance and on out to the sidewalk, taken to the local police station—and all because he accepted literally the proclamation that in America all people are created equal.

It is twenty-two years later, September 23, 1965. The fourth day of the strike. We drive along busy Glenwood Street, César and I. The center line of the street is like the center of no-man's-land on a battlefield. On one side of the street are the little Filipino and Mexican cafes filled with strikers. On the other side the railroad and the packing sheds, not very busy now that we have almost emptied the fields of workers, and a few company men give us scathing looks as we drive past.

As I drive along, César seems deep in thought. I wonder what he is thinking, what the hundred problems are that are on his mind, no doubt tricky and involved legal processes involving unions that I do not even faintly understand—the pressure he must be under!

"Look," he says with a sudden grin, "that little girl." I turn to see a six-year-old Mexican girl bobbing away from us along the sidewalk, her pigtail swinging from side to side like a clock pendulum gone berserk; as she hurries onward on her unknown mission it seems almost to lift her skyward like the whirling blades of a helicopter. So these were the momentous thoughts!

He's always noticing little things along the road that escape me—and writers are supposed to be observant. Is this a great man's way of relaxing? Perhaps it is one test of high intelligence to be able to throw one's self wholeheartedly into a cause, and yet still have another part of the mind free to live a normal life with all its concerns and sensations. Other times he surprises me during moments of high import by discussing a multitude of things that have no bearing on the strike: women, the duties and necessities of marriage, child-rearing, the passing scenery. Or when problems are pressing, he takes time off to practice zany judo chops with his young sons, "Birdie" and "Babo."

Then, as we drive along, almost as an afterthought: "Oh yes—we must picket Máximo Martínez' house tonight."

Perhaps the two incidents cited above give some hint as to the diverse and seemingly contradictory aspects of César Chávez' personality. A man with a healthy sense of his own worth and with a correspondingly intense drive to see that he and his kind are treated as equals, he yet has a disarming simplicity, down-to-earthness, and interest in the ordinary things of life that have an ingratiating effect on almost all people with whom he comes in contact.

César Estrada Chávez was born in Yuma, Arizona, thirty-eight years ago, into a family of five children which barely eked out a living on their father's small farm near the banks of the Colo-rado River. When he was ten years old his hard-working father finally went broke, and there was no alternative but to take to the road, doing the only thing they knew how to do—farm work. They became migrants, and entered the stream of workers that followed the crops from Arizona to northern California and back, barely scraping by as they endured the scorching heat of summer and the bitter cold of winter in ramshackle huts or their broken-down car. School was, to say the least, irregular and haphazard. When the perpetually impoverished family finally settled in Brawley, and managed to establish that as sort of a home base for a few years, young César was to suffer the humiliation of segregated schools with second-class equipment. In spite of these humiliations, he liked school, was an alert and receptive student, but the necessity of helping support his struggling family forced him to drop out during the eighth grade to work as a migrant.

But the learning process for César Chávez did not stop there. He continued to read avidly when he was not working, and most of all he kept his eyes open and learned many social lessons that are not taught in public schools.

"Those early days when we first came to California were rough," César recalls.

We were really green, and whenever a labor contractor told us something, we fell for it hook, line and sinker. We didn't know the ropes yet and we got hooked every time. I remember the first year we ended up in the fall picking wine grapes for a contractor near Fresno. They were bad grapes, there were very few bunches on the vines, and we were the only family working in the field. But we were too green to wonder why we were the only ones, you see. After the first week of work my father asked the contractor for his pay. "I can't pay you yet because I haven't been paid by the winery," the contractor told my father. But we were broke, absolutely broke with nothing at all to eat, so the contractor finally gave us twenty dollars, and said we'd get a big check later when the winery paid him. We worked for seven weeks like that, and each payday the contractor said he couldn't pay us because the winery hadn't paid him yet. At the end of the seventh week we went to the contractor's house and it was empty—he owed us for seven weeks pay, and we haven't seen him to this day.

We were desperate. We ran into another labor contractor in Fresno. "There is lots of money in the cotton near Mendota," he told us. It was late November by now and it was cold and raining almost every day. Because of the rain, there was almost no work at all. That winter of 1938 I had to walk to school barefoot through the mud we were so poor. There was a school and there was an annex. The Mexican-American kids went to the annex—it was just another name for a segregated school. After school we fished in the canal and cut wild mustard greens—otherwise we would have starved. Everyone else left the camp we were living in, but we had no money for transportation. When everyone else left they shut off the lights, so we sat around in the dark. We finally got a few dollars from some relatives in Arizona and bought enough gas for our old Studebaker to get us to Los Angeles. Our car broke down in L.A. and my mother sold crocheting on the street to raise the money for enough gas to get to Brawley. We lived three days in our car in Brawley before we could find a house we could afford to rent.

Next winter we were stranded in Oxnard and had to spend the winter in a tent. We were the only people there living in a tent and everyone ridiculed us. We went to bed at dusk because there was no light. My mother and father got up at 5:30 in the morning to go pick peas. It cost seventy cents to go to the fields and back, and some days they did not even make enough for their transportation. To help out, my brother and I started looking along the highway for empty cigarette packages for the tinfoil. Every day we would look for cigarette packages, and we made a huge ball of tinfoil that weighed eighteen pounds. Then we sold it to a Mexican junk dealer for enough money to buy a pair of tennis shoes and two sweatshirts.

Two days before Christmas a Mexican-American woman who owned a few small shacks near there saw our tent in the rain and felt sorry for us, so she let us live in one of her shacks. Every Christmas this woman put on some Christmas skits in her home, and this Christmas she asked my mother and father to play two of the parts in a skit about the Christ child, in place of the man and woman who usually played the parts. My father and mother played the parts, and the other man and his wife were so angry they never spoke to the woman again.

Well, we finally learned the ropes. We learned where the crops were and when they needed workers, and we learned little tricks like living under bridges and things like that. Once we'd learned the ropes, we began helping other green families like we had been, so they wouldn't have it as rough as we did.

About 1939 we were living in San Jose. One of the old CIO unions began organizing workers in the dried fruit industry, so my father and my uncle became members. Sometimes the men would meet at our house and I remember seeing their picket signs and hearing them talk. They had a strike and my father and uncle picketed at night. It made a deep impression on me. But of course they lost the strike and that was the end of the union. But from that time on my father joined every new agricultural union that came along—often he was the first one to join—and when I was nineteen I joined the National Agricultural Workers Union. But it didn't have any more success than any of the other farm workers unions.

After he left home César continued to follow the crops. He mingled with whites and learned that they had problems too, and that prejudice was not an inborn human quality but something which could be overcome; he gained a new devotion to working people of all races and beliefs. In Delano, he met and married a Mexican-American girl who shared his dedication to the cause of the farm worker, and they worked together in the fields up and down the state and began to raise a family as best they could.

In 1950 they went to live in his former home of San Jose, where they worked in apricot and prune orchards. It was here that César Chávez was to meet one of the two men who were to change his life radically. It was a fateful day when scholarly Father Donald McDonnell of the nearby mission church knocked on the Chávez door on a routine round of visits to the poor people living in his neighborhood. César recalls that Father McDonnell, an expert linguist who spoke not only English and Spanish, but Chinese, Japanese, German, and Portuguese, ". . . sat with me past midnight telling me about social justice and the Church's stand on farm labor and reading from the encyclicals of Pope Leo XIII in which he upheld labor unions. I would do anything to get the Father to tell me more about labor history. I began going to the bracero camps with him to help with Mass, to the city jail with him to talk to prisoners, anything to be with him so that he could tell me more about the farm labor movement."

It was Father McDonnell who one night in 1952 introduced César to Fred Ross of the Community Service Organization, a new social-service group of predominantly Spanish-speaking people which was trying to educate needy people to help themselves with their social and economic problems. Ross was struck at once by young Chávez' engaging personality and leadership qualities, and hired him at a salary of $35 a week to help organize CSO chapters throughout the state.

Ross' confidence was not misplaced. In a comparatively short space of time Chávez had helped build CSO into a powerful organization with chapters in both California and Arizona, and by the late fifties he had become general director of the entire organization.

As head of CSO, César Chávez involved the organization in a direct head-on confrontation with the power structure that gave it real meaning and which threatened to shake the foundations of the feudalistic elements in California's economy. Learning that local farm workers in Oxnard were not able to get jobs because growers were illegally using braceros instead, he daily over a period of several months led a group of workers to the office of the local growers' association, and daily filed a complaint with the California Farm Placement Service when they were not hired, filing over 1,100 complaints in all. He finally succeeded in getting an inspector from the Labor Department to force growers to hire local workers instead of the Mexican nationals. But as soon as the inspector left, the locals were fired and braceros taken back again. After this ridiculous process had transpired time and time again, Chávez finally one day led a huge group of local workers to the fields, and arranged to have the march covered by the newspapers and TV as he provided documentary evidence that braceros were being used while available local workers could not find jobs. This incident triggered a complete investigation of the Farm Placement Service, its chief and two other men resigned under pressure, and an assistant chief was dismissed when it was proven he had accepted bribes from growers. One man—and a Mexican-American at that—had caused a statewide upheaval in California agriculture.

But inevitably, when people are helped to advance themselves in society, some of them forget or ignore their past, and some of the CSO members whom Chávez had helped to elevate themselves in the community later balked when Chávez, at a CSO convention, proposed that the CSO continue to use its influence to help poor farm workers. When conservative elements in the CSO refused to support him, Chávez in 1961 resigned his position as director in order to devote all his efforts to helping farm workers. About the same time, he also turned down an offer of a $21,000-a-year job with the Peace Corps as director of the Corps for four Latin American nations. If no one else would help the farm worker, how could he ignore him?

Instead, Chávez took a $1.25-an-hour job pruning grape vines in his wife's home town of Delano, and began spending all his spare time traveling up and down the San Joaquin Valley talking to farm workers, getting their opinions, laying the groundwork for the establishment of the Farm Workers Association.

By September, 1962, he had contacted thousands of farm workers, mostly Mexican-Americans, and felt at last that the time was ripe to call an organizational meeting. But his long service with the CSO had taught him that the poor farm worker had more problems than just the size of his salary, and the new organization was to be based upon a new and broader concept of a union as an association of workers to help the member with all his needs, social as well as economic. The new organization proposed to provide insurance for its members, a credit union (the first for farm workers), and to help them with such problems as translation from Spanish to English, securing welfare and other benefits due, medical problems, etc. The Farm Workers Association had an immediate grass-roots appeal, and since its organizational meeting on September 26, 1962, has been growing steadily and spreading its influence throughout the entire state of California. César Chávez, with his $50-a-week salary as general director, became the only farm labor organizer in California's history whose salary was paid directly by the workers he had organized.

What is the secret of Chávez' success in a field where national unions with hundreds of thousands of dollars behind them have failed? Scott Fitzgerald, in an autobiographical novel, once wrote that he didn't have the two assets most valuable to a man, animal magnetism and money, but that he possessed the next most valuable, intelligence and good looks. César Chávez goes him one better, for he undoubtedly has a great deal of personal magnetism which is probably the single greatest key to his success, as well as an undeniably keen intelligence and exceedingly pleasant if not handsome appearance. There is something arrestingly candid about him when one first meets him, a convincing lack of affectation and what seems an undeniably sincere interest in the other person's problems; he is one of those persons one feels he has known all his life.

He has an extremely tactful and considerate manner of giving orders so that one finds himself almost doing the thing required as if he had thought of it himself: "Why don't you take this down to the post office and mail it? Why don't we have the volunteers distribute leaflets this afternoon? It might be a good idea if you picketed the Caratan Ranch tomorrow...."

Next to the quality of personal magnetism, probably the most remarkable thing about him is his coolness under pressure. I have never once seen him lose his temper and explode in anger, in spite of the extreme pressure he is under, although I am told he once kicked two high-ranking government officials out of his home when they persisted in wasting his time with proposals detrimental to the farm worker.

He has an excellent and very boyish sense of humor, and really seems completely devoid of any feeling of superiority or of being part of a special elite. Tennessee Williams, in reply to an interviewer's question, once said that a person couldn't help changed by fame and publicity, and it is difficult not to agree him, but in the case of César Chávez the signs have not bec~ evident. If this is an act, it is a magnificent one.

Of course he is not perfect—assuming people could agree o~ what perfect is—and by definition a person who is intensely partisan is intolerant of certain things. In César's case, as more than one person has observed, he tends to be intolerant—because he is so intensely committed himself—of people who do not fight as hard as he is fighting to improve economic and social conditions, and to fail to be sympathetic when they are not willing to have their families undergo certain privations for "la causa." I remember an occasion upon which he subtly reprimanded me in a restaurant for ordering an expensive breakfast of sausage and eggs while he had more modest fare, when I felt it was none of his business.

Whether César Chávez will become the Martin Luther King of the Mexican-Americans remains to be seen. While he has penned no brilliant essays like King's, he has demonstrated remarkable leadership qualities, and there is no one else of his stature in sight in the Mexican-American community.

Of other labor leaders, the one he says who has impressed him most is John L. Lewis; of contemporaries, his favorite is Walter Reuther. As for himself, he says he never has visualized himself as a great labor leader, nor does he plan to stay on indefinitely once his mission has been accomplished and the farm workers have union recognition and can earn a decent living like other workers.

"Even when our work succeeds, I don't want to hang on forever. What I would really like is to be alone somewhere—in Mexico, or in the mountains—and have time to read all the classics that there are in English and Spanish."